Wands

HITLER LIVES

HITLER LIVES –

and the generals die

PIERRE GALANTE

with Eugène Silianoff

Translated from the French by Mark Howson and Cary Ryan

SIDGWICK & JACKSON
LONDON

First published in Great Britain in 1982 by Sidgwick & Jackson Limited.

First published in USA under the title *Operation Valkyrie: The German Generals' Plot Against Hitler* in 1981 by Harper & Row, Publishers, Inc.

This work was first published in France under the title *Hitler est-il mort?* © Librairie Plon—Paris-Match, 1981.

ISBN 0-283-98672-7

Printed and bound in Great Britain by Mansell (Bookbinders) Ltd., Witham, Essex
for Sidgwick & Jackson Limited
1 Tavistock Chambers, Bloomsbury Way, London WC1A 2SG

Contents

Acknowledgments   vii

Preface   ix

1. *July 20, 1944: The Wolf's Lair*   1

2. *July 20, 1944: Paris*   17

3. *1934–1935: The Army Swears Fealty*   31

4. *1936–1937: "They Call Him Hermann"*   39

5. *1938: "A Swine, But a Lucky Swine"*   47

6. *1939: First Soldier of the Reich*   74

7. *1940: "I Can Force Them to Obey Me"*   86

8. *1941: "We Have Nothing to Fear from the Americans"*   99

9. *1942: "The Russians Are Done For"*   118

10. *1942–1943: Stalingrad*   142

11. *1943: Infernal Machines*   161

12. *1944: "When the Oxcart Gets Stuck in the Mud"*   190

13. *July 20, 1944: Exercise Completed*   207

14. *After July 20, 1944: The Last Knights*   217

15. *March 1945–May 1945: "In the Best Interests of the Nation"*   237

Appendix: Interview with General Heusinger   248

Glossary of German Military Terms   256

Sources   258

Bibliography   265

Index   267

Photographs follow pages 100 and 196

Maps

The Battle of France, 1940   93

Operation Barbarossa, 1941–1942   102

The Eastern Front After Stalingrad, 1943–1945   149

D-Day and the Liberation of France, June 1944–1945   198

Acknowledgments

I would like to express my profoundest gratitude to General Adolf Heusinger for his valuable, exclusive, and enriching cooperation, and to Frau Heusinger for her warm and gracious hospitality on innumerable occasions.

To my friend Louis François-Poncet, without whose aid and encouragement this book could never have been written.

To Mlle Jacqueline Sarrazin and the Berger-Levrault Library for allowing me to consult their files on Hitler and the German high command.

To Roger Thérond, managing editor of *Paris-Match*, who inspired me to write this book.

To John Toland and Oron J. Hale for their sheer kindness.

To George Wagner, Robert Wolfe, and William H. Cunliffe of the National Archives and Records Service.

To General von Witzleben, in Munich; Fräulein von Hofacker, in Paris; Herr von Hase, in Bonn; and to Michel Tournier, of the Académie Goncourt, in Paris.

Eugène Silianoff and I wish to give a special vote of thanks to Dr. Helmuth Krausnick, director of the Institute for Contemporary History in Munich; to his assistant, Fräulein Dr. von Kotze, and to their colleagues Dr. Broschat, Dr. Auerbach, and Frau Violet, chief librarian of the Institute, as well as to Dr. Hans Stercken, former director of the Federal Center for Political Education in Bonn.

Preface

*You must realize that the generals who occupied key positions
refused to engage in any kind of subversive activity until
they had made certain of Hitler's death.*

—GENERAL ADOLF HEUSINGER

Born in Lower Saxony, near Hannover, in 1897, Adolf Heusinger served
in the First World War as a second lieutenant until he was taken prisoner
by the English in 1917. He spent the next two and a half years in a
POW camp. From 1927 to 1931 he attended the War College, and in
1932 he was promoted from first lieutenant to captain in the Reichswehr,
the (theoretically) restricted 100,000-man army provided for in the Versailles Treaty. After marking time for seventeen years as a lieutenant,
Heusinger achieved rapid promotion; he became a general in less than
ten years. During his four-year tenure as operations chief of OKH he
met with Hitler between six and seven hundred times, primarily at the
midday military briefings at OKW headquarters. Suspected of complicity
in the events of July 20, 1944, he was arrested by the Gestapo, and
shortly after his release he gave himself up to the Americans. Once
again it was several years before he regained his freedom. He subsequently served as a military adviser to the West German Defense Ministry.

In 1952 he was asked by General Eisenhower, "How is it that you
never succeeded in getting rid of Hitler?"

"He came to power quite legally," Heusinger replied. "If I asked
you to get rid of Truman, would you do it?"

In 1957 General Heusinger was appointed inspector general of the
Bundeswehr, and finally, from 1960 until 1964, he served as president
of the Military Commission of NATO, which has its headquarters in
the Pentagon. Today General Heusinger is retired; he and his wife live
in Cologne, surrounded by their children and grandchildren. He has
never forgotten that he has spent almost six years of his life in prison
camps.

All the scenes and events described in this book at which General Heusinger was present were reconstructed by him shortly after the collapse of the Third Reich in May 1945, from extensive notes he had compiled during the course of the war. Descriptions of conditions at the front are based on eyewitness testimony—letters and transcribed conversations that General Heusinger has preserved in his personal archives; attitudes and opinions attributed to individuals or factions in the German military are also based on written memoranda of staff meetings and personal conversations prepared by General Heusinger during his tenure as chief of the Operations Section of OKH from 1940 until July 20, 1944.

Some of the material that concerns Hitler and the general staff, and some of General Heusinger's own observations, were originally included, in somewhat different form, in a short account of the subject General Heusinger wrote after the war entitled *Befehl im Widerstreit: Schick-sals-stunde der Deutschen Armee, 1923–1945* ("Command in Conflict: The German Army's Hour of Decision"). This work is not available in English, however, and the material presented here has been revised and updated to include information that was still classified when General Heusinger's original account appeared in 1947. (As for the background and authenticity of scenes involving Claus von Stauffenberg, Fabian von Schlabrendorff, and other actors in the Valkyrie drama, see Sources.)

HITLER LIVES

1.

July 20, 1944: The Wolf's Lair

On the night of July 19, 1944, Hitler stayed up until two in the morning, as was his custom. After the midnight conference broke up, he continued to hold forth for the benefit of two of his four secretaries, Frau Johanna Wolf and Frau Christa Schröder. Before bidding them good night, he announced, "I have a feeling of foreboding, but it is critical that nothing happen to me. I have neither the right nor the time to fall ill." After he had swallowed the narcotic sleeping potion that was prepared for him every night on the orders of his personal physician, Dr. Theo Morell, Hitler finally went off to bed.

As always, his valet, Heinz Linge, who had been in his service for over ten years, was waiting to hand him his nightshirt and put away his field-gray uniform. (Hitler never slept in pajamas, and no one, not even Linge, had ever seen him naked, or even stripped to the waist, a fact that gave rise to a great deal of amused speculation on the part of his entourage.) The Führer indulged his taste for luxurious surroundings and bourgeois comfort only at the Berghof, the chalet in Berchtesgaden he shared with Eva Braun; the decor of the Wolf's Lair here in Rastenburg was starkly functional. His bedroom was furnished with almost monastic simplicity; Gertraud Junge, one of his private secretaries, remembers it as very much like a bedroom in a youth hostel—a wooden bedstead, a wardrobe, a chair, a bedside table with a few books and magazines, and four bare walls. Marshal von Bock, who had once caught a glimpse of the Führer's private quarters, commented approvingly, "This is something that the men at the front should see."

Hitler had complete confidence in the invaluable Linge; he remarked to Himmler some time later, "After the war Linge will be made chief of protocol and head of my personal staff." Linge's head was quite turned by all this; he liked to think of himself as a gentleman in waiting at the court of Frederick the Great (a monarch with whom Hitler also felt a great affinity).

On this particular night Hitler had left instructions to be awakened at nine o'clock, an hour earlier than usual, since he was expecting a visit from his good friend Benito Mussolini,[1] who was due to arrive at Rastenburg in the early afternoon of the twentieth. (Thus, the first of the day's military briefing sessions, usually held at 1:00 PM, would have to be pushed forward.) Hitler's personal staff, the "family circle," as he called them, noticed that he seemed exceptionally nervous that morning. Hitler was never really at ease in his East Prussian command post; he missed the pure air of the Eagle's Nest at Berchtesgaden and the mountains of Bavaria.

Rastenburg (now Ketrzijn, in Poland) was a small town of some 17,000 inhabitants in the Königsberg region, a plain studded with lakes and small valleys and covered with gloomy forests of pine, oak, and beech. Before the war the town itself had been notable chiefly for its fourteenth century church and its castle, which had once housed a banner of Teutonic Knights, and as a center of light industry, including several canneries and a ham-curing plant. The townspeople spent their Sundays singing, dancing, and drinking beer at the Karlshof Café in the nearby Görlitz Forest; more formal entertainments—the East Prussian equivalents of square dances, turkey shoots, and county fairs—were held in a spacious meadow not far from the café.

After the fall of 1940, however, the forest was off limits to civilians, the Karlshof was requisitioned as a billet for an SS detachment, and a landing strip was constructed at the edge of the forest. In November 1940 Dr. Fritz Todt, Hitler's expert on fortifications and military engineering, in consultation with a panel of specialists and with Hitler's aide Lieutenant Colonel Engel, chose the Görlitz Forest as the site of Hitler's northern command post, the *Wolfsschanze*—the "Wolf's Lair." (The wolf, which figures prominently in Teutonic mythology, became Hitler's personal totemic animal; the OKH command post during the Battle of France was called *Wolfsschlucht* ("Wolf Gorge"), and a similar command post for the eastern front, *Werwolf* ("Werewolf"), was later established at Vinnitsa in the Ukraine. In fact, the name Adolf itself is a contraction of *Adelwolf*, "noble wolf.")

Hitler insisted that the construction be completed quickly, for the very compelling reason that he had already decided to launch an attack on the Soviet Union. The local people were informed that the site would

1. Deposed by the Fascist Council of state, arrested, and then dramatically rescued by SS commandos, the former Duce was now the puppet ruler of the so-called Italian Social Republic in German-occupied Lombardy. [Tr.]

eventually be occupied by the Askania chemical works, which would have accounted for the elaborate security and the formidable antiaircraft defenses.

On June 22, 1941, the day Germany attacked the Soviet Union, Reichsmarshal Hermann Goering began to set up his own establishment in a nearby hunting lodge at Rominten. At the entrance to this vast game preserve of almost a hundred square miles the inscription *Natur-schutzgebiet Rominten Heide* ("Rominten Heath Wildlife Sanctuary") was carved in Gothic letters over the gateway of undressed logs. The Reichs-marshal's arrival at Rominten was always signaled by the arrival of enormous quantities of foodstuffs and provisions, and a great deal of commotion among his domestic staff. Goering was a lavish host who kept perpetual open house, and while at Rominten he could indulge his two great pleasures—hunting the stag and eating its flesh—to the fullest.

In 1943, after Stalingrad, the Wolf's Lair became Hitler's permanent GHQ. The command post itself was surrounded by a five-acre tract of forest divided into three security zones and was accessible only by a single road. The outer zone contained the barracks for the Organisation Todt construction workers and the troops guarding the perimeter, most of them from the Waffen SS Leibstandarte, Gross Deutschland, and Das Reich divisions. The landing strip and a small railroad station with three locomotives (a full head of steam was kept up in all of them at all times) were also located in the outer zone, which was over a mile wide and liberally sown with land mines.

The second zone contained the barracks, blockhouses, and bunkers occupied by the army officers and Propaganda Ministry employees who were attached to Armed Forces High Command (OKW), including the residence of Marshal Wilhelm Keitel, the OKW chief of staff. This zone was also provided with a mess hall, several movie theaters, and a sauna, storage areas for archives and files, and a telecommunications center, presided over by the chief signals officer, General Erich Fellgie-bel.

The third zone was reserved for Hitler himself, his family circle, and the officers of his personal staff. The Führer's inner sanctum was surrounded by two rings of barbed wire separated by a mine field; the inner ring of wire was electrified, and sentinels with savage guard dogs were posted every thirty yards. Hitler and his staff were lodged in a modest one-story concrete bunker, carefully camouflaged to blend in with the surrounding forest floor.

At the center of the bunker was the conference room in which the military briefing sessions were held. The white walls were covered with maps, and the furnishings consisted simply of a massive wooden table and a number of rather uncomfortable chairs. To the left of the conference room were several small reception rooms where the Führer received foreign chiefs of state and other dignitaries, and German officers who had distinguished themselves for gallantry whom he wished to decorate personally. To the right of the conference room was Hitler's suite, accessible only to the privileged members of the family circle.

On the morning of July 20 the air was thick and the heat stifling. In the town of Rastenburg the sidewalks were filled with long files of housewives in shapeless dresses who had already begun the day's vigil outside the empty shop windows. At the Wolf's Lair Hitler decided to meet with his general staff in the *Lagebaracke* ("situation barracks"), which had the advantage of having a great many windows that could be left open to catch the breeze. The barracks was actually a sort of wooden chalet which had been built in 1941; in May 1944 the outer walls were encased in a thick shell of concrete and daubed with green and brown paint, the colors of the forest; the camouflage netting on the roof was filled with leafy branches and clumps of moss. Against this strange backdrop workmen from the Organisation Todt still busied themselves with their task of construction and concealment.

Berlin

On the night of July 19, as on so many previous nights, Berlin had been the target of an intense Allied bombing raid. In the early morning the volunteer flak crews of the city's air defense were still helping the survivors of last night's raid pick through the rubble of their houses and salvage what they could of their clothing and furniture. The day was already oppressively hot, which would only plunge the Berliners even deeper into the fatalistic torpor into which many of them had sunk after so many sleepless nights spent in cellars and subway tunnels.

Just after sunrise a field-gray Volkswagen made its way toward the center of the city. The driver was Lieutenant Werner von Haeften, orderly officer to his silent passenger, Colonel Count Claus von Stauffenberg, recently attached to the staff of General Fromm's newly organized Replacement Army. (Derisively known as the "ersatz army," this was actually no more than a miscellaneous collection of over- and underage conscripts, wounded combat veterans like Stauffenberg himself, and reassigned noncombatants who were expected to furnish Hitler with his final line of defense against the Soviet invader.)

Tall, well-bred, but with an air of rather careless elegance, Stauffenberg was the son of one of the most prestigious old families of south Germany, traditionally Catholic and separatist. A devout Catholic himself, Stauffenberg was a member of the mystical circle that surrounded the poet Stefan George during the thirties. Stauffenberg's high seriousness and aristocratic bearing made such a profound impression that when he joined the conspiracy to destory Hitler and the Nazi movement, he was admitted to the first rank, alongside such figures as Marshal Erwin von Witzleben and General Ludwig Beck; the economist Carl Friedrich Goerdeler (mayor of Leipzig until 1936); Julius Leber (former vice-president of the Federation of German Trade Unions); Count Clement August von Galen, the Catholic bishop of Münster; Pastor Eugen Gerstenmaier, an influential leader of the Protestant ecumenical movement; Count Friedrich von der Schulenburg, former ambassador to Moscow; and Ulrich von Hassell, former ambassador to Rome.

At dawn, after the Volkswagen had gone barely half a mile, Stauffenberg asked Haeften to turn into a street near the main highway that would take them into the center of Berlin. The car stopped at a small chapel; the door was still locked at this early hour of the morning. Stauffenberg's knock was answered by Chaplain Wehrle,[2] who recognized him immediately, since Stauffenberg had called on him about ten days earlier to ask him a rather curious question: "Father, can the Church grant absolution to a murderer who has taken the life of a tyrant?" The chaplain replied prudently that, to the best of his knowledge, according to canon law only the Pope could grant absolution in such a case, but that he would have to make further inquiries before he could give a definite answer. On the morning of the twentieth Chaplain Wehrle had still not informed himself fully on this point, but in any case Stauffenberg simply wished to collect his thoughts and to pray for his wife, Nina, and their three sons.

"I leave them in your hands," he had said to his brother Berthold that morning before setting out for Berlin. His wife and sons were cur-

2. Chaplain Wehrle later provided this account to a Nazi People's Court, which sentenced him to hang for his failure to denounce Stauffenberg, since, in the court's opinion, this conversation should have provided him with ample evidence of Stauffenberg's "criminal intent." Chaplain Wehrle's defense was based on the doctrine of the secret of the confessional, but this was rejected by the court.

rently staying in a small country house in Württemburg. He always carried their photographs with him, but he had still not found the courage to tell Nina that he had decided to stake everything on the outcome of that day's events; in any case, the outcome should be clear in a few hours' time.

A gray Heinkel III was waiting for them at Rangsdorf airfield; the plane had been supplied by the General Army Office, whose chief, General Friedrich Olbricht, was one of the leaders of the military conspiracy in Berlin. Before leaving for Rastenburg, Stauffenberg announced, "This is more than we dared hope for; fate has offered us this opportunity, and I would not refuse it for anything in the world. I have searched my conscience, before God and before myself. This man is evil incarnate." Stauffenberg and Haeften climbed into the passengers' seats behind the pilot; the bomb in Stauffenberg's briefcase had already been tested by their fellow conspirators on the eastern front. There were two kilograms of explosive inside the metal casing; the detonator was believed to be foolproof—an inch-and-a-half-long tube containing a glass capsule filled with acid. The bomb was armed by breaking the capsule with pincers; the acid would dissolve a thin metal strip that held back the firing pin. The bomb would explode ten minutes after the capsule was broken.

The Wolf's Lair

The plane touched down on the Rastenburg landing strip at 10:15 AM. Stauffenberg ordered the pilot to wait so that he could take them back to Berlin: "Be ready to take off by noon."

Two days earlier General Beck had urged him at the end of their last meeting: "Promise me that you will leave before the explosion. You're indispensable here, as you know, if the Valkyrie plan is to be carried out. You're the only one who knows how our liaison with the army is going to be worked out in detail."

Operation Valkyrie had originally been drawn up by the Wehrmacht, with Hitler's approval, to allow for any contingency that would place the Reich in imminent danger—Hitler's death, an Allied invasion, or an insurrection (presumably of Russian slave laborers). The conspirators, of course, had introduced certain modifications: The army would seize power in Berlin, and military commanders would take whatever steps were necessary to secure the districts under their command. As soon as word came of Hitler's death, the conspirators planned to implement Valkyrie, to occupy the key strategic points and communications centers of Berlin (notably the main radio transmitter), arrest Goebbels, and proclaim General Beck provisional chief of state until a legally constituted civilian government could be installed. The ultimate purpose of the conspiracy was to offer the Western Allies an immediate ceasefire as the prelude to a negotiated peace. The war was irretrievably lost for Germany, and every day, every hour that passed only increased the toll of victims on both sides who had been sacrificed to the bloodlust of a madman.

A car was waiting at the landing field to carry Stauffenberg and Haeften through the security cordon to the Führer's inner circle. They climbed into the back seat, Stauffenberg clutching his precious tawny-leather briefcase in his lap, and set off through the dense forest toward the outer zone. Shortly before they reached the first checkpoint, he asked the driver to stop. He had decided that one kilogram of explosives would be enough to destroy the underground conference room; he removed the other packet of explosives from the metal casing and tucked it away behind the back seat of the car. The briefcase would be lighter, thus less conspicuous and easier to carry.

Stauffenberg was waved through the various checkpoints with no difficulty. His official pass had been signed by General Fromm, and his decorations, his appearance—he had lost most of his left forearm, his left eye, and three fingers of his right hand during the Tunisian campaign—and his aristocratic bearing inspired deference and respect. Stauffenberg and Haeften shared a late breakfast in the officers' canteen with Captain von Mollendorf, adjutant to the camp commandant, then Stauffenberg sought out General Fellgiebel, who was charged with the vital mission of cutting all communications with the outside world as soon as the bomb had exploded and he had informed the conspirators in Berlin. At noon Stauffenberg reported to Marshal Keitel.

"The briefing will take place earlier than planned," Keitel informed him. "Make your report as brief as possible." He added another recommendation: "Don't make the report on the Replacement Army too pessimistic. The Führer will be receiving Mussolini right afterward; he mustn't be put under too much nervous strain." Then Keitel gave him some unexpected and disturbing news—the briefing would take place not in the conference room in the bunker but in the adjoining *Lagebaracke*. The explosive charge might not be sufficient in a building whose wooden walls would not offer as much resistance to the blast; the best chance for success would be to place the bomb as close as possible to Hitler. By now it was twelve twenty.

"Let's go," said Keitel.

Stauffenberg asked permission to take a few moments to wash up before going in to the conference, then, quickly realizing that the barracks latrine would not be a propitious place in which to arm the bomb, he asked if it would be possible for him to change his shirt; Keitel's aide showed him to his own room. Stauffenberg broke the acid capsule with a pair of pliers while Keitel waited impatiently outside the door—"Let's go, hurry up!" When Stauffenberg came out into the corridor, Keitel's aide offered to carry his briefcase; first Stauffenberg refused, then handed over the briefcase. "I want to sit as close to the Führer as possible," he said. "My hearing is very bad."

In the center of the conference room stood an enormous oak table, some fifteen or twenty feet long, supported by thick wooden panels placed crosswise at either end. Near the door were several smaller tables for briefcases and folders. The briefing had begun punctually at noon. Hitler sat with his back to the door. To his right was Lieutenant General Adolf Heusinger, the only one of the general staff officers present who was aware that an attempt was being planned on Hitler's life; his friend General Henning von Tresckow, now in Russia, had been unable to warn him that the twentieth was to be *der Tag*—though Heusinger still suspected that something was up. To Heusinger's right stood Vice-Admiral von Puttkamer, General Bodenschatz, the stenographer Berger—"Hitler's double"—and a number of other high-ranking officers. At Hitler's left were General Alfred Jodl, his deputy, General Warlimont, and SS aide-de-camp, and SS Captain Fegelein, who was married to Eva Braun's sister. Goering and Reichsführer Heinrich Himmler did not attend the briefing; they were represented by their liaison officers, Bodenschatz and Fegelein. In fact, Goering seldom left his personal HQ, some thirty miles away, unless it was absolutely necessary.

Hitler opened the briefing by asking, "Is there any news from the Romanian front?"

"Aside from a few local engagements," General Heusinger replied, "all is quiet."

"Do we know where the Russian armored columns are?"

"Our ground reconnaissance has lost sight of them for several days; it's possible that they are still in their former positions, unless they have already set out toward Lemberg—"

"And don't we have anything from aerial reconnaissance?" Hitler broke in.

"Unfortunately, no," Heusinger went on. "Russian fighter activity has been so heavy that very few of our observers have been able to get through."

"And what is the overall situation on the eastern front, Heusinger?"

"Increasingly strained. It will be almost impossible to prevent a junction of the two main Russian penetrations of our front. Our reserves are spent, and we will have to start drawing on the forces of the General Government." [3]

At that moment Marshal Keitel, followed by Colonel von Stauffenberg, entered the conference room and saluted. Hitler turned rapidly in his chair and returned the salute, but he appeared not to recognize Stauffenberg, whom he had met before on only a few occasions. Keitel, obsequious as always, suggested, "My Führer, perhaps now Colonel von Stauffenberg could present his report on the possibilities of mobilizing the Replacement Army . . ."

"No, first I want to hear what the situation is along the rest of the front. We'll come back to that later."

Stauffenberg whispered to Keitel, "Herr Feldmarschall, I have to make an urgent call to Berlin . . ."

Keitel simply nodded, and Stauffenberg approached Colonel Brandt, who was standing near Hitler. "Colonel, I'll leave my briefcase with you." He slid the briefcase under the table and left the room; he had decided to wait out the next few critical minutes in General Fellgiebel's telecommunications post.

Meanwhile Hitler and several staff officers had gone over to examine Heusinger's maps; Hitler returned to his place at the table, and Colonel Brandt, hampered by Stauffenberg's bulky briefcase, pushed it away with his foot and knocked it over. He reached down and set it upright again, a little farther from Hitler's end of the table. Heusinger resumed his pessimistic report: The 13th Army Corps was doomed to encirclement by the Russians.

"The General Government's forces will fight their way through to relieve them!" Hitler proclaimed.

"We will have to deploy them along a defensive line," Heusinger replied, "since they are incapable of mounting an attack."

By this time Stauffenberg was hurrying toward the waiting staff car.

"The situation in the East Prussian sector is increasingly critical," Heusinger was saying. "The Russians are drawing closer. A major Russian striking force to the west of the Duna is wheeling around toward

---

3. The Nazi administration in Central Poland, which had not been formally annexed into the Reich. [Tr.]

the north. If we don't withdraw our army group around Lake Peipus, a catastrophe—"

It was exactly 12:42 PM. A violent explosion instantly reduced the oak table to a cloud of splinters. The maps were incinerated, and jets of flame surged up on all sides. The men gathered around the table were knocked off their feet or thrown through the open windows. Above the screams and curses Keitel, who was unharmed, was heard crying out, "Where is the Führer?" Heusinger had blacked out for several seconds; when he came to, he found himself lying on his back next to the unconscious form of the Führer. "I have to get out of here," Heusinger said to himself as he crawled painfully to the doorway and dragged himself outside. His uniform was in tatters; his face, his body, and his legs were burned, both eardrums were broken, and his right hand and arm were riddled with splinters of wood. Berger, Hitler's amanuensis, Colonel Brandt, and General Korten, chief of the Luftwaffe General Staff, were mortally wounded. General Rudolf Schmundt, Hitler's chief adjutant, had lost a leg, and would die shortly afterward. All the other officers present were more or less seriously injured, but if the bomb had exploded in the underground bunker, it is almost certain that all of them would have been killed outright. Hitler, his uniform trousers in rags, rose shakily to his feet and collapsed into the arms of the faithful Keitel. He was carried to his quarters, his wounds were dressed, and before long he was ready to change into a fresh uniform in time to receive Mussolini. Hitler had received a rude shock, but his wounds were superficial.

Stauffenberg and Haeften had reached the staff car by the time the bomb exploded. Stauffenberg saw the ambulances arrive, the corpsmen rushing toward the barracks door, and he was convinced that there could have been no survivors, that Hitler had been killed. The staff car sped off toward the first checkpoint; the guards at the barrier, who had heard the explosion, found it rather curious that Stauffenberg was leaving in such a hurry. They had already received orders to let no one out of the compound, but Stauffenberg insisted that he had his own orders and that his mission was extremely urgent. Once again Stauffenberg's self-assurance, his decorations—and his empty sleeve and his blind eye— disarmed their suspicions. The barrier was raised, and he was allowed to pass. At the last checkpoint on the perimeter of the Wolf's Lair he insisted on being allowed to speak to Captain von Mollendorf, with whom he had breakfasted a few hours before. Mollendorf was hesitant at first, then finally gave the order that Stauffenberg and Haeften be allowed to proceed. As they drove toward the landing strip, the driver of the car noticed that Haeften took the remaining packet of explosives, which Stauffenberg had left behind the back seat—and which might very well have changed the outcome of the events that followed—and threw it into the woods. At the landing strip Stauffenberg put through a call to OKH headquarters in Berlin and confirmed what Fellgiebel had already told them: The bomb had exploded, and the first stage of Operation Valkyrie should be set in motion immediately.

At one fifteen Stauffenberg and Haeften took off for Berlin. At first it was assumed that one of the construction workers from the Organisation Todt had planted the bomb, and only later was it noticed that Stauffenberg had been the only officer to leave the conference room before the explosion. The Luftwaffe was ordered, belatedly, to intercept and shoot down the Heinkel III. Himmler had summoned a team of SD investigators to the Wolf's Lair and ordered Stauffenberg's arrest as soon as he touched down. Fellgiebel had succeeded in cutting off all communication for almost an hour, but as soon as Hitler demanded to be put through to Berlin, Fellgiebel was forced to comply. Stauffenberg's flight back to Berlin was uneventful· the plane landed at Rangsdorf airfield at 3:30 PM.

Berlin

General Olbricht and General Beck were waiting for Stauffenberg's return at the building on the Bendlerstrasse that housed the Defense Ministry and OKH headquarters in Berlin. The telephone rang shortly after 1:00 PM, and General Fellgiebel's voice came over the wire. "The bomb has exploded. Hitler is dead." This was the message they had hoped for. Olbricht reported to the office of General Friedrich Fromm, his commanding officer, and informed him that the Führer had been assassinated and that the Valkyrie plan should be put into effect.

"Who told you all this?" Fromm asked.

"Fellgiebel."

But Fromm refused to proclaim martial law on the strength of a single uncorroborated report. He put through a call to Rastenburg; the central switchboard was working by now, and Keitel answered the call. Fromm told him of the rumors that were circulating in Berlin.

"Is Hitler really dead?" he asked.

"The Führer is alive," Keitel replied complacently, "barely wounded at all. In fact, he is going to be receiving Mussolini this afternoon."

Keitel also had a question for Fromm: "Where is Stauffenberg?"

"He hasn't come back yet."

Olbricht suggested to Beck that they begin according to plan by contacting Count Wolf von Helldorf, the Berlin prefect of police. Helldorf was deeply distressed: The only "plan" that Olbricht's staff had supplied him with was an outdated map that had been drawn up in 1942, even though many of the public buildings marked on the map had been destroyed by Allied bombs and many government offices had been evacuated from Berlin. No attempt had been made to estimate the strength of the SS garrison or even their deployment throughout the city. No code had been agreed upon, no arrangements had been made for transportation—even for the conspirators in Berlin itself, most of whom did not even have their own cars and would have to ride the subways or the city buses if they wanted to transmit orders or simply keep track of what the others were up to. They had not taken the possibility into account that Hitler might escape an assassination attempt unharmed or merely wounded; now the glaring defects in the Valkyrie plan were becoming all too apparent.

Beck prudently ordered Olbricht to inform Helldorf at police headquarters that there was still some doubt that Hitler had actually been killed. This was too much for Olbricht—"Keitel's lying!" he shouted. In any case it was decided to do nothing further until Stauffenberg had returned from Rastenburg.

As soon as Stauffenberg's plane landed at Rangsdorf field, he called the Bendlerstrasse, where all the officers of the general staff who had thrown in their lot with the conspiracy were beginning to gather. The duty officer who took the call was surprised to hear him announce himself as "General von Stauffenberg," and at the end of their brief conversation he asked if Stauffenberg was to be congratulated on his promotion. "Yes," came the reply, "I became a general today."

It was after four o'clock when Stauffenberg finally arrived at the Bendlerstrasse, and he was astonished to discover that the others had essentially postponed the coup until after his arrival; three hours had been lost, even though it had been decided that they would have to execute the Valkyrie plan immediately before the Waffen SS units in Berlin could retaliate. In fact it would not be long before the radio announced the failure of the assassination attempt. Stauffenberg was unable to conceal his fury; he began to rage: "They're lying! Keitel's lying! Hitler is dead!"

But Stauffenberg was charged with a double responsibility—not just of delivering the bomb to the Wolf's Lair but of coordinating military operations in Berlin as well—and clearly this had been a serious blunder. Whether Hitler was alive or dead, the explosion had left the conspirators with no hope of retreat. The most elementary logic would have dictated that instead of awaiting Stauffenberg's return, the staff officers at the Bendlerstrasse should have acted immediately, to take full advantage of the element of surprise, which—now more than ever, since Hitler had survived the blast—was clearly essential to the success of their enterprise.

Frau Gertraud Junge, the only one of Hitler's secretaries who is still alive, has provided us with the sequel to Stauffenberg's flight from the Wolf's Lair. Now in her sixties, Frau Junge is still an attractive woman; forty years ago she was the embodiment of "Aryan womanhood"—tall, thin, and graceful, with fair skin and blue eyes. When she was twenty, she married one of Hitler's aides; her husband was killed on the Russian front, and today she lives alone in a Munich suburb that was once much favored by painters, poets, and even a few revolutionaries—including Hitler and Lenin in their early years. Frau Junge spoke calmly, almost with detachment, of the events of July 20, 1944:

"That morning after breakfast I wrote a letter to a friend, and then I went out to meet my colleague Gerda Christian. We took our bicycles and went swimming in a small lake in the forbidden zone. We were quite casual about this, since there had never been an air raid or even an alert, even though the Russians and the Americans both knew perfectly well where the Führer's GHQ was located. This always puzzled us, and to this day I've never understood why this was so. We returned to GHQ before noon, since sometimes the Führer would have something for one or the other of us to do, and Gerda and I were both on duty that day. Frau Johanna Wolf, the senior secretary, and Frau Christa Schröder were taking the day off, since they had been on call during the night of the nineteenth and the early morning of the twentieth. When he was at the Wolf's Lair, the Führer liked to chat with his secretaries and his little 'circle of intimates,' often until two o'clock in the morning. 'I've had enough,' he used to say, 'of listening to people who only want to talk about the war and politics.' The conversation was informal; he reminisced about his youth and happier days, and he particularly loved to talk about his dogs.

"When we approached the bunker and the barracks, we realized that the conference was still going on. All the cars were still parked next to the barracks, which was often used to house guests who arrived unexpectedly or in great numbers. Everything was quiet. We went back to our rooms, and I had just started a letter to my husband at the front when I heard a terrible explosion. Still, that didn't really frighten me, since a stag or a roebuck would sometimes set off a land mine in the forest. Sometimes they tested experimental weapons there as well. But a few moments later I heard someone shouting hysterically for a doctor, and I ran out toward the spot where the sound of the explosion had come from. I took a little path through the woods that led to the bunker, and suddenly, just before I reached the barracks, I ran into two officers—Generals Jodl and Walzenecker, I think it was. They were bleeding and their clothes were torn. The other secretaries had caught up with me by now, but we weren't allowed to come any closer.

"By now we understood that something very serious had happened. Major Otto Günsche, one of Hitler's aides, who had been a witness at our wedding, was the first one to explain to us what had happened: 'You mustn't be alarmed. A bomb has gone off. The Führer is unharmed. You will be able to go and see him, and carry on with your work later today, since he's already returned to his bunker.' We still weren't allowed to go near the site of the explosion, so we went back to join the Führer, who was in the anteroom of the bunker, with Martin Bormann, I think, at his side. The Führer looked very strange. His hair was standing on end, like quills on a hedgehog, and his clothes were in tatters. But in spite of all that he was ecstatic—after all, hadn't he survived? 'It was Providence that spared me. This proves that I'm on the right track. I feel that this is the confirmation of all my work.' Later I thought to myself, What a shame that they failed! Perhaps the fate of Germany wouldn't have been so terrible, and Hitler himself would be remembered by history as a victim rather than an archcriminal.

"As for the assassination attempt itself, it was thought at first that the culprit was one of the laborers who had been working around the barracks, that one of them had brought in the explosives and planted them under the floor. Hitler pointed out once again how Providence had spared his life, since if he had ordered the conference to be held in the bunker, he would already have left this world behind."

There has been some controversy surrounding this point which Frau Junge has helped to clarify. A number of writers have asserted that it was quite unusual for the daily conference to be held in the barracks, as it was on that day, rather than in the bunker, so that the day's routine business could be cleared up before Mussolini arrived in the early afternoon. Certain writers have even claimed that the daily conferences were never held in the barracks. However, Frau Junge was quite clear on this point: "They were indeed held there on several occasions, but Stauffenberg, who attended very rarely, couldn't have known that the conference would not take place in the bunker. . . .

"Hitler was still with us in the anteroom when Heinz Linge, his valet, came looking for him. 'My Führer, you should change. The Duce will be here at three o'clock.' 'You're right,' Hitler replied, and he went off to his quarters. That evening, when Gerda Christian and I were on duty, he told us how he had sent his shredded trousers off to Eva Braun, so she would be quite convinced that his life had been spared in spite of the violence of the blast. He was particularly energetic that evening, and we got the impression that his adventure had been quite invigorating. He was like quicksilver! Even though he was so overburdened with problems at that time, the effects of his unexpected escape from death were entirely beneficial. Before Mussolini left the Wolf's Lair, Hitler showed him the ruins of the barracks and said, "You see, there's nothing left of it, and yet I got out without a scratch.'

"In fact, he had injured his shoulder, and he thrust his right hand between the buttons of his tunic, like Napoleon. Curiously enough, it was while he was giving Mussolini a detailed recital of the day's events that it was realized that the only person who was missing at the time of the explosion was Stauffenberg, who had left the barracks a few minutes earlier to make a telephone call. In his book, which was published just after his death, Heinz Linge claims that his master had hit on Stauffenberg immediately, thanks to his extraordinary intuition, even before the idea had crossed the minds of the investigators. I don't believe that at all, since right after the explosion we spoke with one of Hitler's orderlies, a thin young man called Mondel, who was madly proud to have actually witnessed what had just occurred. He had been present when the Führer remarked, 'Stauffenberg was lucky. He was the only one who wasn't in there.' This reminded them of the telephone call he was supposed to have made, and they asked the switchboard operator if he had seen Stauffenberg. 'He came in here, as a matter of fact,' was the answer, 'and he went right out again.'

"This put things in an entirely different light, and their suspicions immediately fell on Stauffenberg, whereas until then everyone was convinced that it must have been one of the laborers working around the barracks. Everything fell into place very quickly after that, and by that evening, when Hitler recorded his radio address, he knew that a clique of army officers had been responsible.

"We learned that Stauffenberg had rushed off to find General Erich Fellgiebel and then waited in the telecommunications center until the bomb exploded. He got into his car right away and drove off to the landing strip. When he drove past the barracks he could see that the building had been utterly destroyed and that lifeless bodies were strewn on the ground around it, so he might well have supposed that his mission had been entirely successful."

2.

July 20, 1944: Paris

In Paris, as in Prussia, the air was heavy and humid, and the sky stormy on the night of July 19. By morning the summer heat had already become unbearable. At the Hôtel Majestic on the avenue Kléber the administrative machinery of the German military government was running smoothly. The conspirators in Paris had decided not to communicate with one another, and there was nothing for them to do but wait. General Karl Heinrich von Stülpnagel, military governor of Occupied France, was under tremendous nervous strain, though he was at great pains to conceal it. He joined a small group of fellow officers for lunch at the nearby Hôtel Raphaël, as he did every day, but his companions noticed that he seemed abnormally preoccupied. Usually a brilliant conversationalist, today he was taciturn and remote; he glanced at his wristwatch frequently. At two o'clock he excused himself, explaining that he had an urgent matter to attend to. He walked up to the terrace on the hotel roof and began to pace back and forth, his eyes fixed on the pavement. He caught sight of Professor Wilhelm Weniger, author of *Goethe and the Generals,* and greeted him with particular warmth. Weniger would never see him again.

Born in 1886, Karl Heinrich von Stülpnagel finished the First World War as a captain on the Imperial General Staff. He was promoted rapidly during the Weimar years, and on February 3, 1938, at the age of fifty-two, he was appointed to the post of deputy quartermaster general, then quartermaster general—one of the most prestigious positions on the staff of the Army High Command, the topmost rung of the military hierarchy.[1] In 1939 he sided with a predominantly Prussian faction among the generals (he himself was a Hessian, from Darmstadt) who were firmly opposed to an attack on the West. He favored a diplomatic solution to the "Polish question," which would mean that Germany

---

1. Unlike his American or British namesake, the quartermaster general *(Oberquartiermeister I)* of the German army was largely responsible for the overall strategic and operational planning of a campaign, not just transport and supply. [Tr.]

would have to reach some sort of an understanding with the French and the British, and he considered Hitler irresponsible and fully capable of the worst excesses.

Stülpnagel was one of those rare individuals who are able to reconcile great erudition with an agile and supple intellect. He discharged his duties as military governor of Occupied France with the greatest possible restraint for the most part—though the placards posted in the streets of Paris announcing the execution of hostages rounded up by the Gestapo bore his signature. His secretary, Countess Podewils, recalls that he lived modestly and discreetly; he never attended the banquets and fashionable receptions arranged by upper-crust Parisian collaborationists. He preferred the officers' mess at the Hôtel Raphaël, where he dined frequently with his friend Ernst Jünger, an officer on his personal staff who was in close touch with many of the conspirators but was not directly involved in their undertaking.

Born in Heidelberg in 1895, Jünger had served in the French Foreign Legion as well as the Imperial Army; he was a much decorated combat soldier during the First World War and one of the few major writers of the postwar period tolerated by the Nazi regime, primarily because he wrote his early novels, *The Storm of Steel* (1920) and *Fire and Blood* (1925), as a sort of Nietzschean defense of the nobility of warfare. (Today Jünger remains a committed writer, affirming the rights of the individual against the encroachments of a mechanized society in such novels as *The Glass Bees* [1961], and a passionate spokesman for the ecology movement.) Stülpnagel and Jünger's favorite topics of conversation were two subjects in which both men were keenly interested—botany and Byzantine history.

Stülpnagel was born into the hereditary officer caste—he was nicknamed "the Blond" to distinguish him from several of his relatives who were also called General von Stülpnagel—but he valued his friends and associates for their intellectual attainments rather than their military prowess. More of a scholar than a warrior by temperament, he preferred the company of philosophers and mathematicians. For all that, though, he was still a general who knew how to command, a diplomat who knew how to negotiate, and a political pragmatist who had never lost sight of the reality of Nazi Germany.

Now, in July 1944, Jünger noted that "he seems tired; one of his habitual gestures—he repeatedly presses his right hand against the small of his back, as if to stiffen his spine or thrust out his chest—reveals the sort of anxiety that has taken hold of him, and this can be read clearly in his face."

There were times when Stülpnagel became skeptical and disillusioned and decided to withdraw his support from a venture that seemed
so hopeless. Then it was only the energetic efforts of Lieutenant Colonel
Cäsar von Hofacker, Stauffenberg's cousin, that won him back to the
conspiracy. Hofacker was the perfect type of the Swabian gentleman[2]—
energetic, cultivated, passionately devoted to the ideal of justice—and
a courageous pilot as well, the only officer of the Luftwaffe who was
to take an active part in the conspiracy. Born in Württemberg in 1896,
Hofacker had served in civilian life as general counsel to Thyssen's steel
manufacturers' combine. Like his cousin Stauffenberg in Berlin, he was
the guiding spirit of the Valkyrie conspiracy in Paris. On July 19 he
had told Stülpnagel, "There is only one chance in ten that we will succeed, but we must still go through with it. We can't allow ourselves to
be deferred by the thought that we may be fulfilling our oath on the
scaffold, for if we fail, we won't escape the hangman."

By three o'clock on the afternoon of July 20 the conspirators on
Stülpnagel's staff were almost in despair. At four o'clock Baron von
Teuchert, a civilian adviser to the military government and one of the
first to be won over to their cause, was scheduled to confer with a group
of officials who were responsible for the welfare of French refugees.
The meeting had scarcely begun when he was called out again: Hofacker
was standing in the corridor, his eyes shining; his voice trembled with
emotion. "Hitler is dead. The explosion was frightful." He had just
gotten a telephone call from Stauffenberg, who supplied no other details.
Teuchert clasped both Hofacker's hands in his, then hurried off to find
Walter von Bargatzki, another of the conspirators, to pass on Stauffenberg's message. On the way he encountered a civilian who greeted him
with the Nazi salute and a punctilious "Heil Hitler!" Teuchert simply
burst out laughing. The civilian was dumbstruck, and he naturally assumed that Teuchert had taken leave of his senses.

It was not until a short time later that Stülpnagel received official
confirmation from Berlin—the two-word message "Exercise completed,"
the signal that Stauffenberg's mission had been successful. The moment
had finally arrived to put the Valkyrie plan into effect in France, and
within minutes the anteroom of Stülpnagel's office was filled with expec-
tant officers and officials. Hofacker was the first to arrive, since he intended to present his credentials in Vichy the next day as the ambassador

---

2. Swabia is a region of southwestern Germany with strong literary and cultural traditions; its inhabitants, rather like the Scots, have the reputation of being industrious, philo-
sophical, and extremely tenacious of purpose. Several other officers who were associated
with the July conspiracy were Swabians, including Rommel and Hans Speidel. [Tr.]

of the new government of Germany, and time was already pressing. Stülpnagel telephoned his orderly officer, who passed on his urgent summons to Colonel von Linstow, his chief of staff, General Oberhauser, chief signals officer, and Dr. Michel, chief of the military administration. When they arrived, Stülpnagel simply repeated the message—"Exercise completed"—and they set off immediately on their various missions. The telephone had not stopped ringing. Stülpnagel sent an urgent summons to General von Boineburg-Langsfeld, commander of the Greater Paris military district, whose cooperation would be critical to the success of the Valkyrie plan.

Countess Podewils was astonished by all this activity; she knew nothing of the conspiracy, and the general was reluctant to enlighten her for fear of compromising her. After his visitors had been shown into the inner office, he appeared in the doorway to offer her a word of explanation, plausible if untrue: "Gauleiter Sauckel's [3] been making trouble for us again—he wants this year's class of French conscripts called up for labor service immediately. Apparently he has no idea of what's been happening in Normandy."

Stülpnagel had just been in touch with the Bendlerstrasse group and given his personal assurances to General Beck. Now he stood behind his desk and addressed his visitors: "There has been a coup d'état, an attempt on the Führer's life. The SS and SD men in Paris will have to be arrested. Do not hesitate to use force if they resist." General von Boineburg came to attention and clicked his heels. Stülpnagel spread out a map showing the current dispositions of SS detachments and SD posts in Paris. "Is that quite clear?"

"Perfectly clear," Boineburg replied, and the revolution, set in motion from above, was under way.

At about 6:00 PM, when he was finally alone in his office, Stülpnagel received a call on the direct line to the chief signal officer. General Fromm, Stauffenberg's commanding officer, had put through the call, but a moment later Stülpnagel found himself speaking to General Beck once again.

"Stülpnagel, are you aware of what's happened in the last few hours?"

"Yes."

3. Fritz Sauckel, Nazi gauleiter of Thuringia and Hitler's "Plenipotentiary General for the Allocation of Labor"—i.e., the chief organizer of forced-labor drafts throughout occupied Europe. The Allies had launched a major offensive in Normandy just three days earlier, on the seventeenth, and a follow-up attack was expected imminently. [Tr.]

"In that case I must ask you if you are still with us."

"General, I await only the opportunity," Stülpnagel replied unhesitatingly.

"The blow has been struck, but we still don't have any exact information on the outcome. . . . Are you still with us, no matter what comes of it?"

"Yes, I've ordered the arrest of all the SS officers and SD men in Paris. We can rely on our troops here, as well as their commanding officers."

Apparently reassured by this, Beck added, "In any event, the die is cast. It's impossible to turn back now."

"I'm with you," Stülpnagel repeated, but Beck had another critical matter to take up with him. "What will Kluge do?"

Stülpnagel advised Beck to speak to Kluge himself and put the question to him directly.

Field Marshal Günther Hans von Kluge had replaced Rundstedt as chief of Western Army Command at the beginning of July; since July 17 he had also assumed command of Rommel's Army Group B in Normandy. Nicknamed *der kluge Hans* ("Clever Hans"),[4] Kluge was, in 1944, one of the army's most popular commanders, along with Rommel, Rundstedt, and Manstein. He had been in touch with the military opposition since 1942, but he had never committed himself wholeheartedly. Though he was a brave soldier and an exceptionally able tactician, he suffered from a fundamental weakness of character that made him very susceptible, easily influenced. In addition, he felt a personal sense of obligation to the Führer, who had loaded him down with honors and decorations; moreover, Kluge, like a number of other commanders, had been granted a special stipend of 250,000 Deutschmarks.

On July 9 Colonel von Hofacker was dispatched from Paris as Stülpnagel's emissary to army group headquarters at La Roche–Guyon, where Rommel welcomed him with open arms while Kluge, still temporizing, did not receive him at all. And on July 17 Rommel's staff car was strafed by British planes on a back road in Normandy. Critically wounded, Rommel was lost both to the army and the conspiracy, and, as far as the conspirators were concerned, Kluge remained an unknown quantity.

4. A punning allusion to Clever Hans, the famous performing stallion who appeared to spell out messages and do simple arithmetic by tapping with his front hoof, actually in response to subtle, perhaps involuntary cues from his master. [Tr.]

Shortly after his conversation with Beck, Stülpnagel received a message from General Speidel, formerly Rommel's and now Kluge's ADC at La Roche–Guyon: "The field marshal requests that you and your chief of staff report to his headquarters no later than 2000 hours."

"Very well," replied Stülpnagel. "I'll be there."

General Boineburg had already prepared for his night's work by putting the 1st Guards Regiment on full alert, since he felt that the regiment's commanding officer, Lieutenant Colonel von Kraewell, could be trusted implicitly. As usual in this revolution of administrators and desk officers, the order was relayed by telephone from the Hôtel Majestic to the regiment's bivouac at the École Militaire. While Boineburg was shown his way back to his own command post at the Hôtel Meurice on the rue de Rivoli, Countess Podewils—by now a knowing and active participant in the conspiracy—put through a call to Lieutenant Colonel von Kraewell requesting him to report to command headquarters. He had not been told that his regiment had been selected to disarm and arrest the SS officers and SD agents in Paris.

The routine business of the military governor's staff was over for the day; the offices and corridors of the Hôtel Majestic were slowly emptying out. Not a word of the portentous events of the afternoon had left Stülpnagel's inner office, and the conspirators themselves kept the strictest silence. By 7:00 PM the Majestic was almost deserted, though several sections of the governor's staff still had a full night's work ahead of them. Their first priority was to convene a kind of drumhead war-crimes tribunal—the crimes and atrocities committed by the SD and the Gestapo were regarded as an unforgivable affront to the honor of the army and the German nation; Stülpnagel was determined to mete out swift and certain justice.

Before she left for the day, Countess Podewils had arranged for two cars to be brought around, and at 7:20 PM the sentries presented arms as Stülpnagel and three other officers appeared in the massive doorway of the Majestic. "La Roche–Guyon," Stülpnagel called out to the drivers. In a short while his troops in Paris would be moving into action, but he still had no clear idea of what Kluge's intentions were or whether the commander in chief of the land forces on the western front would finally rally to the conspiracy.

The original fortress of La Roche–Guyon dated back to the Viking invasion of Normandy, and it later guarded the frontiers of the Norman dukes against the kings of France. In 1943 Ernst Jünger visited the castle with Dr. Baumgart, Stülpnagel's orderly officer, and was enchanted. Consequently, in the spring of 1944, when Rommel was searching for a site for his army group headquarters in the event of an Allied landing on the Channel coast, Stülpnagel passed on the recommendation. With Rommel out of action, Kluge had arrived on July 18 to assume his command.

On the afternoon of the twentieth, Kluge returned from a tour of the front, dusty and dripping with sweat. He was told that his chief of staff, General Blumentritt, had telephoned from Army Group B headquarters in Saint-Germain about two thirty; apparently there had been an attempt on the Führer's life. "Nothing else?" Kluge replied impassively. "Thank you." As soon as he was called upon to make a decision that involved some personal risk, Kluge began to temporize. Later that afternoon he received a call from Berlin. It was Fromm, calling for General Beck, who had decided to take Stülpnagel's advice and confront Kluge directly. Beck outlined the measures that had already been taken in Berlin and throughout the territories of the Reich. Kluge merely took note of all this, without volunteering any opinion, and Beck was compelled to press the point: "Kluge, listen to me—it's essential that you support the operation that's been launched in Berlin." But first Kluge insisted on an answer to the critical question, "Is Hitler dead?" At that moment a staff officer appeared in his office with the text of a communiqué that had been broadcast over Radio Berlin at six thirty, announcing that an attempt had been made on the Führer's life but that he had survived unscathed.

Kluge glanced through the communiqué, again with no visible display of emotion, then returned to his conversation with Beck. "What is the exact situation at GHQ [Rastenburg] right now?"

"That," Beck replied, "will be of little consequence the moment we decide to take action. I'm going to put the question to you in no uncertain terms, Kluge: Do you approve of what we're doing here and do you agree to be guided by me?" Again Kluge managed to evade the question by bringing up the matter of the communiqué, and Beck continued to press for a direct answer: "So that there cannot possibly be any doubt, let me remind you of our previous conversations and of our mutual understanding, and let me ask you again if I have your unconditional support?"

Kluge had not forgotten about these conversations, but the failure of the attempt on Hitler's life had considerably changed the situation. "I should consult with my staff," Kluge finally announced. "I'll call you back in half an hour."

In fact Kluge would not speak to General Beck again; a few moments later he received another call, from General von Falkenhausen, who had been relieved of his post as military governor of Belgium and Northern France a few days earlier at the insistence of Martin Bormann and replaced by a civilian Nazi gauleiter. However, he was allowed to remain at his headquarters outside Brussels, and several hours earlier, at six o'clock, he too had been contacted by General Beck. "I couldn't hear very well, but at least I understood that the Führer is dead and all the other reports are false. Then we were cut off." Kluge replied that he did not believe that Hitler had been killed, but in fact the emotional shock of the Radio Berlin broadcast had only heightened his sense of uncertainty and indecision. Between 7:00 and 8:00 PM he received a telegram from Marshall von Witzleben in Berlin: "The Führer is dead. Carry out your instructions as planned." It was signed "Supreme Commander of the Wehrmacht."

At that moment there was no more reason to hesitate. The radio broadcast had undoubtedly been nothing more than one of Goebbels' tricks. Now Kluge was finally prepared to throw in his lot with the conspirators and to put himself completely at Beck's disposal.

The telephone rang once more. His aide Colonel Zimmermann informed him that a second telegram, signed by Marshal Keitel, had just arrived. "Hitler is not dead. He's even had a conference with Mussolini just now." Kluge reversed his tack once again, remarking to Blumentritt that there was nothing to do but wait. "Try and find out what's true and what's not. Until then we'll have to carry on as though nothing had happened." Blumentritt's initial inquiries failed to bring in any more information, and Kluge decided to put through a call to Camp Anna at Mauersee in Masuria, not far from Rastenburg, OKH headquarters for the eastern front. Blumentritt managed to get through to General Stieff, chief of the organizational section of OKH and one of the prime movers of the conspiracy. Still, Stieff was too much of a soldier to resort to tactical deception or bold improvisation; he simply spoke the truth without regard to the consequences: "Hitler is not dead—his wounds are very superficial." Stieff even went on to tell Kluge that there could be no possible doubt of this; at that very moment there were officers with him who had actually seen Hitler that afternoon, after the explosion. It appeared that Goebbels' radio broadcast had told the truth.

After his conversation with Stieff, Kluge executed his final about-face. Marshal von Witzleben's blunt proclamation had momentarily brought him around to the conspiracy, but after being confronted with

Stieff's equally blunt and apparently more accurate testimony, he prudently stepped back into the ranks. "Well, then," he observed to his aides with a shrug of his shoulders, apparently both relieved and disappointed at the way events had worked themselves out, "the plot has failed." Speidel would take charge of all the routine business of the army group headquarters that evening.

"Starting with the summer of '43," Kluge told Blumentritt, "Beck and Witzleben sent emissaries to me in Smolensk. After I'd given some thought to the matter, I broke off all discussions with them. Then they went to see Guderian and he showed them to the door. We should have reported this to the appropriate authorities, of course, but what honorable man would do such a thing?"

Stülpnagel and his companions were still on the road to La Roche–Guyon. The governor was counting heavily on Hofacker's eloquence and dash to win over the wavering field marshal, whether Hitler was dead or not. Stülpnagel had already given the signal for the uprising to begin in France, but it would have to be Kluge, the commander in chief on the western front, who would provide the crucial momentum. Colonel von Linstow had remained in Paris to supervise the roundup of the Nazi loyalists; the entire Greater Paris military district had been put on full alert, and the telephone exchange at its headquarters in the Hôtel Meurice was overwhelmed with calls. General von Boineburg had decided to wait until nightfall, though Stülpnagel had urged him to act immediately. "This way," Boineburg pointed out, "we won't have to gratify the Parisians with the spectacle of Germans arresting their fellow countrymen. Besides, it will be better to move against the SS and the SD when they're concentrated in their barracks—we can just throw out our nets and haul them in."

At dusk the second battalion of the 1st Guards Regiment set out from the École Militaire. Officers and platoon leaders had already carried out a full-scale rehearsal of the operation, all possible contingencies had been taken into account, and the chances for success seemed excellent.

What appeared to be no more than a routine troop movement passed almost unnoticed in a city that was preoccupied with staying alive as best it could. Shortages and requisitions were becoming increasingly severe: Since gasoline was no longer available, the tourist buses had been outfitted with charcoal-burning boilers—*gazogènes*. An adult's daily ration was down to one thousand calories. The prefect of police announced that conscripted laborers would be allotted an additional eighty grams of fat a day, but he had also ordered the arrest of a number of bakers accused of sequestering flour and selling bread on the black market. Draconian penalties were enforced against retailers who tried to obstruct the fair distribution of fruits and vegetables (notably rutabagas). Finally, the prefect declared that it was imperative that everyone whose presence was no longer actually necessary—particularly women and children—leave the city as quickly as possible because of the dangers of air raids and malnutrition. They were expected to leave "either by utilizing whatever means of transportation may still be in operation or that they themselves can provide, including bicycles, or on foot."

On July 20 the Parisian press announced that electricity would be severely restricted between July 23 and 30—there would be no household current before 11:00 PM, the *métro* would not run on Sundays, and all theaters and cinemas would be closed. They also informed their readers that "the slower pace of urban life due to the electricity shortage has revealed how much the economic life of the city is dependent on artificial expedients. . . . A Parisian, M. Jacques Arthuys, has devised a method whereby sunlight may be collected on the roof of a building and reflected by a system of mirrors from room to room, even, if you wish, to the basement, and diffused by means of lenses throughout every room." For the moment, at least, a few cabarets, patronized mainly by well-connected collaborators and German officers, were still offering first-class entertainment—the great jazz guitarist Django Reinhardt at La Roulotte on the place Pigalle, the popular torch singer Leo Marjane at Le Beaulieu, who was said to be very susceptible to the Aryan charms of the occupation forces. At the Elysée-Club on the rue Arsène Houssaye a whimsical young man called Yves Montand, who had recently arrived from Marseille by way of the nightclubs on the Cote d'Azur, packed the house every night with his ersatz cowboy ballads; Edith Piaf had scored another triumph at the Salle Pleyel; the film *The Murderer Lives at Number 21* was setting new box-office records; and finally, of course, there was the war. . . .

Paris Soir (now merely another conduit of Goebbels' Propaganda Ministry) dutifully reported the military communiqués from both fronts. "After an intense aerial bombardment the British Second Army launched a powerful attack to the east of the Orne . . . Hand-to-hand fighting between elements of the American First Army and German parachutists near Sainte-Croix and within two kilometers of Saint-Lô. . . . In Italy the fighting around the Mediterranean port of Livorno in Tuscany grows heavier by the hour. . . . . The American secretary of war has completed his inspection tour of the Normandy theater of operations. . . . Cardinal Spellman, archbishop of New York, was granted an audience with the pope in Rome. . . . On the Russian front between Brody and Tarnopol, in the face of tenacious German resistance, Marshal Zhukov has thrown fresh divisions into the line. . . ."

And finally this "clarification" of the official policy toward the Jews who had been deported to Germany was provided by Herr Sundermann, vice-president of the Reich Press Chamber: "As far as the sequestration of the Jews and their integration into the European labor force is concerned, we have acted humanely. The elderly, and all other Jews who have distinguished themselves by their individual accomplishments, have been exempted from labor service. Jewish laborers are allotted the same quarters and the same rations as any other group."

Soon the capital was totally blacked out. Boineburg was preparing to spring the trap on the SD and the SS just as Stülpnagel and Hofacker arrived at LaRoche–Guyon, along with Dr. Horst, Speidel's son-in-law, and Dr. Baumgart, Stülpnagel's orderly officer. Kluge greeted them stiffly, which did not augur well for the success of their mission, though Blumentritt was cordial. Hofacker spoke first, setting out the background of the conspiracy, analyzing the reasons that had compelled the conspirators to decide on an attempt on Hitler's life. "Since the autumn of '43," he said, "I've been acting as liaison between Beck and his circle in Berlin, my cousin Stauffenberg's circle, and the movement that General Stülpnagel directed in Paris." Kluge listened unresponsively, and the air grew thick as night slowly crept into the room. "But it doesn't much matter what happens in Berlin," Hofacker said, raising his voice and staring fixedly at Kluge. "What counts are the decisions that we're about to make here in France. I appeal to you, Marshal von Kluge, to take action on behalf of our country as Rommel would have done. I spoke to him in this very place on the ninth. Free yourself from Hitler's spell and put yourself at the head of our movement in the west!"

Kluge was unmoved by this ardent call to arms. He got slowly to his feet, took a few steps, and said: "Gentlemen, the attempt on the Führer's life has failed."

Stülpnagel turned pale, then flushed. "Herr Feldmarschall, I thought that you were already aware of that."

"I did not have the slightest clue," Kluge replied coldly.

Stülpnagel felt as if he were suffocating; an abyss seemed to be opening up in front of him.

"Now, gentlemen, may I ask you to accompany me into the dining room?" Kluge suggested blandly.

Stülpnagel was overwhelmed by this show of unconcern and asked Kluge straight out if he was aware that there were many officers who had allowed themselves to become implicated in the conspiracy only because of the position Kluge had taken in the past and because of his verbal attacks on Hitler. But Kluge seemed to have put all that behind him; he ate heartily and regaled his guests with his reminiscences of the eastern front. Stülpnagel and Hofacker sat at the long, old mahogany table lit with tapers and stared down at their plates; they scarcely touched their food. Suddenly Stülpnagel looked up at Kluge: "I'd like to have a word with you in private." Puzzled, Kluge seemed to be collecting his thoughts for a moment. Then he got up and motioned Stülpnagel into a small adjoining drawing room.

Several moments later the door was thrown open and Kluge called to Blumentritt, his voice throbbing with rage: "General Oberg and the rest of the SD are going to be arrested—if they haven't been already. Stülpnagel gave the order for this before he left Paris, without consulting his superior officer—an unprecedented act of insubordination!" Stülpnagel stood by silently, his hands behind his back, while Kluge dealt the deathblow to the coup in Paris: "Telephone right away. This order must be countermanded, or I shall not be answerable for the consequences."

Blumentritt called Linstow and reported back that the operation was already under way; it was impossible to pull back. Kluge's face was crimson. "Why didn't you consult me? I wasn't able to join you—no more than Blumentritt."

This was the simple truth—Kluge and his chief of staff had not returned from their daily tour of the front until almost six o'clock. But if Stülpnagel had exceeded his authority, this was only because he intended to present Kluge with a fait accompli. He realized that he was dealing with an indecisive, faltering character, and he hoped that a bold and irreversible stroke like this would overcome Kluge's hesitation.

When Kluge bade his visitors good night at eleven o'clock, he said to Stülpnagel, "Go back to Paris and release your prisoners. You alone must bear the responsibility for what you've done."

At this Stülpnagel recovered his nerve: "Quite impossible! We can't turn back. What's done is done."

Hofacker tried to intercede for his commander: "Herr Feldmarschall, your honor is at stake. The honor of the entire army and the destiny of millions of men are in your hands."

"Yes," Kluge's voice trailed off tonelessly. "If only the swine were dead." He turned to Stülpnagel once more. "Consider yourself relieved of duty.

"We have to do something to help him," Blumentritt muttered to his chief, and Kluge accompanied Stülpnagel to the doorway and dismissed him with this advice: "Get into civilian clothes and disappear." This was not the right sort of remark to make to a great captain like Stülpnagel. As he was about to get into his staff car, he turned and raised his right hand to the visor of his cap and snapped a military salute to his commander in chief. This was the first time the two men had parted without shaking hands.

At 10:30 PM the shock troops of the 1st Guards Regiment were deployed around the Gestapo barracks. The directorate of the Nazi terror in Paris was about to be subdued by stealth and force of arms, and they would offer no more resistance than most of their helpless victims had offered them. The Gestapo chiefs had complacently declined to take any special security precautions after the news of the assassination attempt reached them, and by midnight every Gestapo agent in Paris had been swept up in General Boineburg's dragnet.

Brigadier General Brehmer commanded the troops who were ordered to arrest the ranking officers of the SS. To avoid attracting too much attention from the population, Brehmer decided not to interfere with normal civilian traffic. General Boineburg had arrived to supervise the operation; he found Brehmer's battalion drawn up on the narrow drive that ran along the avenue Foch, not far from the newly constructed buildings on the boulevard Lannes, where the Gestapo was billeted. The windows were brilliantly lit, and it was apparent that all was calm within; the sentries outside—most of them volunteers from the occupied countries in the east—were pacing through their normal rounds. The troops of the 1st Guards Regiment did not seem to be surprised by the fact that they were about to move against the Gestapo. "We're finally going to break those filthy bastards' balls for them" was the prevailing sentiment in the ranks. Whistles shrilled out in the darkness; the trucks and scout cars carrying the assault troops moved to their assigned assembly points. Another whistle blast and the troops jumped down to the pavement and followed their officers into the SS billets and police stations commandeered by the SD. In every case the surprise was total.

The troops burst in on the SS officers, revolvers in hand, and called out for them to give themselves up. The SD agents among them were searched for weapons and taken into custody. Stülpnagel had left instructions that the troops should not hesitate to use their weapons if the quarry offered resistance, and General Brehmer passed this order on to the troops, but the entire operation was carried out without a shot being fired. The prisoners climbed obediently into the waiting trucks, and by shortly after midnight twelve hundred SS men were lodged behind bars in the military prison at Fresnes—whose other inmates had been moved elsewhere to accommodate them—and in an old fort on the outskirts of the city, near Saint-Denis. A council of war would assemble at first light to determine which of the prisoners would be brought up on capital charges and, if found guilty, shot by a firing squad.

The headquarters of the Waffen SS detachments in Paris, commanded by General Oberg, was near the boulevard Lannes and the troops' assembly point on the avenue Foch. Oberg was still in his office, working in his shirt sleeves, since the night was so hot and humid. He was talking to Otto Abetz[5] on the telephone when General Brehmer burst into the room with his revolver drawn. Oberg, naturally quite indignant at this, leaped to his feet and demanded an explanation. Brehmer replied that there had been a coup d'état in Berlin and that he had come to arrest him. Oberg assumed that there had been some sort of misunderstanding that would be quickly cleared up; he followed Brehmer out of his office and ordered his guards to hand over their weapons.

The ranking officers of the SS were arrested on avenue Foch by Lieutenant Colonel von Kraewell. He ordered the SD duty officer to assemble his colleagues in one of the offices, where Kraewell's troops disarmed them one by one. However, the chief of the SD in Paris, SS General Knochen, was not among them; one of his staff called him at the nightclub where he was spending the evening, Knochen dutifully returned to his headquarters and was arrested as soon as he crossed the threshold. Knochen was taken to the Hôtel Continental on the rue Castiglione to join the other high-ranking SS prisoners.

5. Hitler's ambassador to France, whom he had charged with carrying out a program of Franco-German "cooperation."

3.

1934–1935: The Army Swears Fealty

In Berlin on the night of August 2, 1934, the generals of the Reichswehr, the officers of the general staff and of the garrisons, and all their troops were drawn up in ranks in the torchlit Königsplatz. Marshal von Hindenburg, the president of the Reich, was dead, and, by special decree of the Reich Cabinet, he would be succeeded by the Führer and chancellor of the Reich, Adolf Hitler.[1] Hitler would thus automatically assume the title of supreme commander of the armed forces as well. The newly installed supreme commander immediately arranged for a new oath of allegiance to be administered to every man in the Reichswehr:

Before God I swear absolute obedience to the Führer of the Reich and of the German people, Adolf Hitler, supreme commander of the Wehrmacht. As a brave soldier I will be prepared at all times to lay down my life for this oath.

From that moment on this oath of "absolute obedience" would become the dominant motif of the history of the military opposition, since in the future any criticism of the Führer, to say nothing of outright insubordination, could be legally construed as treason. The text was almost identical to that of the previous oath that had been administered to the Reichswehr under Hindenburg on December 2, 1931, and the generals, officers, and soldiers had not immediately realized that there had been two essential changes—they had solemnly raised their right hands (the officers grasping the flag in their left hands) and sworn personal fealty to Adolf Hitler; the Hindenburg oath had simply bound them "to serve the people and the Fatherland honorably and faithfully."

During the period of national despair that followed the defeat of 1918, Marshal von Hindenburg continued to enjoy considerable prestige

---

1. The Weimar constitution provided that a president who died in office would be provisionally succeeded by the president of the Supreme Court until new elections could be held, and theoretically the cabinet did not have the authority to issue such a decree; however, this technical oversight was universally ignored, and Hitler's accession was overwhelmingly endorsed by the German people in a plebiscite on August 19.

as the victor of Tannenberg,[2] the embodiment of the great traditions of the Imperial Army, and even became a sort of remote but benevolent father figure for the German people (in much the same way that the French people looked to Marshal Pétain to restore the national honor after the fall of France in 1940). In 1925, when Hindenburg was elected to his first term as Reichspresident, he had evinced the greatest respect for the Weimar constitution. Yet in 1932 he allowed Franz von Papen to convince him that he should invite Hitler into the government. Baron Kurt von Hammerstein, commander in chief of the Reichswehr, had objected: "You're not going to make that fellow, that corporal, your chancellor?" to which Hindenburg replied angrily, "Don't meddle in politics—you should be more concerned with looking after your army and making sure they make a better showing in the next maneuver!"

On February 1, 1934, Hammerstein was replaced by General von Fritsch. On June 30 Hitler's former comrade-in-arms Ernst Röhm, chief of the SA, and General von Sleicher, among many others, were shot down by SS gunmen in the bloody purge of old enemies and inconvenient friends that became known as "the Night of the Long Knives."[3] (We asked Louis François-Poncet, the son of Ambassador André François-Poncet, how many men had dared to stand up to Hitler's terrible rages. François-Poncet replied that to his knowledge only four had ever allowed themselves to become embroiled in violent arguments with Hitler: Ernst Röhm, the veteran Nazi politico Gregor Strasser, Strasser's younger brother Otto, and his own father, the French ambassador. The first two paid for their imprudence with their lives in 1934; Otto Strasser fled the country in 1933. But Ambassador François-Poncet was a privileged foreign guest, and his courage seems to have won him Hitler's respect, since according to the records of Hitler's "table talk" kept by Martin Bormann, Hitler frequently complained that Germany did not have any diplomats of his caliber.) On July 30 Hindenburg sent off a congratulatory telegram to Hitler: "I would like to state that, according to the reports I have received, by your decisive and courageous personal

2. Decisive battle in August 1914 in which German forces commanded by Hindenburg and Ludendorff repulsed an attempted Russian invasion of East Prussia [Tr.]

3. Steicher, Hitler's predecessor as chancellor, had actively opposed Hitler's assumption of "emergency powers" in 1933. Sleicher and Röhm were said to be plotting an insurrection, which served as the official pretext for the purge. In fact, Hitler regarded Röhm as a potential rival, and Röhm's radical political opinions were deeply distrusted by the general staff, who persuaded Hitler to liquidate Röhm and effectively disband his private army of storm troopers. [Tr.]

intervention you have snuffed out the last sparks of treason and delivered the German people from a grave peril. I wish to express my most profound gratitude."

What sort of man was Hindenburg? To all appearances he was a typical representative of the generation that had grown to adulthood under Wilhelm I, the first emperor of the unified German Reich. He read the Bible every evening, lived frugally, and hated luxury and ostentation. In fact, he was something of a miser. (He agreed to announce his candidacy in 1925 only after he was assured that he could continue to draw his marshal's pension while serving as Reichspresident.) After the war he received an estate at Neudeck in East Prussia as a gift of the nation, which made him a Junker in his own right, complete with all the prejudices of the East Prussian squirearchy. What sort of pressures, then, must have been brought to bear on him before he would send such an effusive message to Hitler, a man whom he deeply distrusted and even despised? André François-Poncet, the French ambassador to Berlin during the thirties, has attempted to provide an answer to this question in his memoirs:

"Given the marshal's personal feelings and the situation of his protégé Papen—who had been compromised by his dealings with some of those who had been shot by the Gestapo and thus had only narrowly escaped the same fate—Hindenburg could not have written or signed such a telegram of his own free will. The old man had certainly been intimidated and duped by the threats that had been made against his son, his secretary, Meissner, his family, and himself."

But Hindenburg, who was born in 1847, was already seventy-eight when he was elected president of the Weimar Republic and eighty when Hitler came to power. His notion of exercising supreme executive authority, at least according to popular rumor, was simply to sign every piece of paper that was set in front of him. According to one story, a cleaning woman in Hindenburg's office retrieved a scrap of paper from the floor and was about to replace it on his desk. Meissner was horrified. "Throw that in the wastebasket! Otherwise the Old Man's going to sign it into law!" Other such stories hinted rather broadly that the old marshal's mind was not as keen as it once had been. When it was proposed that Germany, like France, England, and the United States, might have her own Tomb of the Unknown Soldier, Hindenburg is supposed to have retorted, "Nonsense! In Germany we know who *all* our soldiers are!"

At any rate it seems clear that during the final critical years of the republic the Reichspresident was no more than a complaisant figurehead.

With Hitler raging unchecked, Hindenburg could only nod his approval, and those Germans who still hoped that the hero of Tannenberg would rise up and save the Reich from her greatest peril were to be cruelly disillusioned.

"The Gestapo had already shown what they were capable of," wrote Ambassador François-Poncet. "They had begun the reign of terror. All power was in their hands; from that time on the German people would live in fear, and the concentration camp, from which no one ever returned, was only the lesser of the evils that awaited them.

"The Reichswehr may have imagined that there was something to be gained from this tragic episode. In reality the policies of General von Blomberg, the minister of defense, were to prove disastrous. Hitler may have offered them Röhm's head as a token of submission, but he had no real intention of submitting to the power of the Reichswehr, of becoming the docile instrument of the generals. He realized that the general staff was an enemy camp, that the generals would use him to serve their own purposes—to provide the Reich with a strong army— but they could never be won over. He knew instinctively that this clique of Junkers and conservative army officers represented a permanent threat to his authority, and he had every intention of checking them or eliminating them outright."

Early in July Hindenburg left for his estate at Neudeck, ostensibly for a brief vacation, but it was clear that the "Old Man"—*der alte Herr*— would not be returning to Berlin. Louis François-Poncet relates this story as it was told to him by his father: "At the end of July the family physician, the well-known Professor Sauerbruch, paid a call on the marshal. 'Is Friend Hein in the house yet?" the old man asked. ['Friend Hein' is the familiar name for death in German folklore.] 'No,' the professor replied, 'but he's strolling around in the garden.' " The marshal died on August 2, 1934, at nine o'clock in the morning, according to the official bulletin. "But hadn't he died earlier?" suggested André François-Poncet. "Didn't they delay the announcement for a day or two?" In fact a number of other last-minute arrangements seem to have been made in a remarkably short time, apart from the Reichswehr oath-taking ceremony. Hindenburg's death was announced at noon; at the same time it was announced that the Reich Cabinet had already enacted a decree, effective immediately, which merged the offices of Reichspresident (the chief executive of the Weimar Republic) and chancellor (the prime minister under the empire); thus Hitler would assume the powers and duties of the president, though he made it known on the following day that he would allow the title of Reichspresident (which he rejected as "too democratic") to fall into disuse. He preferred the style of *Führer und Kanzler des Deutschen Reiches.*

On August 2 Goebbels announced that no will had been found. Then, rather abruptly, on August 15 Papen brought Hitler a sealed envelope—the marshal's political testament—which Colonel Oskar von Hindenburg had stumbled upon eleven days after his father's death. The first part of the testament had been drawn up in Hannover in 1919; the second part was dated May 1, 1934, and contained a remarkable tribute to his successor:

I thank Providence that I have been permitted to live out the twilight of my life during these years in which we have once again grown strong. My chancellor, Adolf Hitler, and his movement have taken the decisive step and brought unity and internal harmony to the German people. . . . I bid farewell to my people secure in the hope that everything I desired in 1919 and was slowly brought to fruition by January 30, 1933 [when Hitler became chancellor] will continue to develop toward the ultimate goal, when our historic mission will have been fully and utterly accomplished. Inspired by my faith in the future of the Father-land, I will close my eyes peacefully for the last time.

Of course the contrast could hardly be more apparent between these effusive phrases and the pungent opinions the marshal is known to have held shortly before his death. His strong personal distaste for Hitler had made him extremely reluctant to request him to form a government in 1933, and it is inconceivable that Hindenburg—a lifelong monarchist at heart—could have confided the destiny of the German people to the man whom he customarily referred to as "that Bohemian corporal." (This was simply another instance of the old marshal's chronic mental vagueness. Hitler, of course, was an Austrian, not a Czech. Hindenburg had confused Hitler's birthplace, Branau-am-Inn, near the Bavarian border, with a different Branau, in northern Bohemia, where he had campaigned as a young officer almost seventy years before.)

"In August of 1934," Louis François-Poncet recalls, "the rumor began to spread that the testament was a forgery. The second section had supposedly been drafted by the same person who had assisted Hindenburg in composing his memoirs a short time before. The original text had expressed his regret at leaving Germany in the hands of a man who inspired such profound misgivings, gave assurances of his fidelity to his emperor, and designated Papen as the worthiest of his potential successors. The substitution of the forged testament could only have been carried off with the complicity of Colonel von Hindenburg—whose gambling debts were paid off very promptly—Meissner, and Papen himself. In addition, Colonel von Hindenburg was promoted to major general shortly afterward, Meissner threw in his lot with Hitler, and Papen emerged from limbo to become an ambassador and had all sorts of honors and attentions lavished on him by the regime." Certainly it is also a curious coincidence that the discovery of the missing testament was made public only on the day before the plebiscite in which the German people were asked to approve the assumption of the duties of the presidency by their Führer and chancellor, Adolf Hitler.

But Hitler had already secured the allegiance of the Reichswehr by a simpler stratagem, and now the generals could not defy him without forfeiting their honor as officers. Still, one of their number, General Ludwig Beck, chief of the general staff, considered to be the ablest officer in the Reichswehr, deeply resented the political ambush into which he and his fellow officers had fallen. He foresaw the consequences of Hitler's bloodless coup d'état, which had been arranged with the zealous cooperation of General von Blomberg. After the ceremony in the Königsplatz, Beck strode off through the deserted streets of the capital, remarking to a companion, "This is one of the most tragic days of my life." Though the officer corps as a whole still looked to Hitler as a guarantor of their lost prestige, Beck had little use for the Nazi ideology, still less for Hitler's obvious intentions of using the military to serve his own political designs.

General Beck was a tall, thin man with fine, straight features and an alert and remarkably benevolent expression; he was endowed with an inflexible will and an exceptionally acute intelligence. Both in appearance and temperament he seemed more like a philosopher or a distinguished scholar than a career army officer. His every word revealed his total mastery of his emotions; he always expressed himself incisively and with great subtlety and tact—one of his greatest talents was the ability to smooth over a dispute without giving offense or causing resentment on the part of the officer he had ruled against.

But this paragon of military virtue was not a Junker, or even a Prussian, by birth; he was descended from a line of Hessian army officers, though his father had been a civil engineer by profession and a businessman, the owner of an iron mine in the Rhineland. Ludwig Beck and his two brothers grew up in a beautiful house whose windows overlooked the Rhine. After finishing secondary school in Wiesbaden, he chose to follow the traditional family career of arms and served in various capacities as a general staff officer during the First World War. (In 1917 his commanding officer was General Count Friedrich von der Schulenburg, who was to be his lifelong friend and stand by his side in the conspiracy against Hitler.) After Germany's rearmament Lieutenant General Beck was appointed chief of the reorganized general staff in 1934 and promoted to the rank of colonel general *(Generaloberst)*, which prompted him to write to a friend, "I have truly been forced to accept this honor against my will. They simply want the corpse to be laid out in a handsome coffin."

The new commander in chief of the army was General Count Werner von Fritsch. Born in 1880, the same year as Beck, Fritsch was to all appearances a caricature of the haughty, "correct" Prussian general— red face, strident high-pitched voice, impeccably tailored uniform, monocle tightly screwed into one eye. A confirmed bachelor, he was rarely seen at official functions or in society drawing rooms. He seemed to prefer the company of horses to human beings and could usually be found at a horse show or the racetrack. However, this unapproachable Prussian facade concealed a lively intelligence and a much more sympathetic nature than Fritsch's misanthropic habits and prickly manner suggested.

The officer corps was confident that two such clear-sighted chieftains as Beck and Fritsch would manage somehow to keep Hitler from risking their brand-new army in any dangerous foreign adventures. The Führer was still unsure of himself in military matters; he seemed diffident and ill at ease in the presence of his generals and staff officers, who distinctly lacked the sort of tumultuous enthusiasm which his geopolitical monologues always elicited from the Nazi Party faithful. Still, Hitler had the officers in the provincial garrisons solidly behind him; rearmament had brought rapid promotions and a general increase in matériel and morale for the officers of the Reichswehr, who were for the most part ignorant of or indifferent to the larger issues and preoccupied only with their own immediate interests.

Only the officers of the Berlin garrison and the general staff itself were fully aware of Hitler's real intentions, of his program of internal and external aggression; almost all these men had served under the Kaiser and remained staunch monarchists. In Berlin, the most politically turbulent and the most cosmopolitan of German cities, the officer corps mingled with diplomats, correspondents, and other well-informed foreigners who had already penetrated the secrets of the Gestapo and the concentration camps. The camp at Oranienburg was only forty miles from Berlin, and the screams of tortured political prisoners could be heard in the Prinz Albrechtstrasse, outside Gestapo headquarters. It was in Berlin that the various opposition groups would eventually form a coalition, but so far Hitler had met with nothing but success in his rapid climb to supreme power. On March 15, 1935, Hitler reintroduced compulsory military service for all adult males. The rich industrial enclave of the Saar, under French administration since 1919, was reunited with the Fatherland as the result of an almost unanimous plebiscite.

On the evening of March 7, 1936, Hitler ordered the army into the demilitarized zone of the Rhineland. "He, did not sleep at all that night," General Heusinger recalls. "He was eaten up with worry, and if the French had made a move, he would have recalled the troops. That would have been a serious blow to his prestige."

4.

1936–1937: "They Call Him Hermann"

In that same year, 1936, a very courageous man named Carl Friedrich Goerdeler, mayor of Leipzig, openly defied the regime by protesting vigorously against the persecution of the Jews. Goerdeler has already crossed swords with Berlin in 1933, when he refused to raise the swastika flag over the Leipzig town hall. A similar controversy arose three years later, when the Nazis insisted that the city authorities remove the statue of Felix Mendelssohn from the square in front of the municipal concert hall, the Leipziger Gewandhaus, where Mendelssohn (a Jew, and thus a cultural eyesore as far as the Nazis were concerned) had been resident conductor from 1835 until his death in 1847. Goerdeler protested energetically to Berlin, and Mendelssohn was granted a reprieve. However, as soon as Goerdeler left the city to deliver a lecture in Stockholm, the Nazi deputy mayor took matters into his own hands; Goerdeler returned to find an empty pedestal in the Gewandhaus square, and once again he appealed to Berlin to have his deputy dismissed. This time his request was refused, and Goerdeler resigned and drafted his own political testament, which he confided to a trusted friend for release when Goerdeler felt the time was ripe or in the event of his "accidental death." Though Goerdeler had remained a monarchist and right-wing Nationalist throughout the Weimar years, this testament was nothing less than a manifesto calling for the restoration of party democracy.

Goerdeler was born on July 31, 1884, in Schneidemühl (now Pila in Poland), near the city of Posen (Poznán), into a family of East Prussian magistrates and civil servants. As one of six children, he was obliged to finish his studies rather hurriedly, first at the Königsberg gymnasium, then at the law faculty at Tübingen. He served as a captain on the eastern front, and after his return to civilian life decided to abandon his hopes of a political career, since he felt that there would be no place for a conservative of the old school in the Weimar Republic. However, he was impressed by President Friedrich Ebert's Social Democratic program and he went on to serve in several posts in Prussian municipal government. Ebert, who had been elected by the Reichstag in 1919, governed Germany with a firm hand. His policy was to stamp out extremism both on the right and the left; though he dealt more harshly with the Spartacist revolutionary uprising in Berlin, it was the right-wing Nationalists' unrelenting attacks on his patriotism and personal integrity that helped to bring about his death in 1925, at the age of fifty-four.

Goerdeler continued his political career, first as deputy mayor of Königsberg, then as mayor of Leipzig in 1930 and director of the government Price Bureau (a post he also resigned in 1936). After his withdrawal from political life, and with three sons and two daughters to put through school, he decided to scout out the large industrial combines and was finally hired by the Bosch firm, manufacturers of electrical equipment. The firm was sympathetic to Goerdeler's anti-Nazi crusade and frequently sent him on foreign assignments.

In the summer of 1937 Beck visited General Gamelin, chief of the French General staff. Like the vast majority of generals who had taken part in the First World War, neither Beck nor Gamelin had any intention of embarking on a second. This was what Hitler failed to understand when he promised his generals, "I shall bring you what you desire most—decorations, promotions, glory. . . ." In fact what Beck and Gamelin and their colleagues desired most was to finish their careers without having to send their troops into battle. But among Hitler's chief henchmen there was only one who was not an ardent warhawk, though this was a not inconsiderable exception—Hermann Goering, Luftwaffe chief and soon to be designated as Hitler's successor. A former officer in the Kaiser's army, an ace fighter pilot during the First World War, Goering had become rich and respected, loaded down with honors, and, like the generals, he wanted nothing more than peace. André François-Poncet has left us a description of Goering at the height of his powers: "He loves protocol, punctilio, and publicity, and he is a great ornament of the fashionable world. He finds it very much to his liking to make a grand entrance in all his glory, in all his vastness and splendor, and revels in the curious—often ironic if not actually envious—glances that he attracts with his handsome uniforms covered with gold braid, his decorations, and his jewels. During the early years of the regime the Nazi leaders held themselves aloof and kept their distance from the foreign diplomatic community, but around 1936 they were instructed to show themselves more in society. Goering had already anticipated this order, made contact with the foreign diplomatic corps, and arranged a series of receptions and sumptuous banquets in their honor."

Goering's family background was a great deal more comfortable than most of his party comrades'. His father had been a diplomat and a colonial administrator, at one time governor of German South West Africa; Goering himself was destined for a career in the army, but during the First World War he left the infantry for the newly organized air corps, distinguished himself as a courageous fighter pilot, and took command of his squadron after Baron von Richthofen's death. After the war he became a commercial pilot for Lufthansa, flying passengers and cargo between Germany and Sweden. One night his plane was forced down by engine failure; he made an emergency landing on the grounds of a Swedish castle, and was cordially welcomed by the master of the house and the beautiful Baroness Karin von Kantzow, who was soon to become Goering's first wife after she divorced her husband and followed the dashing young flier back to Germany.

"Goering's face was quite handsome," recalls Louis François-Poncet, "with regular, expressive features, a 'Grecian profile,' and clear, cold eyes. But he was tormented by obesity; he subjected himself to all sorts of drastic cures, lost sixty pounds in one month, gained back seventy a month later. He had also become addicted to morphine after he was wounded during the war.

"He had a quick, supple mind but was not a really cultured man. He was completely amoral, never let scruples of conscience stand in his way, but was still capable of the most romantic gestures and fits of extreme generosity. His greatest weakness was his vanity—he could never have enough titles or decorations. He had an eye for fine pictures and tapestries, beautifully bound books, but he was fascinated by precious stones. He often carried handfuls of gems around with him in a small buckskin pouch. He would dig his fingers greedily into this pouch—full of amethysts, opals, aquamarines, jade, amber, and tourmalines—since he had apparently been told that they would discharge the accumulated static electricity in his body, which would calm his nerves and act as a sort of alchemical tranquilizer. He loved money, but only for the sake of the pleasures it could bring him—which he indulged in to the hilt."

Goering was won over to the Nazi cause after he heard Hitler speak at a rally in Munich; he joined the Party, took part in the "Beerhall Putsch" of 1923, and had fallen, severely wounded, at Hitler's side when the police opened fire. His wife, Karin, had spirited him off to Italy, and unlike Hitler and several other leading lights of the Party, he escaped arrest, though he could not return to Germany until a general amnesty was granted four years later. (Karin remained behind in Sweden; she died of tuberculosis in 1931.) In the late twenties, with the resurgence of the Nazi movement, Goering became Hitler's chief lieutenant and one of his closest advisers. He personally took charge of the June '34 blood purge in Berlin; it was he who created the Gestapo and the concentration camps, who declared, "I'll see to it that anyone that shoots down a Communist will not go to prison."

He was totally devoted to Hitler, would never think of betraying the Führer, but was definitely not averse to criticizing him occasionally. This led to several stormy passages between them, after which Goering, very sensitive to a rebuke, would stalk off to brood over his injuries. However, Hitler always summoned him back, clapped him on the shoulder, and called him *"mein braver Hermann,"* while Goering flushed with pleasure. The roll of Goering's honors and titles grew longer—president of the Prussian State Council, president of the Reichstag, air minister, minister for economic affairs, director of the Hermann Goering State Enterprises (an enormous factory complex), and chief huntsman and master forester of the Reich. He had been a captain when he met Hitler in 1921; after 1933 he was quickly promoted to general, then field marshal, and later Hitler created a new rank for him that he would not have to share with anyone: *Reichsmarschall des Grossdeutschen Reiches,* Reichsmarshal of the Greater German Reich.

In contrast to Hitler, Goering delighted in extravagant uniforms, which he designed himself to suit his own free-ranging imagination. And since the combined salaries of his various official posts were not entirely adequate to his needs, he advanced himself handsome dividends from the factories in his economic empire and was not above soliciting commissions on arms contracts from Krupp, Thyssen, and other steel magnates of the Ruhr. (In 1937 he coined the celebrated slogan, "Germany wants guns before butter.")

Goering was as popular with the German people as Goebbels was heartily detested. On one occasion, when Goebbels denounced General Erhard Milch, secretary of the Air Ministry, because Milch's father was a Jew,[1] Goering shot back, "In my ministry *I* decide who's a Jew!" (*"Wer Jude ist, das bestimme ich!"*) This anecdote was immediately seized on by the people of Berlin and repeated endlessly. The cabaret singer Claire

---

1. The allegation may not have been invented by Goebbels. As Milch himself once confided to Mme François-Poncet at a state dinner, "My mother frequently deceived my father, so then, you know . . ."

Waldorf brought the house down every night with a song that gently satirized Goering's craving for decorations:

Hermann heest er—seine Brust is voll lametta . . .

[They call him Hermann—his chest is covered with tinsel . . .]

About sixty miles north of Berlin, near a lake surrounded by forests of pine and birch trees, Goering built the luxurious rural retreat he called Karinhall, in memory of his wife. Her grave was marked by a double line of standing stones, like prehistoric megaliths, that were covered with inscriptions in the Runic alphabet of the early Germans and Norsemen. (Three years after Karin's death Goering married an actress called Emmy Sonnemann, a blond tragedy queen from the classic Weimar stage, no longer young but gracious and unaffected in her manner. Their daughter, who was given the fittingly Nordic name Edda, was born in 1938.)

The original hunting lodge on the site—really nothing more than a log hut—was transformed into a rambling two-story villa; the design was inspired by the Merovingian basilicas of the early Middle Ages, but the interior was fitted out with all the refinements of modern comfort, including a sauna and a universal gym with specially designed equipment that allowed Goering to play a kind of mechanized version of virtually every sport. The great hall itself was a vast, lofty expanse, as high as the nave of a church, whose walls rose up to the roofbeams that topped the second story.

On the morning of December 25, 1937, Goering telephoned Ambassador François-Poncet to invite him and his family to spend Christmas day at Karinhall. "This was a tradition," recalls Louis François-Poncet, "but that year it was especially cold. The roads were iced over and still covered with snow. My father pointed this out to Goering. 'Don't worry,' he replied, 'we'll take care of it. You'll be able to make the trip in perfect safety.' And within the hour a fleet of Luftwaffe trucks and tenders had sprinkled sand and gravel over every inch of the sixty-mile drive from Berlin to Karinhall.

"A Luftwaffe sergeant met us at the gate, and we followed him to the entrance of the villa, where Goering, who had been alerted by the guards, was waiting to greet us on the steps. He was dressed, as always, with studied elegance—a raw-silk shirt, chamois riding breeches, and particolored boots with ebony-colored insteps and light-beige shanks. There was a hunting dagger at his belt in a solid-gold scabbard, the gift of a high government official, and the jeweled ring on his finger would have been worthy of a cardinal.

"Once in the great hall we turned left and made for the grand reception hall. A Christmas tree that touched the ceiling, almost twenty-five feet high, stood in the middle of the hall. Luftwaffe airmen, perched on the rafters, were putting up wreaths and strings of colored lights, and long tables, each covered with a delicate linen cloth, were piled high with gifts for Goering's guests, his family, and his entire household."

This piratical adventurer generally lived a life of bourgeois domesticity, surrounded by his wife, his daughter, his sister, his nephews, and numerous servants. He made it a point of honor to pick out all the Christmas presents personally for the entire household. "I remember," says Louis François-Poncet, "that he had bought embroidered silk panties and brassieres for the chambermaids and the lady's maids, the entire female staff in fact. When I asked him, 'How did you know what size they all wear?' he replied, 'I have an eye for these things!'

"For the younger guests there were lead soldiers: that year French poilus in their horizon-blue greatcoats for us, and Bersaglieri [Italian Alpine troops] for the children of Bernardo Attolico, the Italian ambassador. In the afternoon Goering took us to see his tame lioness, who lived in a deluxe kennel with ceramic-tile walls faced with an iron grille. She was greatly attached to her master and seemed delighted to see him. 'One day,' Goering told us, 'she gave one of my female guests a swipe with her paw that tore off a piece of the woman's backside. So I had to give her to the zoo, but I still came to visit her often. One day when I was getting ready to leave, they weren't quick enough closing the cage door. She ran out and jumped into the back seat of my car. I took her home with me, but now we keep a close watch on her.' Then he took us to see the other animals that roamed free in the park—stags, does, and buffalo. Goering put his hands to his mouth and imitated their calls—the war cry of the old bull, then the mating call of the young buck in rut—and soon the animals came to investigate.

"Finally he led us into a large converted barn that housed his model railroad, a gift of the employees of the Prussian state theaters. The trains were operated from a control panel that looked like the keyboard of a harmonium, and there were almost three miles of track that wound its way through a perfect miniature Bavarian landscape, across meadows, plowed fields, and forests, through towns and villages, through tunnels and across viaducts, all overhung by a mysterious network of fine brass wires. There was a whole assortment of semaphores and signals, spurs and switches, stations and train sheds where trains of various models and countries stood ready to roll out onto the track. Goering walked over to the control panel, and one of his nephews called out, 'Bring out the French train, Uncle Hermann!' This was a PLM locomotive pulling a first-, second-, and third-class carriage—no doubt laid on in my honor. Then another nephew pressed a button, a miniature Stuka slid down one of the wires, and the unfortunate French train fell under a hail of 'real' bombs—they were armed with caps. Goering let out a loud guffaw; we laughed along with him, though you might say that we were not amused, but his nephews were in ecstasy.

"After this small diplomatic incident Goering took us back to the villa for a tour of his various offices. The first was a splendid executive suite, where he carried out his duties as president of the Prussian State Council. 'This is where I receive visitors,' he explained. The next office was more like a miniature command post; and as he crossed the threshold he became the chief of the Luftwaffe general staff. There were portraits of Frederick the Great, Bismarck, and Napoleon hanging on the walls, but the fourth wall, opposite the doorway, was covered by heavy green drapes. I peered behind the curtain and saw a map of Spain stuck full of little flags representing units of the Condor Legion,[2] even though Germany was still denying that she had intervened in the Spanish Civil War. 'This is where I work,' Goering said. Finally he led us into a third office with dark wooden paneling, which reminded me of Dürer's engraving *St. Jerome in His Study*. 'And this,' Goering said, 'is where I sit and think,' to which my father replied, 'You mean, this is where you catch up on your sleep!'

"Goering had fitted out a palace for himself in the Potsdamerplatz district of Berlin where he received diplomats and distinguished foreign visitors. One evening my mother found herself seated at Goering's right at a state dinner; he was wearing a white silk shirt with lace ruffles and wide, billowing sleeves beneath a kind of mauve buckskin surplice and with an emerald as big as a pigeon's egg dangling from a heavy gold chain. She mentioned how much she admired his art collection. 'It wasn't all that easy to get it here,' he explained. 'I sent my ADC to the curator of the National Museum to ask for some first-rate pictures. My ADC didn't know anything about it, so the curator sent him back here with some ghastly old daubs he'd been keeping in storage. I was beside myself at first, but I went straight back to the museum and took

2. German "volunteers"—eight Luftwaffe squadrons and support troops—sent to assist Franco in 1936. They were responsible for the bombing of Guernica the following year. [Tr.]

the curator by the arm and said, "I'll pick them out myself. You'll send me that one and this one and that one, and if they haven't arrived by five o'clock this afternoon, you'll be tucked up in your little bunk in a concentration camp tonight." I don't have to tell you that every last one of them was present and correct at five o'clock.' "

5.

1938: "A Swine, But a Lucky Swine"

At the beginning of January 1938 Marshal Werner von Blomberg announced his plans for a second marriage. Blomberg was a dapper old gentleman of sixty, tall and thin with a small, wizened face, alert, jovial, and cultured, a widower for many years with grown children. He had decided to marry his secretary, Fräulein Erna Gruhn.

Hitler was deeply indebted to his minister of defense on several accounts. First, he had done everything in his power to keep the officer corps from aligning itself against the new regime; he had maintained the Reichswehr in a state of disciplined, docile neutrality. He had had a hand in the extermination of Röhm and his cronies (which he had also done a great deal to instigate); he was also the principal draftsman of the oath of August 2, 1934. In return for all this he had been awarded a marshal's baton. Hitler thought of Blomberg as a friend, and when Blomberg brought news of his forthcoming marriage, he offered his hearty congratulations.

Several days later, however, Blomberg returned, crestfallen, to ask the Führer to accept his resignation. The Reichswehr had refused to grant permission for his marriage. Beck and Fritsch had informed him that the match was quite unacceptable, and Blomberg had acquiesced. Hitler was outraged—these gentlemen had the audacity to oppose a marriage to which he had given his personal approval. He could not tolerate this sort of insubordination. They simply couldn't face up to the prospect of one of their own marrying a woman of the people.

"These rotten reactionaries, these stupid aristocrats, these Potsdam mummies still think they're living in a society with a class structure—they understand nothing of the Third Reich. I'll bring them into line! I'll break them! I'll sweep them away!" Hitler refused to accept Blomberg's resignation—better than that, he offered to stand as a witness, along with Goering, at Blomberg's wedding. "We'll see the look on their faces then!"

Blomberg was married on January 17, but General von Fritsch—

who was more solicitous of his general officers' morals than of the strength of their character—was adamant in demanding Blomberg's resignation. Fritsch sought out Hitler and announced that it would be impossible for Blomberg to remain minister of defense—not because he had married a woman of the people, which was a perfectly honorable estate, but because he had married a woman whose past was extremely dubious.[1] In the circumstances how could he, General von Fritsch, commander in chief of the army, expect to instill the proper standards of dignity and deportment in his junior officers with such an example before their eyes?

Hitler was furious; he lashed out with a stream of invective. The irascible Fritsch replied in kind, then went on to speak his mind frankly and completely. He denounced the brutality of the Nazi regime, the clumsiness and crudity of its policies, official corruption and inefficiency, the political intrigues that had infected the army, the antireligious propaganda that demoralized the rank-and-file soldier, the provocative foreign policy that threatened to precipitate Germany into a general European war that she was unprepared to fight. Hitler was speechless.

Afterward Fritsch met with Beck and his aide, General Halder. He told them, "I found myself in the presence of a madman, and what is more the symbol of Germany's evil destiny. That destiny will bring us to the brink of the abyss."

Now Hitler's rage was deflected onto the hapless Blomberg, who had dragged the Führer into this farcical muddle and made him appear ridiculous. He decided that Blomberg was unworthy to wear the uniform of a German general, nor would he ever set foot in the Chancellery again. He would be stripped of his rank and compelled to leave the country for a year. This did not mean, however, that Fritsch's intransigence would be overlooked; he had been highly disrespectful of the Führer and it was clear that he was harboring the same disturbing thoughts that Hitler suspected were shared by the majority of the general staff. Nevertheless, Blomberg would have to be replaced as minister of defense, and it seems that Hitler was reluctantly disposed to appoint Fritsch as his successor. He was, after all, a loyal officer, popular with the troops. But at this point Himmler intervened to offer the Führer an opportunity to avenge himself on Fritsch. He claimed that the com-

---

1. In fact, though neither Fritsch nor Hitler was aware of this at the time, the Berlin police had already compiled an astonishing dossier on Frau Blomberg. She had been convicted of prostitution several times, as well as trafficking in pornographic postcards (some of which she had posed for herself). Count Helldorf, the prefect of police, gave the dossier to Keitel, who (for reasons best known to himself) handed it over to Goering.

mander in chief was a homosexual, and that he would produce conclusive evidence of this. Fritsch, of course, was almost speechless with indignation, though not so much so that he was prevented from seeking an immediate audience with Hitler; Goering was also present. Fritsch denied the charge with ferocious energy; he gave his word of honor that he had never even been accused of conduct of that sort. Beck, who was summoned by Hitler, insisted that a military court of honor be convoked, and Fritsch voluntarily resigned his post as commander in chief and placed himself under house arrest until the court had met and handed down its verdict.

At the beginning of the Blomberg affair Goering had sought out Himmler and Reinhard Heydrich, chief of the SD, and together they awaited an opportunity to turn all this to their advantage. On January 25 Goering—who coveted Blomberg's post as minister of defense—met with Hitler, briefed him extensively on Frau Blomberg's and Fritsch's real or supposed transgressions (with the help of a dossier supplied by Heydrich). The Führer was already inclined to credit these accusations, but not to appoint Goering as Blomberg's successor (though Goering was awarded the supreme honor of the outsize Reichsmarshal's baton two years later as compensation).

At 9:00 PM on February 4 a special communiqué announced a sweeping reorganization of the armed forces. Hitler had decided to take personal command of the armed forces of the Reich. The Ministry of Defense as such was abolished, to be replaced by the Wehrmacht High Command (OKW), which would serve as the Führer's general staff. Keitel was appointed OKW chief, with the rank of minister and all the other prerogatives that were previously enjoyed by the minister of defense. General Walther von Brauchitsch replaced Fritsch as commander in chief of the army. Sixteen senior generals were relieved of their commands (sixty generals all together), and a whole battalion of lesser officers found themselves suddenly promoted, demoted, or dismissed outright.

Carl Friedrich Goerdeler was still actively promoting his personal crusade against Hitler; he had made contact with the military opposition at the beginning of 1938, and met frequently with Beck, whom he had an especially high regard for, and Fritsch, to convey to them the impressions he had formed on his trips abroad. The German military attachés in the various capitals he had visited had all assured him that the outbreak of war would be catastrophic for Germany, but Beck and Fritsch could only confirm Hitler's warlike intentions. In London Goerdeler had arranged a meeting with Churchill (then in the political wilderness), but Churchill had apparently received a mysterious phone call that sabotaged the meeting (and convinced Goerdeler that a powerful pro-Nazi faction in Great Britain was already working against him). He did succeed in meeting with Sir Robert Vansittart at the Foreign Office. Goerdeler assured the undersecretary that no one in Germany, apart from Hitler, wanted war and that an opposition group had already formed among the general staff; Sir Robert blandly remarked that that would be an act of high treason. Goerdeler also informed his acquaintances at the Bank of England that he was in close touch with an opposition group that enjoyed the full approval and support of the commander in chief of the army, General von Brauchitsch.

In fact, as soon as Hitler's reshuffling of the high command was announced, the officer corps cautiously began to sound out their new commander in chief. Brauchitsch, at least initially, appeared to be a fairly impressive choice—well educated, serious-minded, high-principled, and free of all of Fritsch's shrill affectations. For that matter, it would seem that he and Hitler would be totally incompatible and that a serious clash of personalities was inevitable. However, Brauchitsch had one serious defect (from his brother officers' point of view); he seemed to lack the nerve to set himself on a collision course with Hitler; he had always served the regime loyally, though without making any special effort to curry favor. He was not especially known for the firmness of his character, and he was not physically strong; he suffered from heart trouble. Worse than that, he had recently married a fanatical Nazi, and it was Hitler himself who had provided the money for the divorce settlement with his first wife. He began to show his gratitude immediately by eliminating from key positions all the officers whom he suspected might be tempted by seditious thoughts. Hitler was well pleased.

Brauchitsch assured Beck and Admiral Wilhelm Canaris, chief of the Abwehr (Military Intelligence), that he would make every effort to ensure that the army would never become the cat's-paw of the Nazi Party and the adventurist and criminal tendencies of its leaders. Still he continued to temporize. When Hans Bernd Gisevius, a well-connected Gestapo official who also happened to be an active member of the opposition, asked to see Brauchitsch in order to discuss the Fritsch case, the commander in chief agreed to receive him.

I was at great pains to convince him [Gisevius wrote later] that we did not expect him to launch a coup d'état or take part in any kind of disloyal maneuver against Hitler. It was essentially a question—in order to avoid any fresh machinations against the Army High Command—of carrying out measures which could be justified after the fact by conclusive documentary evidence. I could be sure of providing this evidence within hours of the operation itself by searching through the treasure vaults of the Gestapo. . . . I outlined a dozen unimpeachable reasons that would allow us to arrest the entire Gestapo clique. The general was visibly pleased to hear me say this. . . . Brauchitsch did not seem to wish the Führer very well; the word *destructive* even escaped his lips at one point.

The general was clearly displeased by the course of our foreign policy "which, in my opinion," I told him, "will inevitably lead to a second world war. . . ." When I said the word *war,* Brauchitsch tapped his temple with his index finger, signifying that Hitler was insane. I came away with the profound conviction that he was going to take action. . . .

Count Helldorf, the Berlin prefect of police, was the next one to seek out Brauchitsch. As a precaution he brought along the dossier on Frau Blomberg as well as a long list of outrages committed by the Gestapo. Brauchitsch listened, then let Helldorf know that he did not consider the Blomberg and Fritsch affairs to be settled and seemed to have a clear idea of where the Gestapo's methods would lead. But it was the indomitable Goerdeler who finally succeeded in pushing Brauchitsch too far. He painted an unsparing picture of the foreign and domestic situation, showed that the threat of war existed but that there was still an honorable way out. Brauchitsch not only agreed, he also seemed to be deeply moved by the end of the interview. Goerdeler was radiant. Brauchitsch still maintained, though, that the final conclusive link was still missing in the Fritsch case. . . .

I expressed my willingness to clarify the matter, and Goerdeler wrote to Brauchitsch that same night asking him to send for me. When Admiral Canaris' adjutant, Colonel Oster, gave the letter to Brauchitsch the next morning, Brauchitsch shouted indignantly that he didn't have the slightest desire to see me. He added that he had nothing against me personally, but he never wanted anything to do with Goerdeler again as long as he lived.

We learned shortly afterward that Brauchitsch had just received a letter saying that one of his relatives had heard an appalling piece of news—Goerdeler had announced during one of his trips to London that there was going to be an internal upheaval in Germany, assisted by the commander in chief of the army. . . . Brauchitsch was furious and threatened to turn the matter over to the Gestapo—the same Brauchitsch who had been in the grip of such enthusiasm during his session with Goerdeler.

He ran straight to the Führer, only to receive a well-deserved rebuff. Hitler declared that it was a stupid business, no more than the same sort of foolish rumors that had been making the rounds for years. Still, he was prepared to order a political investigation in order to soothe the conscientious scruples of the commander in chief. "The Goerdeler affair" had come very close to the dangerous precincts of the Gestapo, though fortunately the intervention of various other interested parties would bring it to a more favorable conclusion. All in all, it would have been impossible to prove that Goerdeler had really been guilty of any treasonable activity.

This incident was to have important consequences, since Brauchitsch's "valiant resolutions" had all melted away when they were exposed to the light of day.

Such, then, [Gisevius concluded] was our hero in gold braid: At first he led us on for months, coldly manipulating civilians so that, at the risk of their lives, they might provide him with a few scraps of useful information. And when at last it was time to do what had to be done, he ran off to the Führer and denounced the men who had helped him the most. Worse than that, he had been counting on the loyalty of the man [Goerdeler] he had just betrayed so wretchedly to the executioner, expecting that he would march off quietly to a concentration camp rather than betray the broken promises of the commander in chief.

"Abandon hope, all ye who would treat with generals" was the bitter moral drawn by Gisevius to the history of their campaign to win Brauchitsch over to the opposition.

As for Goerdeler himself, discouraged by his unprofitable trip to London and further disillusioned by Brauchitsch's treachery, he sought refuge in his beloved city of Königsberg on the wet, sandy plains of East Prussia. "The West most definitely will be taken in by Hitler," he announced to his wife, and shortly afterward he took up his pilgrim's staff once again. However Beck and his brother officers, as well as the civilian opposition groups, were beginning to mistrust Goerdeler's enthusiasm. As much as they admired his courage and patriotism, his "indomitable" fighting spirit, they now had serious misgivings about his discretion.

As for the Fritsch case, the board of inquiry quickly established that General von Fritsch had been framed by the Gestapo in a willful and malicious confusion of identities—it was a Lieutenant Colonel von *Frisch* who had in fact been accused of homosexual offenses in 1935. So much was clear, and Brauchitsch was urged by the conspirators to take action. Hjalmar Schacht, president of the Reichsbank and former minister for economic affairs, tried to make a personal appeal to Brauchitsch, but the commander in chief refused to see him and informed

Beck that they would have to wait until the verdict of the military court
of honor was announced—then they would take the appropriate action.
Brauchitsch was inclined to insist that the court of honor still be convened
and hand down a formal verdict, but Goering and Himmler had scented
danger, and they asked Hitler simply to announce that there had been
a regrettable error. Fritsch—whose enthusiasm for his own cause was
beginning to flag and had to be constantly sustained by Beck in all
this—would not permit his case to be dismissed with a vague disclaimer
of this kind. So the court of honor was convened—Brauchitsch, Admiral
Erich Raeder, as the commanders in chief of the army and navy, two
judges of the supreme military tribunal, with Goering, as the ranking
military officer of the Reich since his latest promotion on February 4,
presiding. But on the morning of their first session on March 11, Hitler
announced that the court would recess until March 17. The reason for
this soon became clear enough—German troops marched into Austria
the next day and received a tumultuous welcome in Vienna. There was
no reaction whatsoever from the Western democracies, which served
only to confirm the wisdom of Hitler's decision. When the court recon-
vened, neither Raeder, Brauchitsch, nor even Fritsch asked any embarrassing questions of the Gestapo. The next day Fritsch was formally
acquitted, but not reinstated in his command. Hitler simply conveyed
his best wishes that Fritsch would quickly be "restored to health," [2]
and shortly afterward appointed him honorary commander of his old
artillery regiment. (In September 1939 Fritsch was killed during the
siege of Warsaw by a bullet fired by an unknown hand—according to
some accounts, while he was hurrying to the aid of his orderly officer,
who had been seriously wounded on the field.)

But now that the verdict had been reached, the time had arrived
for Brauchitsch to take whatever unspecified form of action he was prepared to take; the opposition tried to rekindle his "valiant resolutions,"
but it soon became clear that Brauchitsch was resolute in one thing
only—he was determined to do nothing that might either alert the vigi-
lance of the Gestapo, or flout the ardent National Socialist convictions
of his new wife. The opposition was at first disconcerted, then finally
exasperated by the spectacle of a commander who listened to their plans
for a coup d'état with an attentive ear but seemed to be totally immobilized in the realm of action. It would not be very long before his authority
over the army became a derisory fiction; and worse, he himself was to

2. According to the official communiqué, Fritsch had previously resigned "for reasons
of health."

become the whipping boy who took the blame for the strategic blunders of the supreme commander himself.

On August 10, 1938, Hitler summoned the chiefs of the general staff and senior generals of the Wehrmacht to his GHQ near Berchtesgaden, the "Eagle's Nest." The French historian Jacques Bénoit-Méchin has described the scene perfectly:

The conference room was enormous, and with its cream-colored walls, coffered ceilings, and light wood paneling, rather rustic in character. One wall was covered with a remarkable series of Italian Renaissance paintings; one of them, a Titian, was a gift from Mussolini; the other wall was hung with a seventeenth-century Flemish tapestry representing a battle scene. A grand piano, a large globe, a classical bust, and several leather-covered sofas filled one corner of the room. The immense fireplace, where a great pyre of tree trunks blazed even in summer, faced a row of bay windows looking out over the Salzach Valley and the mountainous amphitheater that rose up to the south. The view was spectacular. In front of the windows stood a table more than six yards long topped with a single slab of porphyry. . . .

Today all the great captains of the Wehrmacht were gathered around this table. Maps of Central Europe were spread out, and Hitler, his face waxen and pale, put on his reading glasses and stabbed with his finger at the space marked "Bohemia." He set out the reasons that had convinced him he must "intervene" in Czechoslovakia. Hitler's manner—that of the infallible potentate and invincible warlord—was disquieting; the generals felt now that their worst fears were about to be realized.

On the twelfth Hitler called up between 300,000 and 400,000 civilian workers to begin construction of the Siegfried Line along the French border. On the fifteenth the army had already assembled for maneuvers, and Hitler took advantage of this opportunity to address his generals and the entire officer corps as well. He took his newly appointed aide, Major Schmundt, aside and explained his view of the situation quite candidly: "These gentlemen should not be meddling in politics. I can look after such things better than they can. . . . General Beck sent me a memorandum advising me not to fight the Czechs and tried to conjure up the specter of a second world war, but I refused to allow him to lecture me. If the generals allow these theories of theirs to undermine their faith and their morale, then I have no further use for them. . . . And the army, like my Party, should put its blind trust in me. I am going to dispense with Beck . . . he may be intelligent, but he really doesn't fit into the age we're living in. . . . Fritsch is another one who belongs on the retired list." And so saying, Hitler went off to inform his officers that he intended to settle the problem of the Sudeten Germans living in the frontier regions of Bohemia by marching on Czechoslovakia.

On the morning of the same day, August 15, 1938, Baron Ewald von Kleist-Schmentzin was preparing to set off on an extremely hazardous mission. The baron, a tall, sandy-haired man with a high forehead, had all the requisites of the typical Junker—he was a monarchist, a former stalwart of the Conservative Nationalist Party, the proprietor of a vast domain beyond the Elbe, even the master of a small castle with a white stone facade that dated from the beginning of the previous century. The approach to the castle led through a spacious tract of carefully tended parkland, surrounded on all sides by the endless, flat plains of Pomerania. In 1934, when his party was disbanded by Hitler, the baron was left with no formal occupation other than the management of his estates, though his influence continued to be felt in the corridors of power in Berlin; his forceful personality always ensured him a respectful hearing in business and financial circles, and he still played a leading role in various organizations of industrialists and entrepreneurs.

Kleist was a devout Christian and a sworn enemy of the Nazi regime. As early as 1929 he had published a pamphlet on the dangers inherent in the National Socialist movement (then emerging into prominence once more after several years of obscurity). The baron was convinced that Hitler's program was directly contrary to all the teachings of civilized morality and religion; his own intellectual creed was that of nineteenth-century humanism, which naturally led him to take his place in the ranks of the opposition. He decided at the outset that it was essential to seek support among influential, like-minded men in foreign countries and to mobilize public opinion abroad. Unfortunately, the baron knew no one in England and could not speak a word of English. A great many of his friends had fallen away from him after he renewed his violent and uncompromising attacks on Hitler, for fear of an equally unrestrained and considerably more damaging counterstroke on the part of the Gestapo.

Admiral Canaris at least appreciated the baron's courage and frankness and valued him for his undoubted abilities and the soundness of his political judgments. Canaris shared Baron von Kleist's pessimism about the future of the Third Reich and recruited him into his unofficial intelligence network. The baron was often closeted with Canaris during his frequent trips to Berlin, but his usefulness as a permanent source of information was limited, since all his comings and goings were duly noted by the Gestapo; whenever he boarded a train at the rural station of Schmentzin near his estate, a railway security officer called ahead to alert Berlin.

Canaris and his associates were clearly hard-pressed to find an independent power in Germany to oppose Hitler and his regime; since 1934 not only had all political parties (save one) been suppressed, but the church, the Wehrmacht, the financial and industrial sector, and the entire apparatus of the government had all fallen under the absolute sway of the Führer. As Canaris had announced at a meeting of his staff, speaking as usual in a low, conspiratorial voice: "The Allies, foreign public opinion, the governments of nations like Great Britain and the United States should come to our aid. War should be avoided at all costs." Then, bringing his index finger to his lips in a familiar gesture, he added, "Don't forget this. We have not been discussing treason but simply a means of guaranteeing the security of the Reich."

Thus the opposition began to make plans to send an envoy to London in April 1938. Ewald von Kleist met with a fellow Junker, Herbert von Bismarck, to discuss the logistics of the mission in the gentlemanly surroundings of the Casino Club in Berlin. In May Kleist called on Admiral Canaris, who had already learned of Hitler's designs on Czechoslovakia. It was crucial to find out whether the English planned to come to the defense of the Czechs. Colonel Hans Oster, Canaris' chief of staff, who was also present, observed that unless Hitler was totally mad, he could not possibly feel sure that a military action against the Czechs would be successful. This opinion was shared by the entire general staff; as one officer put it, "If the Allies energetically alert Hitler to the fact that they will oppose any aggression against Czechoslovakia, or any intervention whatsoever, then Hitler is certain to pull in his claws."

It was at this time that Canaris introduced Ewald von Kleist to General Beck, who was also searching for some way of securing the aid of the Western Allies against Hitler. On May 20 Hitler announced that his new motorized divisions would take part in war games near the Czech frontier. The British were disturbed by this; Ambassador Neville Henderson passed a first warning on to Hitler, and the Führer flew into one of his titanic rages, verging on genuine hysteria. According to legend, this was one of the occasions on which Hitler threw himself to the floor and began to gnaw the carpet. When the fit had passed, he was heard to proclaim, "England, I will never forget this!" He sent for Brauchitsch, ordered that the plans for the "western defense wall" be carried out immediately and that the effective strength of the peacetime army be reinforced. Nevertheless, preparations for an immediate attack on Czechoslovakia were put in abeyance.

On his next visit to Canaris, Kleist learned that the situation had reversed itself again: Hitler was preparing a démarche against the Czechs, an attack that Canaris was convinced would be launched before the end of the year, unless the British made it clear that they were opposed to any form of German intervention. Canaris was eager to inform the British of the existence of "Case Green," the general staff's plan for a military operation against Czechoslovakia. Once again Canaris and Kleist called on Beck, who explained the situation in detail and concluded by saying: "If the British allow Hitler freedom of action, they will be losing their two principal allies in Germany: the general staff and the German people. If you can bring back some concrete proof that Great Britain will go to war in the event of aggression against Czechoslovakia, then I will put an end to this regime."

"And what would you consider to be 'concrete proof'?" asked Kleist.

"A formal undertaking to come to the aid of Czechoslovakia in the event of aggression," Beck replied and went on to say that a forceful statement from the British government to this effect would strengthen his own position with the general staff.

All that remained was for Canaris to get Baron von Kleist to London without arousing the suspicions of the Gestapo or of the British Secret Intelligence Service, who might reasonably be expected to take the baron for a German spy. Canaris promised to provide the baron with a false passport, two if need be. Kleist returned to Schmentzin Castle, where he would remain until he got the go-ahead from Canaris. On the morning of August 15 he received his marching orders, and on the seventeenth a car pulled up to the gate of Berlin's Tempelhof Airport carrying a middle-aged man in a gray suit, Baron Ewald von Kleist, and an army general in full uniform—this was the baron's cousin, whose name was also Ewald von Kleist. The police clicked their heels and waved them through without checking their papers, and the baron climbed aboard a Lufthansa Junkers-52 that would take him to London.

On board the plane an English passenger took the seat behind the baron's; after the plane touched down at Croydon, the Englishman signaled to the police and the customs officers to pass through the civilian in the gray suit. A few moments later he introduced himself to the baron: "My name's H. D. Hanson."

Hanson telephoned the Secret Intelligence Service from a booth at the airport. "Our visitor from Germany has just arrived."

"Bring him in then."

The baron had scarcely arrived in his room at the Park Lane Hotel when Lloyd George, the aging chief of the Liberal Party, appeared to take him to dinner at Claridge's. Neither man spoke the other's language, so their conversation was conducted in French.

"Everything's decided," the baron announced at the outset. "The mobilization plans have been drawn up. X Day has been set. The army group commanders have their orders, and nothing will be able to stop Hitler except a strongly worded, solemn warning from Great Britain." When Lloyd George asked who had sent him to England, the baron answered that it had been "my friends" on the general staff, explaining that there was not a single general in an important post who was not opposed to the idea of war, even Marshal von Reichenau, one of the few generals who had been an enthusiastic partisan of the Nazi regime. (Walther von Reichenau had served as coordinator of land forces in the Defense Ministry until he was replaced by Keitel in 1935.)

Baron von Kleist had carried out his assignment both deftly and courageously. The virile personality of the Prussian squire made a strong impression on his British hosts, and at that time he was doubtless the first German to deliver such a somber and dramatic warning of things to come. He was fully aware of the risk that he and his principals were running by undertaking this quasi-official diplomatic mission: "I have come to you with the halter around my neck," he said, and he met with no one except Lloyd George, Sir Robert Vansittart, and Winston Churchill.

"If Great Britain, in concert with France and Russia, adopts an energetic attitude toward Hitler," Kleist told them, "if she issues a warning that he will be held solely responsible, we can expect that the generals will put Hitler under arrest if they see him persist in his policy of aggression. In addition a British statesman should make an open declaration, aimed especially at German public opinion, which would make it clear that an attack on Czechoslovakia will bring down all the calamities of a second world war on Europe. It will be particularly necessary to leave no doubt in Hitler's mind that this sort of warning is not a bluff, as Ribbentrop has been claiming all along." Without the indirect support that such a firm assertion of British policy would give them, the baron's friends on the general staff "would be incapable of carrying out any action designed to put an end to this reign of terror, and it will be impossible to establish any kind of rational world order with this regime in place."

The baron later met with Churchill at Chartwell and volunteered the opinion that if Hitler were overthrown, then the monarchy would most probably be restored. (Though a staunch patriot and a good Prussian, he did not rule out the possibility of a negotiated settlement of the problem of the Polish Corridor.) He concluded by repeating his request that he might be given a letter addressed to General Beck to take back to Germany.

The British reactions to Baron von Kleist's mission were, characteristically, mixed. Though Sir Robert Vansittart was an avowed enemy of the Nazi regime, since January 1938 his post at the Foreign Office had been purely honorary. Churchill had been out of the government for many years, nor did he have formal ties with any particular party; but he did everything in his power to assist the baron in his mission and to stiffen the resolve of the German opposition group. Churchill told Kleist that there were powerful currents in British public opinion that made him certain that the British would no longer stand by passively if Hitler attempted any further aggressive measures in Central Europe. He cited Prime Minister Chamberlain's declaration of March 24, which was still in force, and later assured himself on this point by putting the question directly to the foreign secretary, Lord Halifax. In addition, Churchill testified to his own strong personal enthusiasm for the formation of a new German government and told the baron that Great Britain, as well as France, might be willing to grant certain concessions as far as the restoration of Germany's former colonies and the conclusion of new trade agreements were concerned. Even the idea of clarifying the knotty problem of the Polish Corridor—which Kleist insisted would be essential—was not rejected outright, although it was Churchill's opinion that the time was not yet ripe to broach this question with the Poles, for fear of driving them into the arms of the Nazis. Finally Churchill promised the baron a letter calculated to encourage his friends in Germany, and he urged Lord Halifax to have a serious warning presented to Hitler in the form of a joint communiqué signed by the British, the Russians, and the French, with the fullest possible support of the United States. In a speech to his constituency on August 27 Churchill described the threatened German invasion of Bohemia as "a crime against civilization and against the liberty of mankind."

But Churchill was speaking only for himself, and the attitude of the man who would have to speak for Great Britain, Neville Chamberlain, was entirely different. In a letter to Halifax he characterized Baron von Kleist as a political enemy of Hitler, blinded by personal hatred: "There are certainly a great many arguments which might be brought to bear against his allegations. We have recently heard other voices from Germany claiming that Hitler's warlike intentions are to be taken seriously and, consequently, this suggests that we should respond to them with gestures of conciliation." Thus Chamberlain refused to make the sort of public declaration desired by Kleist and Churchill, for fear of antagonizing Hitler even further. For his part, Ambassador Henderson in Berlin—whose sympathy with the Nazi regime was well known—refused to take any notice of the warnings issued by the German high command. "Their information," he asserted, "is one-sided, partisan, and intended solely as propaganda against Hitler."

On his return to Germany Baron von Kleist was evidently deeply disappointed with the results of his mission. He reported to Canaris to brief him on his talks with Lloyd George, Vansittart, and Churchill. "I found no one who would be willing to take advantage of this opportunity to risk waging a preventative war. It is my impression that the English want to avoid the outbreak of war this year, and at almost any price." Several days later the baron received the letter that Churchill had promised, which made it clear that if Germany launched a military operation against Czechoslovakia, then sooner or later war would be inevitable, and that after a long, bitter struggle Germany would be cruelly and decisively defeated. Kleist was left to mull over this prophecy with the small circle of German patriots who had made him their emissary to England. Churchill was the only British politician who expressed himself in language that Hitler might have understood, but unfortunately Churchill was not the prime minister.

Less than a month after the baron's clandestine mission, Canaris received a visit from an officer of the Gestapo; his organization had learned that an envoy had recently gone to London and engaged with British politicians in conversations that were no less than treasonable. Canaris was asked to look into this matter. He immediately warned Baron von Kleist that he should prepare a convincing alibi, then sent for the officer who had made the baron's travel arrangements and ordered him to take charge of the investigation: "Of course, our man has nothing to do with any of this. You will be searching elsewhere. I don't want his name brought up in this inquiry." Profoundly discouraged and embittered, Baron von Kleist returned to his Pomeranian estates. The Nazi regime seemed no less secure than it had before his departure for London, and as the baron's cousin, General von Kleist, remarked to him a short time later, "Hitler is a swine, but he's a lucky swine." He was referring, in fact, to Neville Chamberlain's visit to Berchtesgaden on September 15. Chamberlain had requested an interview with Hitler, and Hitler had agreed. How could anyone claim that Hitler was throwing himself blindly into the arena of world conflict when in fact he had immediately agreed to negotiate with the British?

"Can you imagine," cried Hjalmar Schacht, the economic wizard of the Reichsbank, now fallen out of favor, "a prime minister of the British Empire paying a call on that gangster?"—a gangster, in fact, who had risen to supreme power with the help of Schacht and many others like him.

General Beck had already reached the limit of his endurance. He could not accept the fact that the officer corps could submit to the outrageous humiliation that had been inflicted on General von Fritsch with such supine resignation. Now that the blow had fallen, Beck realized that Hitler would have nothing more to fear from his generals, glutted as they were with stipends and decorations. Beck, at least, was determined to strike back, and from that moment on, the drawing room of his home on the Goethestrasse in Berlin would become the principal forum of the conspiracy.

In August, several weeks before Chamberlain's visit to Berchtesgaden, the French ambassador was taking the waters at Bad Gastein in Austria. Goering telephoned Mme François-Poncet several times a week at their summer house in Wannsee, a residential suburb of Berlin. He was most insistent: "When is the ambassador coming back? Something is up, they're preparing a coup. I have to discuss all this with the ambassador." Goering, as we have seen, was content with his wealth and his titles, and, essentially, with things as they were.

Beck tried to see Brauchitsch, who avoided him, then went off on leave, and left Beck to meditate on the situation until his return. Beck found it inconceivable that Hitler might decide to involve Germany in a war without consulting his general staff, but he had learned that the Führer had dictated a memo to Keitel in April in which he made it clear that he expected to exercise supreme command of the Wehrmacht in fact as well as in name. When Brauchitsch returned to Berlin, Beck handed him a memorandum he had drafted himself, with the approval of his fellow generals, in which he expressed the opinion that war—"even a blitzkrieg"—would entail the risk of economic collapse for Germany and for all Europe. In addition he believed that the army was simply not ready for war. Brauchitsch passed this memorandum on to Hitler, though very reluctantly. Hitler was indignant and ordered Beck to retract these opinions, which Beck refused to do. Meanwhile the Czech crisis was becoming more serious every day; Hitler's vaunted concern for the "ethnic Germans" of the Sudetenland had become a pretext for naked aggression.

Hitler agreed to grant Beck an audience, the course of which was predictably stormy. Beck requested an assurance that there would be no serious diplomatic provocations without consultation with the general staff. Hitler pointed out that Beck's role as chief of the general staff was purely to carry out his orders and requested him to do so without further discussion. "All this talk of 'shared responsibilities' has been going on for too long. The general staff reports on problems of military command and nothing more—that goes for its chief as well." Beck replied that he could not pass on an order he disapproved of, and he immediately sent in his resignation. Hitler was somewhat embarrassed by this—he disliked his officers' resigning of their own free will; he preferred to keep the initiative in such matters himself. He asked Brauchitsch to intercede with Beck and try to persuade him to withdraw his resignation. Beck replied that he had intended it as a gesture of protest; he had hoped to preserve the general staff's right of consultation and to put an end to the rapid erosion of the generals' authority. He was counting on other generals to follow his example, but his resignation would serve its purpose only if the esprit de corps of the German high command were actually as staunch as Beck wished it to be, and the reality was something quite different. In addition, if his resignation was to have the desired impact of a political bombshell, it would have to be made public immediately. This Hitler refused to do for some time, and Beck unfortunately did not press the point. Beck, like so many other officers, felt shackled by the personal oath of allegiance he had sworn to Hitler, and in any case the discontented elements in the officer corps were not entirely sympathetic with Beck's *beau geste*. If all the opponents of the regime who held important posts were to resign, they said, then the field would be clear for the Nazis. Beck, who was always optimistic in his evaluation of the strength and tenacity of the opposition, replied that he knew that his successor would feel just as he did.

Pleading that the increase in international tension had forced his hand, Hitler soon presented Beck with his successor in the person of General Franz Halder. General Heinz Guderian had been his first choice, but he was worried that Guderian might prove too difficult to manage. It was only at the last moment that he chose Halder, in spite of the fact that Halder was a practicing Catholic, which Hitler found detestable. And although Halder's talents as a military theorist were universally recognized, Hitler was certainly aware that Halder was less highly respected for his firmness of character. He was not a warrior but a bureaucrat, a desk officer who enlivened his leisure moments with mathematics and botany.

If Halder was altogether unmoved in the beginning by National Socialist propaganda, he was visibly swayed by the efforts of members of the opposition to win him over to their side. As far as Halder was concerned, the butchery of June 30, 1934, the "Night of the Long Knives," had exposed Hitler for the monster he was. On August 6 he sent Beck a letter cataloging the excesses of the Nazi regime in every sphere of national life. When, during the eventful month of March 1938, Hans Bernd Gisevius encountered General Halder, he was struck by the ferocity of his language: "That criminal Hitler is deliberately dragging us into a war, no doubt in order to gratify his pathological sexual impulses and his blood lust. He is one of those revolutionary absolutists who feel that everything that he sees around him when he comes to power must be destroyed." As a Catholic, General Halder saw Hitler as an amoral creature for whom truth was an illusion, who only acknowledged the reality of power and material gain. He saw Hitler not only as the gravedigger of his country but also as the incarnation of all the evils of the world. Unfortunately, however, General Halder was not a man of action, for all the vehemence of his opinions, and he was less concerned with the national crisis—according to Gisevius, at least—than with the creases in his uniform: "He never crosses his legs without spreading out his handkerchief to protect the crimson stripe on his trousers—the very model of the reluctant general."

Halder was born in 1882 into an old Bavarian military family. At first glance he might have been taken for a natty little schoolmaster with his inexpressive features, his pince-nez, and his brush-cut haircut. He lived in the Berlin suburb of Zehlendorf, in a house that was as modest and unpretentious as its owner—visitors found that the general himself always answered the door. But one's impression of him improved with better acquaintance, when his sensitivity and intelligence were revealed. A true expert on military affairs, he was a worthy representative of the staff generals of the old school. Serious-minded, conscientious, he made a thorough study of every dossier that arrived on his desk and carried out his assigned duties to perfection. His mind was critical, austere, precise, unprejudiced, and receptive to political and historical problems; his thinking was methodical and so rational as to be dry and bloodless; his judgment, in certain respects at least, was more objective than Beck's. Though his physical appearance was rather unprepossessing, he was actually a man of great vitality with an unflagging capacity for work. Everyone who knew him concurred in describing his nature as sensitive and even inclined to weakness and sentimentality; he clearly lacked the single-minded tenacity of his predecessor. Halder was painfully aware of this failing in himself, even tortured by his inability to make bold decisions and especially to carry them out. As soon as he became chief of the general staff, he gave ample evidence of this diffident, overcautious side to his character. Goerdeler, for example, he felt had compromised himself by his rashness and indiscretion, and Halder made a point of avoiding him, much as Brauchitsch had done. His prudent overtures to the opposition group were strictly for the purpose of gathering information; he asked Admiral Canaris if the Case Green plans for an invasion of Czechoslovakia represented pure bluff or actual preparations for war. Canaris, who was aware of Halder's vacillating temperament, thought it best to answer that the Abwehr did not report on political matters.

Admiral Canaris was an elusive, enigmatic figure, though this seems appropriate in the chief of military counterintelligence. Baron von Weizsäcker, prominent in the Foreign Ministry and a fellow conspirator, wrote: "He exemplifies two qualities that are rarely found together in Germany—intellect allied with cunning, and a total absence of bad faith. All his guile is entirely put to the service of those causes he believes to be just." Canaris left the navy to reorganize the Abwehr in 1935, and he was to remain its chief until July 1944. He was born in the Rhineland. His family, of Greek origin, had migrated first to Lake Como and finally settled in the wine district of Bernkaste in the Moselle Valley at the beginning of the nineteenth century. Canaris himself preferred not to be reminded of his foreign heritage, though the Mediterranean always had a strong attraction for him. He was also extremely self-conscious about his size—his nickname was "the Little Admiral"—and he would often remark to his wife after a reception or a state dinner, "Once again I was the shortest one there."

Canaris carried himself gracefully; his gestures were sharp and precise. He seemed always to feel the cold, and he wore a coat even at the height of summer. His pockets were stuffed full of all sorts of medical nostrums, powders, tablets, and lozenges, which he offered freely to anyone he happened to be talking to. He was extremely courteous to strangers, and more than that, evidence presented at the Nuremberg trials revealed that he had intervened personally to save a number of lives, including those of General Giraud and General Weygand. He did not form attachments easily, had no friends or confidants, and seemed to be really close to no one but his dogs. As a good intelligence officer, he had the gift of making others open up to him without revealing anything of himself.

His wife recalled that one evening while she was watching him reading in front of the fire, he asked, "What are you thinking about?"

"About you."

"About me? Why think about me? I'm the most insignificant man in the world."

Ten years after his death she said, "Whenever I tried to define him in words, I could never manage to do it. I could only say that he was a simple, modest person; he liked horses, dogs, history books, and good novels. Still, an analysis of his handwriting brought out serious contradictions—an almost neurotic sensitivity combined with a great deal of energy, a kind of tenacity that verged on stubbornness."

The Little Admiral's closest professional associate was Colonel Oster, Abwehr chief of staff. Oster was born in 1887; most of his male forebears had been Protestant pastors in Alsace. He joined the Abwehr at its inception with the rank of major. Schooled in the Prussian tradition of discipline, he was revolted by the massacres of June 30, 1934, and began at this early date to conspire against the regime. The Abwehr furnished the perfect cover for Oster's conspiratorial activities; nowhere else outside the Nazi inner circle could he have kept so well informed on what Hitler was up to. Colonel Oster served primarily as a liaison between the military and the civilian opposition groups. It was he who introduced Goerdeler and Dr. Schacht to General Beck, and he had taken it upon himself to supply General Halder with the sort of information he had requested as soon as the general appeared to be ready to take action.

Oster was a jovial man who loved life, enjoyed riding and good company, and set a tireless pace for his colleagues and subordinates. They recalled him sitting behind his desk carrying on four simultaneous conversations on four different telephones in a bravura display of intelligence coordination. In fact his private intelligence network gave him at least forty-eight hours' advance warning before Hitler was supposed to give the order to mobilize in September 1938. Oster's mission was thus to alert the other conspirators, first of all General von Witzleben, commander of the Third Military District, which included Berlin.

Witzleben was born in Breslau (now the Polish city of Wrocław) in 1881; his was a very old Prussian military family. Witzleben was a simple man, not particularly cultured but deeply imbued with all the traditions of the officer corps, and he had never shown any interest in politics. Even the advent of Nazism would probably not have distracted him from more pressing military concerns but for the wholesale purge of the high command and the Fritsch affair, which he felt was an unforgivable affront to the honor of the army.

In August 1938 Oster was attempting to make contact with the generals in the military districts near Berlin who might put their troops at the conspirators' disposal in the event of an anti-Nazi putsch. He approached General von Witzleben and had scarcely begun to explain the reason for his visit—Hitler's preparations for an armed attack on Czechoslovakia—when Witzleben anticipated him by offering his unconditional support to the conspirators. At the end of the interview Witzleben gave Colonel Oster his word: If Halder could reach a decision, they would go along with him; if he was still wavering, they would go ahead without him. In any case Witzleben would put himself under the orders of General Beck.

In response to the growing disaffection of the upper echelons of the army, Hitler had come to regard his generals with increasing mistrust and even hatred. He effectively severed relations with OKH and turned instead to the small coterie of Nazi loyalists in OKW. Hitler feared that he would be betrayed by those old-line staff officers whose function was to know everything and whose duty it was to conceal it. After Beck's resignation he felt that a great burden had been lifted from his shoulders. For a long time he had thought of Beck as a living relic of an outworn military creed, and his impatience quickly gave way to anger when Beck finally felt compelled to voice his own equally blunt opinions. In front of Keitel Hitler referred to his former chief of staff as "the old sniveler" and "the barracks-room lawyer." Beck himself had bid farewell to his officers with these words: "I don't understand politics very well, but I don't have to understand in order to know what has to be done." After his resignation he remained in Berlin, where most of his friends were; he had decided, with the help of his trusted friend Halder, to reduce the unapproachable Brauchitsch by siegecraft if he could not be taken by storm. Beck became a popular figure in the neighborhood—the tall, erect old general who marched straight ahead but always seemed to have a mournful, preoccupied expression. His daughter looked after the house for him, and he gave the impression that he spent all his time reading in his well-stocked library and pottering in the garden. In fact he remained active and extremely well informed. Beck's greatest talent had always been in the art of conversation, persuasion, and personal contact. He was still a leading spirit and highly respected member of an exclusive honorary society and discussion group called the Wednesday Club, which was founded in the eighteenth century as an informal adjunct to the Prussian Academy of Sciences, though the salon later attracted scholars and intellectuals of all sorts. There were never more than sixteen or seventeen members at a given time; a new member was elected only on the death of one of their number. The club met on the second Wednesday of every month; the host of that particular session would prepare a presentation on some topic from his own field of expertise, and the mistress of the house was permitted to join her guests only after the meeting, to announce that dinner was about to be served. This was always a frugal meal, as prescribed by the club rules, so that even the poorest scholar among them could entertain his guests in the same style. The Gestapo had kept Beck under close surveillance since his resignation, but he felt that he could speak freely in such company (which included a Prussian minister of state, a general, and a former ambassador); he knew that Hitler would never dare interfere with the proceedings of the society, no matter how much he detested them for their seditious opinions—for most of Beck's fellow members shared his distaste for the Führer and the Nazi regime.

Shortly after he was installed as the new chief of OKH, Halder informed his friend Beck that he would have no part of any movement that opposed Hitler unless it clearly stood on a firm legal and moral foundation. He insisted on being shown a comprehensive dossier on the crimes committed by the Nazis, on the concentration camps—as if the Gestapo were given to publicizing its exploits. Halder also intended to do nothing without the approval and complete cooperation of his superior, Brauchitsch. Still, the "Czech crisis" seemed to be gradually nudging both of them into the camp of the opposition, and there were other important points to be settled before the conspirators could fix a date for their operation. Brauchitsch, Halder, and a number of others favored bringing Goering into the conspiracy, as a counterweight to Hitler and Himmler, but how could they make contact with the Reichs-marshal without fatally compromising themselves? They learned that at a dinner at the French embassy in early August Goering had candidly addressed the subject of Czechoslovakia in the presence of the French ambassador and a great deal of his beloved French champagne: "See how this Czechoslovakia looks on the map! It flies in the face of reason—it's the inflamed appendix of Europe, and it has to be cut out." He added, "And what would France do in a case like that?"

"Make no mistake about it," Ambassador François-Poncet replied. "France will stand by her commitments."

"So much the worse, then," said Goering.

There was also the question of what to do with Hitler once the putsch had succeeded—some of the conspirators favored immediate ex-ecution, others that he should be made to answer for his crimes before a tribunal, or that he should be sequestered in an insane asylum. Cer-tainly these officers had the power to take Hitler dead or alive, but it would be difficult to reconcile any of these solutions with their oath of allegiance. Halder leaned toward the less compromising alternative of obliterating the Führer in a way that would appear to be the handiwork of some unknown terrorist—for example, blowing up his private train as it was steaming through the open countryside. However, the idea of a military coup seemed to be gaining a foothold. Brauchitsch and Halder would have to prepare a special channel of communications to their key generals; Witzleben would be given a free hand to operate in Berlin. He had already secured the backing of General Erich Hoepner, the commander of an armored division stationed in the Berlin suburbs, and he had not ruled out the possibility of arresting Halder and Brau-chitsch if they tried to back out at the last moment. The plan was for the provisional military government to step down in favor of a new civilian government, in which Dr. Schacht would play a prominent role, as quickly as possible. By now, though, events were moving rather more quickly than they would have liked.

On September 9 Hitler held another council of war at Nuremberg to discuss the final preparations for the Case Green operation against

Czechoslovakia. He was convinced that the French would do nothing to oppose him; the general staff did not agree. Halder felt that Hitler had finally brought them to the edge of the abyss; he met with Brauchitsch, but without making any visible impression on the commander in chief's massive complacency.

On September 15 the conspirators gathered in Halder's apartment to hold their own council of war. Beck, Canaris, Witzleben, Hoepner, and several others were joined by a useful new ally, Count Helldorf, the Berlin prefect of police, who believed that the coup should be launched immediately if war broke out. Canaris had prepared a kind of manifesto addressed to the German people, a complete exposé of the crimes of the Nazis. Canaris spoke quietly, his blue eyes fixed and inexpressive as glass, but the plan he presented seemed to have been drawn up by the sort of dashing, romantic young naval officer that the admiral himself had been many years ago: Canaris would request an audience with Hitler and would arrive at the Chancellery with one of his adjutants, Captain Liedig. Then Canaris would announce that he felt very ill and would leave Captain Liedig at the Chancellery, accompanied by several other officers who would wait in the antechamber. Liedig would ask the Führer's permission to present two of the officers, explaining that they had performed exceptional services for the Reich. Hitler, as was his custom, would get up from his desk to shake hands with them, whereupon they would pinion his arms, hustle him out of the Chancellery through a back entrance, and drive him out to a sanitarium in the suburbs. Meanwhile another group of reinforcements would arrive in the antechamber to deal with the Chancellery staff and Hitler's SS bodyguard. The director of the sanitarium, Dr. Kurt Borhoefferil, was a well-known psychiatrist who was prepared to commit Hitler involuntarily and to sign a certificate stating that Hitler was insane. This document would do a great deal to appease the moral scruples of the officer corps, and Witzleben would proceed to occupy the strategic points of the capital. Goering would be offered the title of Führer, which he undoubtedly would not refuse. Himmler and Rudolf Hess would be arrested immediately, and Goering could be eased out as soon as the situation was secure.

Realistically, however, this plan seemed to pose a great many practical difficulties. Witzleben suggested that it would be much simpler to arrest Hitler as soon as he returned from Nuremberg. They had started to discuss the text of the proclamation that would be addressed to the German people when they were interrupted by an astonishing piece of news being read over the radio—Chamberlain had requested an interview with Hitler, and Hitler had agreed to confer with him at Berchtesgaden; he would proceed there directly from Nuremberg without returning to Berlin. This meant not only a temporary check to Canaris' bold plan but possibly the collapse of the entire conspiracy as well. The raison d'être of the conspiracy, after all, was the removal of Hitler the adventurist warmonger, but Hitler the master diplomatist was another matter. The English appeared to be taking Hitler at face value, or as he himself had predicted, "The English will give way when I shake my fist at them, and when they realize that we intend to see this through to the end."

Several days later the German press announced that the French and British foreign ministers had met in London and devised a new set of proposals that involved further concessions to Germany at the expense of the Czechs. The Western democracies had lost their nerve, and Hitler's position was considerably strengthened. Chamberlain had returned to Germany, however, this time to Bad Godesberg, and there was talk of a breakdown in the negotiations. The foreign offices of Europe were in a frenzy, and the German people became increasingly convinced that war was inevitable. On September 27 Hitler sent an armored division rumbling across Berlin; the Berliners stared suspiciously at the troops in their battle gear, and the expected demonstrations of popular enthusiasm did not materialize. That evening, a certain Major Woeffler, who was attached to the general staff, confided to two of his fellow officers: "The real crisis won't be long in coming now. A great rift is opening up, with a handful of officers of the old Reichswehr on one side and a vast horde of newcomers on the other. There are some good fellows among them, and some pretty unsavory types as well—the Party boys, the careerists who're looking out strictly for themselves, and the ne'er-do-wells who've messed up everything else in their lives. It will take years before you'll get all the lumps out of the batter, and I only hope they give you enough time to get the job done."

"What do you mean *you*? Aren't you in this with us?"

"I haven't said anything about this to anyone, but I'm leaving. Because of my wife's family and the racial laws, they won't let my sons join the Hitler Youth, which leaves them precisely in limbo. I was an officer in the Great War, and I could have stayed on myself, but I have to think of my children. The moment they started persecuting the Jews, my mind was made up. I've been offered a job in the Dutch East Indies, and I'm off."

The German people had also begun to have doubts about their Führer; they were close enough now to the abyss that Fritsch and Halder had seen yawning from afar, and of course the Führer's most strident critics were to be found in the upper echelons of the army. Only Keitel's confidence in Hitler was unshaken: "It is regrettable that the Führer has the entire German nation behind him, with the exception of the senior generals of the army," and in fact even the few loyalist generals lost their footing in the torrent of protest. Never before had Hitler's own position been so dangerously overbalanced, but the Western powers seemed to be unaware of this. In the meantime a comprehensive plan for a military takeover of Berlin had been drawn up, but the conspirators insisted that they would have to have two days' notice before the final orders could be given; Hitler had fixed the date for the invasion of Czechoslovakia for September 30, three days away. On the twenty-eighth Witzleben asked Halder to approach the commander in chief once again. Halder came back to report that Brauchitsch was indignant over Hitler's extortionist approach to diplomacy, but not indignant enough to intervene personally; he preferred to leave things as they were. Yet Halder had still gotten the impression that Brauchitsch would budge if the operation began without him.

Witzleben telephoned Brauchitsch himself from Colonel Oster's office to inform him that all was in readiness; he had only to give the appropriate orders. Brauchitsch managed to evade this direct request for action, saying that he needed more information and he intended to look in at the Chancellery and see what had developed.

Colonel Oster was still monitoring the foreign news broadcasts, which now seemed to be contradicting themselves. The French and the British had appealed to Mussolini to mediate, a representative of the Italian government had telephoned Berlin, and finally came the announcement of the Munich Conference, a diplomatic triumph for Hitler. There was not going to be a war after all. Hitler's intuition had served him well, and his prestige was once again on the ascendant. On October 2 German troops entered the Sudetenland unopposed, and in the army the consensus had decidedly shifted: "The Führer plays a dangerous game, but he wins in the end. He knows instinctively just how far he can press his demands with the West." The moral that others drew from Munich was: "Who was right after all? Chamberlain has given in completely, and once again it seems that Beck was terrified by nothing at all. You can begin to see why the younger officers are skeptical of the old generals. Hitler's authority is growing stronger every year, and even the most diehard critics will have to hold their tongues if the West keeps giving him everything he wants." The conspirators were inclined to blame the Western Allies for this setback, even though they recognized that it was ultimately the responsibility of the German people to settle their own affairs.

"The Munich accords were primarily the handiwork of the English," wrote Ambassador François-Poncet, which is to say that Neville Chamberlain was the principal instigator of the conference. "As for me," François-Poncet went on, "I do not share the optimism which the signing of the treaty of September 29 has kindled in the breasts of certain persons. . . ." In his view, the only restraining influence that still had some effect on Hitler was that of his Italian ally. Mussolini seemed to be sincerely committed to the cause of peace, and he had done a great deal to secure the acceptance of the Munich accords as the final solution to the Czech crisis.

"There is nothing more for us to do in Berlin," observed François-Poncet. "The future is entirely in the hands of Mussolini." Before Munich French interests in Rome were represented only by a chargé d'affaires, but the apparent success of the conference—which inspired such great hopes for the relaxation of tensions between the great powers—convinced the French government to reestablish full diplomatic relations with Fascist Italy.

"Consequently," François-Poncet wrote later, "I began to hope that I might be sent to Rome . . . and when the appointment was announced officially, I received numerous assurances of friendship and regret. . . . Though Ribbentrop nevertheless sent on a report which preceded me to the Italian capital and which made me out to be a very dangerous character . . .

"Hitler decided to say his farewells in an unprecedented manner. He summoned me not to the Chancellery in Berlin or the Berghof, his chalet at Berchtesgaden, but to the Eagle's Nest itself, his nearby Alpine retreat, which until that time had been penetrated only by his intimate circle, and certainly never by a foreigner." The invitation arrived on the evening of October 17, and the ambassador set off the next day for Berchtesgaden accompanied by Captain Stehlin, the air force attaché.

"The Führer gave me a friendly and courteous welcome. He looked pale and exhausted. . . . He expressed his regret at my imminent departure, then we began to speak of politics, the last such conversation that I would have with him." At the end of two hours Hitler rose to see

his guest to the door. "Remember that the democracies are ungrateful,"
Hitler said, "even to their most faithful servant. If you ever find yourself
in difficulties, I'll always be able to get a job for you here."

"Ah! And what sort of job might that be?"

"But I've already found it, and I've even thought of an official title
for you—you will be *Reichsredner* ['Speaker of the Reich']."

It is true that Hitler had always admired the eloquence of the French
ambassador, who during his seven years' tour in Berlin had become
the dean of the Berlin diplomatic corps.

On November 8 Ernst von Rath, the third secretary of the German
Embassy in Paris, was shot by a young German Jewish refugee. Organized
reprisals began the next day; wholesale pogroms, including organized
pillaging of Jewish homes and businesses, were carried out by the SS
and the Gestapo; this was the so-called *Kristallnacht*, "Crystal Night,"
because of the splinters of broken glass that littered the streets in towns
all over Germany. (Curiously enough, the Nazi regime had been fairly
successful in holding the lid down on the rowdier manifestations of
anti-Semitism over the past two years, for fear of a boycott of the Berlin
Olympics.) The conspirators seized on this opportunity to reclaim General Halder for their cause: Oster sent him a voluminous dossier on
the anti-Semitic atrocities of the Nazis. Beck, Canaris, and Ulrich von
Hassell (who had been recalled from the embassy in Rome two years
before) all appealed to him personally; but even an interview with the
energetic Goerdeler left him unmoved. Hitler's diplomatic victory at
Munich had apparently made a deep impression on Halder, and he had
retreated to his earlier cautious position—any sort of illegal undertaking
was categorically ruled out. Brauchitsch had become ever more inaccessible, and, if that was possible, even more susceptible to the fanatical
Nazi influence of his wife.

6.

1939: First Soldier of the Reich

On March 15, 1939, Hitler allowed his gambler's instinct to get the better of him. German troops moved into Prague—in express violation of the Munich accords and all Hitler's assurances that he had no further territorial ambitions in Czechoslovakia—and it seemed that Hitler had overplayed his hand at last. The English had finally realized what sort of adversary they were dealing with, and the occupation of the non-German city of Prague made it almost inevitable that the historically German city of Danzig [1] would be annexed as well. This new threat of war restored the conspiracy to life; the conspirators' immediate objectives were unchanged—to rally Halder, Brauchitsch, and Goering (many of the conspirators were not daunted by Goering's questionable past record of service to the regime, since they felt that Goering's current loyalties were inspired only by fear of Hitler, Himmler, and Heydrich, and thus that he could be won over to their side). On the other hand, the conspiracy suffered a tangible loss when Brauchitsch promoted General von Witzleben to the command of an army group that was stationed in the Frankfurt-am-Main district—which put him well off on the sidelines as far as events in Berlin were concerned. On May 23, during a planning session at the Chancellery, Hitler announced that an attack on Poland might well provoke a wider and more protracted war, but he hoped—and Brauchitsch seemed to second him in this—that a campaign of a few weeks' duration would settle the issue.

Then Hitler turned to a different subject: "Why didn't the French intervene the moment we reoccupied the Rhineland? Why did they allow us to reintroduce conscription? Why didn't they object when we began to build up our Wehrmacht? Why did they just stand idly by while we moved into Austria and Czechoslovakia? Because their entire country is being torn apart by factional struggles . . . their people are worried only about hanging on to their material comforts. Because their army

---

1. Formerly the chief port of East Prussia, designated a "free city" in 1919, at the head of the Polish Corridor, which separated East Prussia from the rest of the German Reich (and now the Polish city of Gdansk).

is ill-prepared, and they lack the will to fight, and their armaments are obsolete. . . . Because the French people are satiated, they want nothing to disturb their repose, they don't want to fight. . . . No one can say how long they'll remain in this torpor, but as chief of state I must assume that the French will attempt to become militarily strong once again. They have plenty of time; I don't. . . ." In fact Hitler's major expansionist adventures—the occupation of the Rhineland, the proclamation of the Anschluss with Austria—were launched while the French government was paralyzed by a cabinet crisis. Hitler's last remark is a cryptic allusion to the real reason for Hitler's impatience. He was convinced, as he once confided to Mme François-Poncet, that he had only ten years to live. This was why, as General Heusinger explained, Hitler was determined to push the timetable forward as far as he could, though he did not expect to be fully prepared for war until 1943.

The time had come once again for the conspirators to regroup and resume the siege of Generals Halder and Brauchitsch. This time their emissary was one of Brauchitsch's cousins, who was a close friend of Hassell's. He had asked Frau von Brauchitsch to pass on the warning that an attack on Poland would bring about a general European war; Brauchitsch listened in silence to his cousin's recital, then replied simply, "Please give my regards to the ambassador." Hassell's next attempt to appeal to Brauchitsch directly was met with similar rebuff; the commander in chief was now ostensibly too busy to receive visitors.

Perhaps the definitive verdict on the state of the army at that time was pronounced by the former commander of the Reichswehr, General Kurt von Hammerstein, a stoic blue-eyed giant who was called the Red General because he had had extensive dealings with the Red Army while secret units of the Reichswehr were bring trained and equipped inside the Soviet Union. He had been dismissed by Hitler in 1934 (to be replaced by the unfortunate Blomberg), but collaborated actively with Beck, Canaris, and Goerdeler in the years that followed. "The German army," he observed in 1939, "is a headless, nerveless body which has been emasculated by the negligence and lassitude of its commanders."

On August 22 Hitler invited his senior generals to Berchtesgaden, where, after an elaborate banquet accompanied by the finest wines, he planned to address them, once again, on the subject of his foreign policy. "Hitler began by summarizing his accomplishments since 1933," General Heusinger recalled, "then went on to say that there were two problems that remained to be dealt with: the colonies and the Polish Corridor.

As far as the colonies were concerned, he hoped to strike a bargain with the English, and in any case, he was not about to fight for them. As far as Danzig and the Corridor were concerned, however, he had decided to settle things right away. The world, he said, had seen a great many demonstrations of his love of peace. He had reached an agreement with the English to limit naval rearmament, he had guaranteed the territorial integrity of France in her present borders and had renounced all claims to Alsace and Lorraine, albeit with a heavy heart. He had shown these other nations that he had no intention of forcing them into another war, and he added, 'I know what war is. I have lived through it in all its wretchedness and suffering, and I wish that the other heads of state were all combat veterans who knew what war really means. . . . If the English intend to support the Poles from behind the scenes, then let them realize that I cannot tolerate any more of this boorish Polish insolence.' And Hitler went on to make the connection clearer: 'If we have to resort to force of arms to prove ourselves right— and I will have the justice of our claims recognized at the point of the sword—then be assured, gentlemen, that I will avoid a second world war. The French will not fight for the sake of the Poles, and England will give way.' "

It was then that Hitler made an extraordinary announcement: "In several days I am going to conclude a nonaggression pact [with the Soviet Union]. You will soon see what an effect that will have on the rest of the world. If it becomes necessary, I am counting on you to crush our Polish enemy with all the impetuous fervor of a young Wehrmacht with the entire German people standing firmly behind it, united by the idea of National Socialism, so that soon the world will be faced with an accomplished fact."

"Not one of us moved," Heusinger recalled. "We were all struck dumb with astonishment. Then someone said, 'Splendid! He's going to do it again!' and someone else answered, 'No, he overestimates his own strength and he underrates the determination of the English—but a pact with the Russians could change everything.' General von Stülpnagel did not hesitate to express his private thoughts: 'He's a madman, he's willing to take any risk, and there won't be any stopping him now.' "

The next day, August 23, Foreign Minister Joachim von Ribbentrop—the man whom François-Poncet called "Hitler's evil genius"—arrived in Moscow to sign the nonaggression pact with the Soviet Union.

The conspirators' reaction to the Hitler-Stalin pact was mixed, though Beck was not alone in defending it as a timely revival of Bismarck's policy of rapprochement with Russia. Still, though they were as yet unaware of its exact provisions, they all felt that the very existence of such a pact meant that war was virtually inevitable.

The French and the British confirmed their earlier guarantees to defend Poland if it was attacked. Beck wrote to Brauchitsch to remind him of the tremendous responsibility he would have to bear if war broke out; Brauchitsch naturally did not reply. Beck then asked Halder to come see him, and Halder, recognizing that events had proved Beck right, came. Halder was now convinced that war with Poland would be only the prelude to worldwide conflict, from which Germany could not possibly emerge victorious. However, Halder still believed that the time for action had not yet arrived, and Beck was forced to conclude that it would be useless to rely on him in the future; General von Witzleben, now commanding Army Group 2, had not wavered in his convictions, but he was still too far from the capital to be of any practical help.

On August 31 Admiral Canaris learned that the order had been given to attack, and on September 1 from the stage of the Kroll Opera House in Berlin, Hitler announced to the Reichstag that Germany was at war with Poland: "From this moment on," he declared, "I am nothing more than the first soldier of the Reich. I have once again put on the uniform that was so dear to me, which I held sacred. I will not put it aside until we have achieved total victory, and if destiny denies us this prize, then I will not survive." Hitler was wearing black uniform trousers and a field-gray jacket with no decoration or badge of rank except a gold party badge, his Iron Cross, First Class, and an eagle on his left sleeve, the insignia of the army.

The German people received this news unenthusiastically but without any particular sense of foreboding. Fortune was still smiling on their Führer, and the Polish campaign was concluded even more rapidly than had been expected, since although England and France had in turn declared war on September 3, their armies made no attempt to come to the defense of the Poles. Once again, Hitler had played a winning hand. Warsaw surrendered on September 29 after a bitter struggle, and Colonel von Greiffenberg, chief of the Operations Section of OKH (who would be succeeded by Heusinger the following year), suggested to Halder that they begin to reroute the troops toward the west: "The situation on the French frontier is appalling. According to our calculations, their troop concentrations should have reached maximum strength some time ago. If they want to come to the aid of Poland, they won't wait a moment longer."

Halder was unconvinced: "The French missed their chance, when it would have been all too easy for them to intervene."

Shortly after the end of the Polish campaign and the army's blitzkrieg victory, Hitler announced to the officers of OKW that he had complete confidence in the generals of the Luftwaffe, which Reichsmarshal Goering fully shared, as well as in the admirals under the command of Grand Admiral Raeder, but "on the other hand, I have misgivings about the generals of the land forces." If fact, the generals had been accusing the SS of committing atrocities during the recent campaign; specifically, SS Totenkopf units [2] operating behind the front lines were reported to have brutally executed a number of Jews and Polish civilians. The Führer waved these charges aside indignantly—these SS units had simply been carrying out their orders. They had been ordered to be ruthless, and ruthless they had been. Case dismissed. By a decree of October 17 special tribunals were established for the SS, presided over by judges appointed by the Führer; the Waffen SS was no longer answerable to the military courts. Thus the generals would have no legal grounds for complaint in the future. The Nazi threat to the autonomy of the Wehrmacht, which the generals thought had been dispelled by the Night of the Long Knives and the purge of the SA in 1934, had finally been reawakened by the "black knights" of the Waffen SS. The storm troopers of the SA had been formidable only in their sheer numbers, but (at least from a Prussian perspective) they were little more than a rabble of ill-equipped, undisciplined street brawlers. In the Waffen SS, on the other hand, the generals were faced with a half-dozen divisions of hand-picked volunteers, superbly trained and lavishly furnished with the latest arms and equipment—and who appeared to be making a bid to beat them at their own game.

On October 6 Hitler's first peace initiative was rejected out of hand by the French and the English; two weeks later Hitler summoned his generals once more to announce that the offensive on the western front would be launched at the beginning of November. Brauchitsch and

---

2. The *Totenkopfverbände* ("Death's-head battalions") served as concentration camp guards and, in partnership with the Gestapo, had already begun the mass roundups and executions of Jews and all Poles whom they deemed "capable of leadership" (intellectuals, Catholic priests, and the nobility). A number of Waffen SS troops were given token prison sentences by the military courts for atrocities committed against civilians until Brauchitsch, after vigorous prompting from Himmler, announced a "general amnesty." [Tr.]

Halder called Hitler's attention to the possibility that bad weather might prevent the Luftwaffe from providing adequate air support. Hitler pondered this, hesitated, then began to berate the generals en masse. They were always trying, he said, to dissuade him from doing anything at all—Brauchitsch in particular. Brauchitsch offered his resignation on the spot, which Hitler refused; he would rather have Brauchitsch than a commander in chief with genuine authority that might rival his own. In any case, the offensive would begin on November 12.

At the headquarters of the Operations Section of OKH at Zossen a number of staff officers, Heusinger among them, discussed the prospects for the offensive: "The Führer regards the English as a Germanic people, but he expects England to come up with a set of proposals that will put an end to the war. If these proposals fail to materialize, then he will try to defeat the French as quickly as possible to force the English to negotiate." But could the French be beaten as easily as the Poles? As far as Hitler was concerned, the answer was yes. Most of the officers Heusinger spoke to were less complacent: "The French armament is much better than the Poles', their commanders are first-rate, and the Maginot Line will allow them to defend their frontiers south of Trier with a minimum of troops. If we follow the old Schlieffen Plan and drive south through Belgium—an eventuality that they must have prepared for—they'll be able to intercept us in force. It won't be a surprise attack this time, and the outcome of that initial encounter will decide the fate of our entire offensive." There was one unknown quantity: the panzers, which would be facing a mechanized adversary for the first time. Would the French armor be overrun as easily as the Polish infantry and cavalry had been? "Our troops have already seen action, and the French don't have much of a will to fight. That is our best hope."

Beck and the others feared that the offensive would fail completely of its objective, and they asked General Georg Thomas, chief of the Economics Section of OKH, to draft a memorandum stating their case and to present it to General Halder. Thomas reported to GHQ at Zossen on November 2. Thomas was respected as a highly capable staff officer, and for some time he had acted as the spokesman of the anti-Hitler faction of the general staff. Halder called him into his office as soon as he had read the memorandum and launched into a discussion of the necessity of forestalling the offensive and of putting an end to a war that could only end badly for Germany. Thomas was astonished by Halder's abrupt reversal—now he was advocating once again that

Hitler be assassinated by means of a carefully staged accident.

Halder sent for Colonel Oster and asked him to review all the arrangements that had been made in September 1938 and then get in touch with his adjutant, General von Stülpnagel. Stülpnagel, unlike his chief, had remained steadfast in his commitment to the conspiracy, and he had familiarized himself with every detail of the existing plan. The watchword was now: Be ready by November 5.

On the morning of the fourth Brauchitsch and Halder flew to the western frontier to confer with the army group commanders. They had essentially agreed to wait for the order to launch the offensive and then refuse to pass this order on to their commanders. Clearly the generals who were to take part (or rather, not to take part) in the offensive would have to be alerted; after that there would be nothing left for them to do but move into action, to turn their guns against the supreme warlord and his black knights.

On November 5 Hitler summoned Brauchitsch to the Chancellery to confirm the attack order for the twelfth and to issue him his final instructions. It would be up to Brauchitsch to make his objections felt, or indeed to refuse to transmit the order at all, and the coup would be as good as launched, or he might choose instead to delay this act of direct defiance until the actual order to attack was in his hands. At any rate Brauchitsch did set forth his objections to Hitler's campaign plan: The enemy still enjoyed numerical superiority; they must not be underestimated by any means. Even though much French equipment was obsolescent, it was still superior to that of the Poles. For the first time the Wehrmacht would be called upon to engage mechanized forces, and the task of the Luftwaffe would accordingly be more difficult. At present there were twenty-four divisions, including several newly raised armored divisions, which were still in the process of formation; the same held true of the engineers and the artillery. Thus, the commander in chief concluded, if the attack could be postponed for a few months, all of these units could be brought up to full strength, the balance between the various branches of the army would be restored, and the prospects for a successful offensive would be greatly improved.

Hitler took this all in without flinching, though his face was taut and drawn, and his slender, expressive fingers, which seemed to be animated by an independent spirit of their own, twitched nervously on his desk. Finally he replied. General Heusinger has supplied us with a report of the ensuing confrontation between the "first soldier of Germany" and the commander in chief of the German army:

"General, I am interrupting you because I do not share your opinion at all. First of all, I set very little stock in the fighting spirit of the French army. A nation's army is the reflection of its people, and thus, even if their officer corps is courageous and well trained, the army itself will not be able to display the sort of resolution that will be asked of them in battle. They don't want to fight and they will collapse quickly enough after the first few setbacks. In addition, they will not be fighting to achieve a greater goal, as we are.

"In the second place, I have been following the course of French rearmament, more closely no doubt than our own military intelligence, and from a practical rather than a theoretical standpoint. The French have been rearming since 1936, but if you count the number of workers employed in their armaments industry—which can be calculated exactly from the unemployment figures and the number of workers engaged in other industries—you can deduce easily enough the number of tanks, heavy guns, and planes that have been produced since 1935—which does not even begin to approach the figures supplied by our general staff. In other words a substantial fraction of the French army's equipment necessarily dates from before 1936 and will not be of any great value in combat.

"In the third place, general, I do not believe that the numerical balance will have shifted in our favor by spring. If we equip twenty-four new divisions, we should expect the enemy to do the same, particularly with the addition of the British Expeditionary Force. Belgium and France will be working feverishly on their fortifications, and nothing will be working in our favor. Whereas now is our best opportunity. Our Western adversaries are still paralyzed by our victory over the Poles. If we give them a good shaking up, they will understand, after we have struck with a series of lightning blows, that they will only be delivering themselves up to an even bloodier holocaust if they choose to continue. I should strike at the west as soon as possible, and this is what I wish to do. Our army stands on the threshold of a victory as decisive as the victory over the Poles. You must put your trust in me."

Brauchitsch remained skeptical. He mentioned the difficulties that the panzer divisions would encounter at least at the outset; the Meuse and the network of canals in Belgium and the Ardennes would prevent their being used as effectively as in Poland, which would entail a loss of momentum. Apart from that, good weather would be the first prerequisite if the offensive were to gain ground rapidly; severe cold, rain, or snow would cause delays which would only benefit the enemy. Thus they would be running the risk that their advance would be totally stalled, and a positional stalemate, reminiscent of the trench warfare of 1914–18, would be the result:

"You yourself, my Führer, know how difficult it is to get these things under way, which is why I'm doubly concerned that we'll be setting off in winter."

Hitler was still not convinced, however: "Put your mind at rest, general; I study the weather report every day, and I have retained the services of a qualified meteorologist. The western winters vary a great deal—mild or bitter, wet or dry—but the cold is not severe enough to cause serious engine trouble, and if there are spells of extremely bad weather, then our enemies will also be stopped in their tracks. In fact, I believe that the French are more susceptible to the cold than we are.

"In any case, general, as soon as we're sure that weather conditions will be favorable, I shall give the order to attack. I have been aware for some time—much longer than you have—of the sort of baleful predictions the general staff have been making about the outcome of my decision." Hitler raised his voice; his face grew pale. "But they will not deflect me from the course I have chosen—no more than they have already done—for the salvation of the German people."

Brauchitsch might have chosen to withdraw discreetly at this point and simply wait for the arrival of der Tag to give the signal for the generals' rising. However, he saw fit to raise one final objection: He told the Führer of his misgivings about the level of training and discipline in the army. He explained that serious shortcomings had been observed in Poland which, quite naturally, could be traced to the rapid expansion of the army and of the officer corps in particular: "They do not display the precision, the competence that they once did, the sort of scrupulous attention to detail in supervising the men. It will take me all winter to put everything in order, especially in the newly raised units. Apart from that, there were a great many incidents in Poland that proved that discipline in the ranks still leaves a great deal to be desired."

But Hitler had heard enough of this; he leaped to his feet and bore down on the general until they were only a few inches apart. "These accusations are monstrous," Hitler shouted, "and they reflect both on the army that you command, general, and on myself. Do you realize that? For six years I have been trying to teach our people, our youth especially, discipline, obedience, and a sense of duty. . . . And you come here today and make these wild accusations. . . . You are telling me that all my work has come to nothing! I've mobilized the entire apparatus of my Party to furnish the army with virile young recruits—and perhaps the world has never seen a finer body of men, and certainly the state of their morale leaves nothing to be desired. And you claim that they have not lived up to our expectations of them? For my part, I shall have to see some documentary evidence of these disciplinary problems that you've been referring to. And I intend to take the most vigorous measures against the persons responsible, particularly the senior officers who have tolerated that sort of thing. As far as the rest of it goes, I want you to deploy your troops for an immediate attack. I bear the sole responsibility, not you, no more than any other commander in chief. You may prepare to attack!''

Hitler grabbed the sheaf of documents that Brauchitsch had placed on his desk, threw them on the floor, and trampled them underfoot. Then he pounced on Brauchitsch himself, snatched the few papers he was still holding on to, and tore them to pieces. There were flecks of foam on Hitler's lips as he manhandled Brauchitsch out the door of his office, and Brauchitsch, moaning and blubbering, was virtually in shock. He had paid the price for speaking the unspeakable, and now he would have to solicit some sort of corroboration of the charges he had made from all his army commanders to save the situation.

A man of firmer character might have taken this extraordinary scene as an additional reason for ridding Germany of a dangerous fanatic and avenged this undignified assault on his honor. Brauchitsch, however, made it the pretext for abdicating all personal responsibility for the final decision. He summoned Halder to his office and told him that he might feel free to carry on, but he himself would not be taking the initiative any longer. With Brauchitsch lending his tacit support, Halder could still set the machinery of the coup in motion, but Halder himself was actually hoping to turn the entire mission over to a willing deputy. He settled on Canaris, who refused. The admiral detested violence and had never been in favor of attempting to assassinate Hitler. But, in any case, the immediate task was to forestall the offensive on November 12, and thus to obtain a commitment from Brauchitsch and Halder that they would refuse to transmit the order to attack.

Beck sent Stülpnagel to announce that he was ready to assume military leadership of the insurrection if that would relieve the commander in chief and the chief of the general staff of all responsibility for the coup. He made one stipulation, however; he wanted assurances that the three army group commanders in the west—Gerd von Rundstedt, Fedor von Bock, and Wilhelm Ritter von Leeb—would not come flying to Hitler's rescue; Witzleben was eager to receive similar guarantees from these three generals. Colonel Oster served as Beck's envoy on these difficult missions, but all the generals he called on seemed to be paralyzed with fear, Rundstedt in particular. This tall, spare, dignified old Junker (born in 1875) felt the deepest contempt for Hitler, "the mad corporal," but he still wished to have nothing whatsoever to do with politics.

"To all appearances," writes the historian Heinrich Uhlig, "Rundstedt was a grand seigneur, the picture of the old-school commander in chief, but he would invariably bend to Hitler's will." Raymond Cartier confirms this judgment in his *Histoire de la deuxième guerre mondiale*: "Rundstedt strictly avoided intrigue of any kind. To be sure, he detested Hitler and permitted his staff to speak of him in the most blasphemous terms. Rundstedt himself never hesitated to show his contempt for Hitler, but though he was aware of the existence of a conspiracy, he refused to recognize or countenance it in any way. His attitude, in the words of General Hans Speidel, was no more than *'eine sarkästische Resignation.'* It never crossed his mind that a Prussian marshal might take up arms against his commander in chief, in the face of the enemy and in wartime, even if that commander in chief was Adolf Hitler."

Oster returned to Berlin to do what he could to keep the shaky structure of the conspiracy from collapsing altogether, but there was nothing more to be done, since every general who held an important command shrank in horror from the responsibility of launching the coup. At least the urgency of Oster's mission was relieved somewhat on November 7, when an unexpected announcement came from OKW: the offensive was to be postponed for several days. Similar announcements were made at regular intervals over the next two weeks.

On November 8 a bomb exploded under the impromptu stage that had been set up in the Munich beerhall where the anniversary of the abortive putsch of 1923 was celebrated every year. The building was partly demolished, several people were killed and wounded, but Hitler had left the premises less than ten minutes before the explosion, prompted, as he was to explain shortly after the event, by an inner voice that compelled him to leave with all possible speed and thus saved his life. The other circumstances of this first serious attempt on Hitler's life are scarcely less mysterious; the official culprit at any rate was a woodworker called Georg Elser, who confessed to having planted the bomb.

At noon on November 23 Hitler summoned all his army commanders to the Chancellery in order to issue a warning. Once again, when confronted by the senior officers of his army, the architects of victory in Poland, he bayed at them like a wild animal. "He barked," Halder wrote in his journal. "He denounced all the generals as representatives of a mentality that had been discredited during the First World War. The concept of knightly honor, he said, had absolutely no meaning for him. He accused the high command of consistently having opposed him in undertakings that were ultimately crowned with success. It was Hitler and Hitler alone who had created the new army, acting against the advice of his generals, and it was to him alone that all the credit for the victory in Poland was due. Now, he concluded, the high command was trying to find some spurious reason to thwart his plans for the offensive in the west, but he would not allow himself to be deflected from his purpose."

But for whatever reason—the heavy rains, the gloomy situation reports submitted by his generals, the inadequate stockpiles of arms and ammunition, or the disinclination of the Italians—the attack was put off once more, until the twenty-sixth, then put off several times more, and finally postponed indefinitely. Nevertheless, the conspirators were still uneasy; the assassination attempt of November 8 had produced no discernible reaction in Germany, which plunged the generals deeper into despair. Now they even began to suspect each other; they no longer dared to meet or to talk on the telephone, and each of them began to reproach the others for their alleged indiscretions.

7.

1940: "I Can Force Them to Obey Me"

Almost three months later, in early February, Hitler sent for General von Manstein. Erich von Lewinski von Manstein was born in Berlin on November 24, 1887. In 1930 Adolf Heusinger was a young officer on Lieutenant Colonel von Manstein's staff; he recalls, "Manstein the Berliner could accomplish in a single night what the other military leaders would take weeks to do. He could see in a flash how an operation should be carried out. His quickness, his capacity for work, and his ability to get things done were exceptional. As a strategist he was a genius—the best of them all." In Heusinger's opinion only Rundstedt and Fedor von Bock were even in the same class; Rommel, he explains, was a tactician, a battlefield commander with an exceptional gift for feeling out the enemy's weak points, but Rommel was not really a strategist.

At the end of this February afternoon in 1940, just as Manstein was leaving the Defense Ministry in the Bendlerstrasse, the following dialogue took place between an officer attached to the OKW operational staff and one of Hitler's aides-de-camp.

"It's a good thing you've brought Manstein to meet the Führer. In my opinion he's the only one who measures up to the problems we'll be faced with in this new world war. . . . Do you know what they talked about?"

"About the offensive in the west exclusively," replied that ADC. "The Führer's been busy with that for weeks. He wants to abandon the old Schlieffen Plan and shift the center of gravity to Rundstedt's army group.[1] He felt hesitant about that, but Manstein agreed with him and that was very reassuring."[2] Hitler's appreciation of Manstein was

1. Army Group A, which, thanks to Guderian, would achieve a decisive breakthrough at Sedan.

2. In fact it was Manstein who came up with the plan, though he and Hitler had apparently been thinking along parallel lines. Hitler took this as a great tribute to his own strategic acumen, and he endorsed Manstein's plan wholeheartedly. The essential idea was to concentrate the bulk of the armored and mechanized units against the northwest bastion of the Maginot Line, so that they could drive a wedge between the French fortifications and the Allied armor deployed to the west. Thus, if the German panzers could

highly qualified, though: "He is certainly very intelligent and an exceptionally gifted strategist, but I still don't have complete confidence in him—he's a devout Protestant." Hitler was uncomfortable with those whom he felt to be his natural superiors, and Himmler did everything possible to feed the Führer's jealousy and mistrust where Manstein was concerned. In later years he was obliged to take the blame even for his successes on the battlefield—Hitler referred to him contemptuously as the "chamber-pot general" after he engineered the remarkably efficient retreat from the Dnieper during the Russian campaign. *and saved the lives of a whole army of men against Hitler's order to remain & die where they were*

When the staff officer asked about the state of Hitler's relations with Brauchitsch, the ADC made a wry face and replied, "Things have been patched up since November as well as could be expected, but the Führer will never forget Brauchitsch's remarks about the lack of discipline in 'his army.' You know he has a memory like an elephant's—and an insult like that is going to stick in the back of his mind forever."

Before launching the offensive in the west, however, Hitler had decided to carry out another, less ambitious operation—the invasion of Norway. A number of generals were openly cynical about Hitler's change of heart, but the navy was quite concerned about the prospect of a confrontation with the British flotilla that patrolled the coast of Norway. Brauchitsch and Halder were not informed until March 5, several weeks after preparations for the invasion, directed by Keitel, Jodl, and General Nikolaus von Falkenhorst, were already under way. "The Führer claims to have proof that the English have designs on Norway, which would justify this decision," Halder observed.

On April 9 German troops moved north into Denmark and Norway. Such resistance as they encountered was quickly subdued, and the massive counterattack on the part of the Royal Navy failed to materialize. Falkenhorst had won the victor's laurels, but he was incautious enough to register a complaint about a Waffen SS regiment that was under his command. Predictably Hitler exploded: "My SS troops are not bad soldiers—it's Falkenhorst who's a bad commanding officer!" and Falkenhorst was soon to disappear from the scene. After the success of the Norwegian campaign the generals refused to listen to any more talk of conspiracy: the Führer's intuition clearly made his leadership infallible.

The French and the British were aware that the Wehrmacht was preparing for a spring offensive in the west. One of Canaris' agents, a

---

break this weakest link in the French defenses and advance to occupy the heavily wooded Ardennes plateau, they could drive on straight through to the Channel, or to Paris.

Many of the alleged war crimes were not proved against him —

prominent Munich lawyer called Joseph Müller, was passing information to the Belgian government by way of his connections in Rome; Oster had a direct channel to the Dutch government, but he could not tell the Dutch or the Belgians anything they had not already suspected, and in any case they were reluctant or unable to do anything to save themselves at this late date. Hitler relieved Brauchitsch of the task of drawing up plans for the invasion of the Low Countries and entrusted it to his faithful servants at OKW, Keitel and Jodl.

At 5:30 AM on May 10, 1940, the blitzkrieg was launched, and even the staunchest of the conspirators did everything in their power to ensure the success of the offensive. On the evening of May 13 at an army command post west of Luxembourg, the commanding general told his chief of staff: "We will find out today whether this operation is going to succeed. If Guderian can force a passage from the Meuse to Sedan, then what once seemed barely possible will have become a reality. This is one day's work that Guderian hasn't exactly been looking forward to."

On their southern flank the French had not budged from their positions. "Every day they hang back, then so much the better for us. The divisions in our second wave are moving right up and wheeling around toward the Maginot Line. Soon the danger will have passed, and it's a miracle that the enemy have let this chance slip through their fingers. This is one maneuver they weren't ready for, and now they're just watching it all go by."

"And what's the word on Bock's army group?"

"The glider assault on Eben-Emaël was a success. The forward elements of the French mechanized columns seem to have pushed on to the east of the River Dyle. . . . Hitler will be pleased by what's happened at Eben-Emaël [3]—that was his idea. He makes plans that fly in the face of all the rules of warfare, but they work for him.

"Bock is about to make contact with the French—wonderful news! They've crossed over into Belgium and fallen into the trap. That means our advance will be all the more decisive." [4] A signals officer appeared

3. In other words, the French mechanized troops (numerically superior to the Germans') had allowed themselves to be decoyed out of an excellent defensive position—and ultimately to be disastrously outflanked by the main German drive to the south. Eben-Emaël, also in Belgium, was a fortress that was successfully stormed by a handful of German glider troops and parachutists—thereby forcing the Allies to abandon still another excellent defensive position, this time in full retreat.

4. Henri Michel, president of the International Committee on the History of the Second World War, summarizes the strategic situation in these words: ". . . the generalissimo of the Anglo-French forces [Gamelin] hardly suspected that in advancing in Belgium

with a personal radiogram for the general; he read it out loud: "Crossed Meuse, broken through at Sedan. Am pressing on toward Laon. At any rate it looks like we've done it. Guderian."

Heinz Guderian—"Heinz the Meteor" as his troops called him after the Battle of France—was born in 1888 in the Prussian town of Kulm (now Chełmno, Poland). He joined the army when he was nineteen, and after the war he became an expert in the theory of mechanized warfare. Guderian was unsparing of his own energies, and he demanded as much from his troops: The standing order was to advance until the last drop of fuel was spent. "Anyway," he explained, "you have to watch out for unit commanders who claim that they've run out of fuel. Usually they have quite enough, but as soon as they get tired, it starts to run out."

On May 17 Colonel Charles de Gaulle was chosen to lead the French counterattack. The 4th Armored Division, reinforced by a battalion of B tanks and two battalions of obsolete R 35 light tanks, succeeded in breaking through to Montcornet, "destroying everything that had not escaped in time." This came as a rude shock to the Germans, but they were able to halt de Gaulle's advance with their light antiaircraft batteries and a few tanks that had recently returned from the refitting sheds in the rear. De Gaulle launched a fresh attack on the nineteenth, and this time the French 4th Armored penetrated to within a few kilometers of Guderian's field HQ, which was virtually unprotected; shortly afterward Guderian dismissed this precarious passage as merely "a few hours' difficulty."

On May 21 Hitler complained that the infantry were not following up on the armored advance closely enough; this was accompanied by a number of scathing observations aimed at Brauchitsch. Nevertheless he announced that the campaign in northern France was over, and it was time to prepare for the second assault, which would force the French to lay down their arms altogether. Brauchitsch suggested a new battle plan, which Hitler agreed to that morning, but by afternoon he had changed his mind. Brauchitsch, routed on the map table once again, retreated in confusion; in any case, even this unbroken string of successes

---

the Allied armies were behaving like a mighty tree that obligingly uproots itself in order to make it easier for the storm to blow it down. It slowly dawned on him that the bulk of the German forces were not to be found in Belgium at all, but farther to the south, where no one expected them to be, in the Ardennes. . . . If [Hitler's] gamble paid off, then victory would be total. The risk was only proportional to the size of the stakes involved. . . ."

had not mitigated Hitler's hostility toward his commander in chief. This greatest triumph of German arms coincided with Brauchitsch's fortieth year in his country's service, but Hitler gave orders that this anniversary should be celebrated as unostentatiously as possible. "That monocled old Junker had never ceased to plead the cause of weakness, and he set himself against all my ideas." Hitler took this opportunity to heap even more abuse on all his generals—"those old fossils, those idiots; I denounce them for their total lack of imagination, for their refusal to accept the National Socialist ideology, for their contempt for the Party and its leaders. They want to trample on all that with their shiny black boots. . . . I can't expect them to understand me, but I can force them to obey me!"

On May 24 Hitler gave Brauchitsch another tongue-lashing because he had transferred the 4th Army from Rundstedt's Army Group A to Bock's Army Group B. Rundstedt ranked very high in Hitler's favor at that time, and Hitler had personally visited Army Group HQ at Charle-ville to offer his congratulations. "You have shown an admirable grasp of my ideas," he told him, and in fact Hitler was prepared to make remarkable allowances in Rundstedt's case: "I know that he is a general of the old Prussian school and he has no love for National Socialism, but he is an excellent soldier." This would not prevent him from being cashiered on three separate occasions over the next five years. Each time Hitler complained that Rundstedt was "an old man who has lost his nerve." "Rundstedt," Heusinger said, "would never have the courage to say to Hitler, 'Resign. Get out,' though this was a liberty that Rund-stedt, as senior marshal, might well have taken."

Brauchitsch proposed an all-out armored attack on the Vimy–Saint-Omer–Gravelines line, along the Channel, in order to put irresistible pressure on the pocket around Dunkirk where the French and the British Expeditionary Force were still holding out. Hitler frowned. "I can't say that I approve, Brauchitsch, because we will have to keep our panzers in reserve for the new battle that is about to be joined. However, I will not make a ruling on this myself; I will leave the final decision to Rundstedt." To appeal to one of his subordinate commanders to resolve this difference of opinion was another grievous affront to the commander in chief—and Rundstedt, naturally, was inclined to agree with the Führer. This resulted in a serious tactical blunder that allowed virtually all the British troops (and nearly two-thirds of the French) to be rescued in the "miracle of Dunkirk."

On the same day, May 24, the order went out to Rundstedt's headquarters: "The main concentration of armored units is not to advance to the west of the line Le Cateau–Laon." The panzers were stopped in their tracks to the south of Dunkirk. When the order was passed on to Major von Tresckow of Rundstedt's staff, he blurted out, "This is pure madness—we have to reach the Channel as soon as possible!" The reaction at OKH headquarters was much the same: "What's the point of this preposterous order? Do we want to build them a golden bridge so they can march straight off the beaches without getting their feet wet? Are we going to let them evacuate their entire expeditionary corps? This is a disgrace!" At this point an OKW staff officer attempted to explain: "This may decide the outcome of the war. Hitler's reasoning is this—he's afraid that our armor may sustain heavy losses in the ditches and hedgerows around Dunkirk; he seems to be thinking of the last war. Then, these armored units won't have the wherewithal for the second phase of the offensive. Also, Goering has guaranteed that the Luftwaffe will prevent the English from evacuating the beaches and ferrying their troops across the Channel. As always, Keitel is keeping his own council. Tonight I had a rather violent difference of opinion with him. . . . At any rate, up until now the Luftwaffe has had a rather undistinguished record in all its operations against naval targets.

"Our people," the OKW officer added, "are getting drunk on promises. The atmosphere is very unpleasant. Yesterday the Führer went off on a long tirade because the Crown Prince's eldest son was killed in action—it was already galling enough that Fritsch was killed at Warsaw. This time he announced that he didn't want anyone else from the old royal families to die for the cause and be resurrected as a heroic legend."

"Mean-spirited," remarked the OKH officer. "The old Prussian ruling class is anathema to him—he even thinks they're dangerous. That's part of the reason why he doesn't get along with Brauchitsch and Manstein."

The 7th Armored Division was the first to reach the Channel. Its commander, General Erwin Rommel, born near Ulm in 1891, the son of a high-school teacher, was not a member of the old Prussian ruling class, and he had given his unconditional allegiance to the Führer. "What a shame," remarked Guderian, "that they stopped me before I got to Boulogne." (Rommel's division was part of Guderian's XIX Army Corps, which was attached to Rundstedt's army group; thus both generals were reined in before they could close with the French and English troops who had fallen back on Dunkirk.)

Why had Hitler issued such an order? He had allowed the British to save their best troops, who would become the elite cadres of the Commonwealth forces. Hitler's explanation—"worn-out troops, short on supplies"—does not seem very compelling, nor do Goering's assurances that the Luftwaffe alone would prevent the evacuation. This was to be the Reichsmarshal's first major setback.

"In fact," Heusinger explained, "Hitler wanted to preserve England at all costs. He didn't hesitate to make statements like, 'We need the English—they're the policemen of the world . . . and we're of the same blood.' "

In addition, in General Heusinger's opinion, the explanations offered by the OKW staff officer were essentially correct. Hitler had seen action in Flanders during the First World War, and he remembered only too clearly how the Belgians had opened the floodgates on the marshy coastal plain and come close to annihilating the right wing of the German army, which was advancing on the French Channel ports from the north. Thus, in 1940, the German panzers were ordered to halt at Le Cateau. Also, Heusinger adds, Hitler still had a great deal of confidence in Goering and the Luftwaffe, and he was well pleased with Goering's guarantee that the British could be destroyed on the beaches without exposing any of his precious panzers to the risks of attacking a heavily entrenched position.

Belgium surrendered on May 25, and the British evacuation plan went into effect immediately. The French and British navies, assisted by hundreds of civilian vessels, succeeded in bringing some 338,000 men off the beaches and out of Dunkirk harbor. By the time the operation was completed on June 4, the Germans were masters of Belgium, the Netherlands, Luxembourg, and all of France north of the Somme. Events began to move even more rapidly now. On June 14 the Germans marched into Paris, which had been declared an open city after the government fled to Bordeaux. Italy declared war on the tenth and attempted to invade the south of France, without making much headway. On June 17 Marshal Pétain succeeded Paul Reynaud as president of the council of state; he asked for an armistice the following day, the same day on which General de Gaulle broadcast his appeal from London to continue the struggle under the banner of the Cross of Lorraine. Pétain's request was granted on the twenty-first, and the formal surrender was concluded on the twenty-fifth. Here are some impressions of the soldiers of the victorious army, recorded by General Heusinger during the last days of the Battle of France:

"The English at Dunkirk proved themselves to be different from

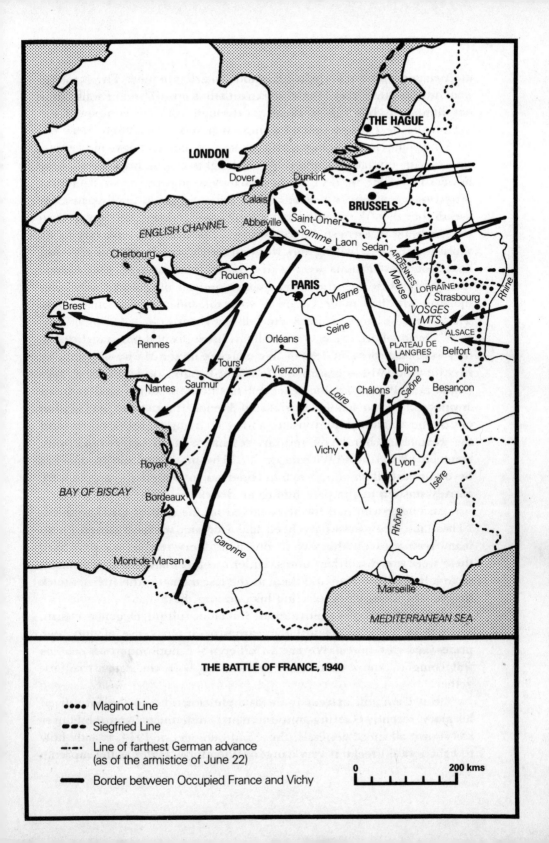

THE BATTLE OF FRANCE, 1940

•••• Maginot Line

▬▬▬ Siegfried Line

▬·▬· Line of farthest German advance
(as of the armistice of June 22)

▬▬▬ Border between Occupied France and Vichy

0   200 kms

the Belgians and the French—tenacious and determined. They realized what was at stake and fought to save their ships. The Luftwaffe took out after them, but a lot of them got through. All their equipment was left on the beaches—a hell of a mess that was! Then there were the forced marches to the Somme. My company commander gave me permission to visit my father's grave on the heights at Combres; I left some flowers there. He would have been happy to join us in our triumphal progress . . . when we reached the Somme, we could finally pause for breath, but then the fighting started up again and this time the French were fighting in earnest. But we kept on advancing . . . moving like a whirlwind under a blazing sun, through a rich, wonderful country—our boys from East Prussia were wide-eyed with amazement. Our morale was good; we were proud and happy—and all our hearts were with the man who had made Germany so great and powerful once again. There were no more skeptics after all our victories."

"Ahead of us," a major recalled, "their front lines had broken; they were leaderless, in despair. We marched up the Marne—an unlucky river for us in 1914—crossed the Plateau de Langres, and took the strongpoints at Belfort from the rear. But fortifications didn't matter to us anymore, or even whole divisions of French troops who had gotten out of the Maginot Line too late and were trying to break out toward the west. They hardly offered any resistance at all before they were marched off to the POW camps. . . . The morale of the troops was beyond praise, their confidence in Hitler was unbounded—people were already starting to compare him to Frederick the Great."

An officer who had formerly served on the staff of OKH recalled: "These last few weeks have been like a dream; we have stored up so many memories on the way to our final overwhelming victory. Still, there were two discordant notes: Hitler's unfortunate decision to bring us to a halt before Dunkirk, then, at the last moment, the Italian attack on France, like Shylock exacting his pound of flesh.

"How this country captivates us! Its classic culture, elegance, charm, and joie de vivre, as against our earnestness, our sense of duty, our pride—and our boots. We are so different—I hope our two peoples will come to know each other so we can walk the same road together.

"But I am still extremely uneasy. Hitler strides to the fore in all his glory; recently Goering announced at a conference, 'Now the Führer has shown all those generals, those old bunglers of 1914, exactly how to fight a war.' I feel it is very dangerous to glorify Hitler as the supreme warlord, since he is still no more than an amateur. I hope he will be able to find his way back to the path of peace. He has the means to do so, but will he be able to stay the course? He will need a Bismarck for that."

Hitler's triumph was complete, and the Germans would profit ruthlessly from the unlimited opportunities for pillaging and "requisitioning" in the conquered territories. On one occasion Hitler drew a line on the map that extended from the Somme through the Ardennes and across Alsace and Lorraine to the Swiss border. All of northern France— as well as Belgium, the Netherlands, and Luxembourg—would be incorporated into the Greater German Reich after the war, and the old Frankish kingdom would be restored, for the first time since the days of Charlemagne. "I am very pleased," Hitler observed, "that the inhabitants of most of this territory have already taken to their heels—that means they will never come back to resettle their land." If Hitler had not planned all this before the war, then, as General Heusinger points out, "His appetite had improved with eating."

Most of the officers of the "opposition" also stood to benefit from the gentle rain of promotions and decorations that descended on the front rank of the Wehrmacht; even Witzleben, as one of the victors of the French campaign, proudly flourished his brand-new marshal's baton.[5] But, as he had before Dunkirk, Hitler felt hesitant about the prospect of an amphibious invasion of England. To maximize their chances of success, it would be best to think of the Channel as simply a very wide river that could be spanned by a bridge of boats, at least until the weather turned in the fall. But when Grand Admiral Raeder was asked if the Royal Navy would be able to cut this vital supply line between the French and English coasts, he replied, "The rearmament of the navy has been

5. On July 19, 1940, Erwin von Witzleben, Gerd von Rundstedt, Fedor von Bock, Walther von Brauchitsch, Wilhelm Keitel, Hans Günther von Kluge, Wilhelm von Leeb, Wilhelm von List, and Walter von Reichenau were all awarded their marshal's baton— though the presentation of Goering's special Reichsmarshal's baton was the climax of the ceremony. By the end of the war Hitler had raised nineteen generals of the land forces to the rank of marshal—the first was Werner von Blomberg in 1936, the last, after a long hiatus, Ferdinand Schörner on April 5, 1945. The youngest of the marshals was Erwin Rommel (born November 15, 1891, promoted to marshal on June 22, 1942), the oldest, Gerd von Rundstedt—though, as we have seen, Rundstedt was to do little or nothing to exploit his position as elder statesman of the Wehrmacht. In fact his inflexible sense of duty was later to involve him in a number of curious moral compromises, and finally would compel him to drain the bitter cup to the dregs. It is curious to note that Manstein, the mastermind of the Ardennes breakthrough in 1940, did not receive the accolade until July 17, 1942; Heinz Guderian, the first and perhaps the greatest exponent of modern mechanized warfare, was passed over altogether and never rose above the rank of general.

too recent for me to offer a guarantee of complete protection"—to which the troops replied with the punning catch phrase, "You don't need wheels [*Räder*] to get across the water." And inevitably Goering announced with characteristic bravado that the Luftwaffe would sweep the English off the seas and bomb them into submission. As for Hitler himself, he was doubtless still privately convinced that he could negotiate a lasting peace with England.

By the end of August it was becoming clear to the officers of the Luftwaffe command in France that Goering's promises were beginning to wear a little threadbare. The question was asked, "Will our bombers still be able to 'bring the English to their knees'?" "I understand that one may have doubts," one of the colonels answered, "but it's dangerous to express them openly." Losses were running well above normal and downed planes were always a total loss, men as well as machines, whereas the English pilots, in most cases, could simply bail out and float back down to their home ground. General Heusinger, recently appointed OKH chief of operations, reviewed the casualty figures for the Battle of Britain and realized very quickly that the British fighters were taking a frightful toll of Goering's armada (thanks in part to the development of radar by the English technician Watson Watt; radar installations were already in place by 1940, in time for the Battle of Britain, so that enemy aircraft could be detected before they reached the English coast). Even during the few brief weeks of the blitzkrieg in France, French fighters had accounted for eight hundred German planes.

On the Channel coast near Cap Gris-Nez, where the chalky cliffs of Dover on the other shore seem so close that one could almost reach out and touch them, Marshal Brauchitsch conferred with several of his generals:

"We are confronted with a new problem, that of defeating the English on the battlefield. The sacrifices that an invasion would entail are certainly less grave than those of a war of several years' duration. . . . But the Führer doesn't seem to be willing to engage them face to face, since he still expects to reduce them by air power alone. He would prefer to avoid the risks of an amphibious assault, but one day he'll thank us for having prepared the way with all the means at our disposal. As soon as we've gotten across, our worries will be over. To be sure, the English have managed—thanks to that disastrous order to use only our infantry to drive them back to the Channel ports—to bring back their troops—such as they are—but they don't have the matériel, their units are not properly organized, and they don't have the trained reserves.

"And what of the empire?" The question was rhetorical, and Brauchitsch provided the answer himself: "Churchill wants to fight on, at all costs, but I doubt that the people will follow him, or that the empire will survive without London—with its heart cut from its body. The enemy will be driven out of Europe altogether, which will give us a considerable advantage, and events will take an even more favorable tack if we succeed in driving them out of the Mediterranean as well."

On October 28, 1940, at OKH headquarters at Fontainebleau, General Heusinger and a liaison officer from the war staff of the navy were poring over the situation maps—both had already come to the conclusion that the Wehrmacht had let the summer, and then the fall, slip by without accomplishing any important objective. At first the war seemed to be won, demobilization plans had already been drawn up, and the German people were already beguiling themselves with dreams of peace. Hitler was expected to offer terms to the English—since Goering had failed to make good on his bold promises to bomb England into submission, and it had begun to seem that the Luftwaffe itself was nothing more than another of his artfully constructed bluffs. Next Hitler had threatened the English with invasion, and finally scratched the operation altogether. . . . What else could be done? Hitler could step up the submarine warfare in the Atlantic. Infiltrate the Arab world, and the British Empire would begin to totter. His Italian ally could help by opening up a corridor to the Mediterranean. Brauchitsch was also looking to the south—he had been calling for an attack on Gibraltar, though he also wanted to take Malta and ensure the direct sea route to Libya. Goering would have to be won over to this project.

"Then our three supreme commanders [Brauchitsch, Raeder, and Goering] would have a joint operation to work on," Heusinger observed, "which is as it should be. The three branches of the Wehrmacht must stop working in isolation, with no liaison and no coordination of policy and outlook."

"Unfortunately," the naval officer began, "the Führer wants to hold all the reins himself—he distrusts the idea of his generals' working together." At that moment an orderly officer appeared with a telegram for General Heusinger: Italian troops in Albania had crossed the Greek frontier.

"That's just splendid!" Heusinger said. "First they start a war in an insignificant corner of the Balkans and now they're pushing on into

Greece without consulting OKW. Why didn't they attack Malta instead? This simply shows how urgent it is that we join in a common struggle against the English, with comprehensive strategic objectives that our ally must adhere to at all costs. What good is Keitel then? He's the master strategist, or at least he's supposed to be. . . . It's time for our commanders in chief to start pulling together."

On December 18, 1940, three weeks after Soviet Foreign Minister Molotov's most recent visit to Berlin, Hitler drafted one of the most famous documents in military history. Molotov's stated objectives—resumption of the war against Finland, southward expansion toward the Balkans and the Bosphorus—were interpreted by Hitler as the opening gambit in a Soviet game of encirclement. His Directive Number 21, an eight-page program for the conquest of the east—"Operation Barbarossa"—began with these words: "The Wehrmacht must have the capability to crush the Soviet Union in a brief campaign. . . . If the opportunity presents itself, I shall give the order to begin troop concentration at least eight weeks before the operation is launched. All preparations that will require more time should be undertaken immediately in order that they may be completed by May 15, 1941. The greatest precautions shall be taken so as not to arouse any suspicion whatsoever. . . ."

At Zossen, the headquarters of the OKH general staff, the Barbarossa directive caused a certain amount of concern. There would be enormous risks involved, and General Friedrich Paulus took it upon himself to point out the disproportion between the endless expanses of the Russian plain and the comparatively meager forces that the Wehrmacht would have at its disposal. However, Hitler's recent successes in France seemed only to have increased his self-assurance in the role of supreme warlord. But in fact he took the generals' warnings to be prompted by their lack of confidence in him; dissent was taken to be a reflection on his military abilities—though Hitler still seems to have been troubled by serious misgivings of his own. So far he had not dealt successfully with the English, either as a soldier or as a diplomat, he still insisted on the vital importance of the empire in the geopolitical scheme of things, and he was clearly ambivalent about this fratricidal struggle between two kindred peoples. He was groping for a military solution, approving and discarding campaign plans, marshaling and dispersing his forces. He had not dared to strike a decisive blow, either an amphibious assault on England itself or an attack on Gibraltar.

8.

1941: "We Have Nothing to Fear from the Americans"

Hitler received Mussolini at the Berghof on January 19, 1941, for a two-day strategy session, in the course of which Hitler made this remarkable observation: "If the Americans enter the war, we have nothing to fear from them." And in fact, in Hitler's picture of the world, North America might just as well not have existed. Hitler, who had never traveled outside of Europe, regarded the United States as a feckless, spendthrift nation which had been plundered by capitalism, polarized by economic crisis, corrupted by the Jews, blighted by materialism, and stupefied by Hollywood, a high standard of living, and baseball. The country was governed by an enemy of the Third Reich, Franklin Delano Roosevelt, passionate in his hatred but powerless to act on it. "America," Hitler said, "had too bad an experience in the First World War; she won't be tempted to intervene in Europe again."

Though he was perfectly well informed on the strategic situation in Europe, Hitler still had only a vague and confused idea of the American military potential. The gearing up of war production in the United States did not make any impression on him at all, and the sluggish trickle of material aid that reached the English only confirmed his idea of American powerlessness. This was a conviction he was to uphold with an obstinacy that verged on total blindness. In the same way he derisively dismissed the British as "a great power with no soldiers, like her American cousins." The Commonwealth and its vast network of political and economic interests were incomprehensible to him, and he was quite ignorant of the workings of the English and American governments. "Hitler had not the vaguest notion of the Anglo-Saxon ideal," wrote Raymond Cartier, "and he flatly denied its existence. He foolishly saw only pure materialism in those countries, where the imperatives of morality and religion play an important role."

But for all this, Hitler's adversaries in Germany were not having any easier a time of it. They had thought that fatigue, privation, and enemy bombing raids would sap the morale of the German people and thus swell their own ranks. In fact they were steadily being thinned out by desertion, for it appeared that no attempt to overthrow such a successful and supremely gifted leader could ever be welcomed or understood by the people.

In 1941 Goerdeler was still traveling to Sweden and Switzerland under the convenient cover of his job with the Bosch electrical firm. He spent most of his free time trying to send warnings of the coming danger to his friends in America and in establishing new contacts—notably with Allen Dulles, who had recently been dispatched to Bern on a very special mission. No one offered Goerdeler the least encouragement, though Dulles had taken his warnings seriously enough and sent back to Washington a detailed report on the German resistance movement. There was no longer any point in trying to convince the generals of Hitler's malevolent intentions when he had just—though reluctantly to be sure—lavished medals, brilliant promotions, and stipends on them all. Next to this the prophecies of General Beck, a worn-out old Prussian pottering in his garden, could not be expected to count for very much.

11

On the morning of May 10, 1941, a Sunday, a mysterious prisoner was lodged at Maryhill Barracks in Glasgow. He gave his name as Alfred Horn and asked to be allowed to speak with the Duke of Hamilton personally. The duke himself, then serving as a wing commander at a nearby RAF base, arrived at the barracks the next morning. The man he had come to meet was tall, thin, and pale, with brown hair, thick eyebrows, prominent cheekbones, and a hagridden expression; there were dark circles under his eyes, which were deeply sunken into his skull.

"Don't you recognize me?" he asked. "You had lunch at my house during the Olympic Games in Berlin in 1936. I am Rudolf Hess."

It took several moments for the duke to recall that Rudolf Hess was the deputy chief of the Nazi Party and that he had indeed met him in Berlin in 1936. Hess explained that he had taken off from Augsburg the night before in a twin-engine Messerschmitt 110 fighter plane and that he had intended to set down on the duke's estate at Dungavel. However, he was afraid of being shot down by the antiaircraft batteries and decided to bail out instead. He had asked to see the duke because he knew him to be one of those reasonable men in British public life who might help him to accomplish his heart's (and his Führer's) greatest desire, to put an end to the fratricidal struggle between their two coun-

Reichspresident Paul von Hindenburg and his son, Colonel (later General) von Hindenburg. (The helmeted regulars of the Reichswehr are drawn up on the near side of the motorcade, the paramilitary Brown shirts of the SA on the far side.)

André François-Poncet meets Hitler and Goering at a reception at the Chancellery of the Third Reich. On the following day a bouquet of roses arrived for Mme François-Poncet, accompanied by the visiting cards of the evening guests of honor. *(Archives of Louis François-Poncet)*

Adolf Hitler
Deutscher Reichskanzler

Hermann Göring
Reichsminister der Luftfahrt und Oberbefehlshaber der Luftwaffe
Reichstagspräsident
Preußischer Ministerpräsident
Reichsforstmeister
Generalfeldmarschall

The Old Guard and the tribunes of the New Order in the former imperial box of the Berlin Opera House: (second from left to right) Rudolf Hess, Hermann Goering, Marshal August von Mackensen (a hero of the First World War), Hitler, and General (later Marshal) Werner von Blomberg. *(Archives of Louis François-Poncet)*

OKW versus OKH—Hitler, Keitel, Halder, and Brauchitsch.

General Ludwig Beck, resigned as Chief of Staff in 1938, the gray eminence of the military opposition, and the Valkyrie conspirators' choice to succeed Hitler as provisional chief of state *(Reichsverweser)*. *(Archives of Paris-Match)*

Marshal Erwin von Witzleben, the only marshal of the Wehrmacht to rally to the conspiracy; distrusted by Hitler and placed on the inactive list in the early forties, returned as commander in chief for a day on July 20. *(Ullstein)*

Admiral Wilhelm Canaris, spymaster of the Abwehr, cooperated actively with the Allies and the German military opposition, fell victim first to Himmler's ambition in 1943 and finally to Hitler's thirst for vengeance in April 1945. *(Ullstein)*

General Karl Heinrich von Stülpnagel, military governor of Northern France, guiding spirit of the Paris conspiracy, and tragic hero of July 20. *(Ullstein)*

Marshal Gerd von Rundstedt, senior soldier of the Third Reich. Though he was treated shabbily by Hitler, he refused to take sides with his fellow officers of the "Prussian opposition." *(Ullstein)*

Marshal Walther von Brauchitsch on the Russian front in 1941, the Indian summer of Operation Barbarossa. *(Ullstein)*

tries. . . . The duke refused to hear any more. He was not entirely convinced that "Alfred Horn" was really who he claimed to be, and he saw no reason why he should be exchanging diplomatic pourparlers with this envoy who had literally dropped out of the clouds.

Subsequently a representative of the Foreign Office, Sir Ivone Kirkpatrick, formally identified Hess and took down his lengthy deposition. Hess declared that he had made the flight on his own initiative, but he was certain that he was not just speaking for himself in expressing the Führer's sincerest wish and innermost conviction—Germany would guarantee the territorial integrity of the British Empire, offer an alliance against the jealous machinations of the Americans, and in return ask only for a free hand on the continent of Europe.

Who was Rudolf Hess? He was born in Alexandria in 1894, joined the National Socialist Party in 1920, and became Hitler's private secretary in 1925, his deputy in 1933, and his designated successor, next in line after Goering, in 1939, which made him the number-three man in the Reich. The assumptions underlying Hess's bizarre peace mission in 1941 were not entirely unfounded; in 1936, the year of the Berlin Olympics, there were certain British aristocrats who still regarded Hitler and his formidable Party as the eventual means of vanquishing the threat of international communism, a potential ally in a kind of holy war against Soviet Russia.

In May 1941, when Hess arrived in Scotland, British morale was at its lowest ebb. The intermittent bombing raids on London had reached a final peak in April, the Royal Navy was continually harassed by U-boats in the Atlantic, in Africa General Rommel was marching from strength to strength, and General Sigmund von List had overrun Yugoslavia and Greece in the space of a few weeks. Hess thought that the Duke of Windsor might be able to negotiate a separate peace, but, as Lord Granard [1] remarked to us, "Hess did not understand the English."

Beaverbrook, who was then serving in Churchill's War Cabinet, was convinced that Hess really did have Hitler's backing. He immediately conferred with Churchill, who ordered Hess to be sequestered before he could speak to the press. Churchill was fearful of the consequences if the public learned the purpose of Hess's mission; a "peace scare"

---

1. An Irish peer who had worked as a young reporter on the *Daily Express* and was a close friend of Lord Beaverbrook's. At the time of Hess's flight he was an officer in the RAF and later served with the SIS.

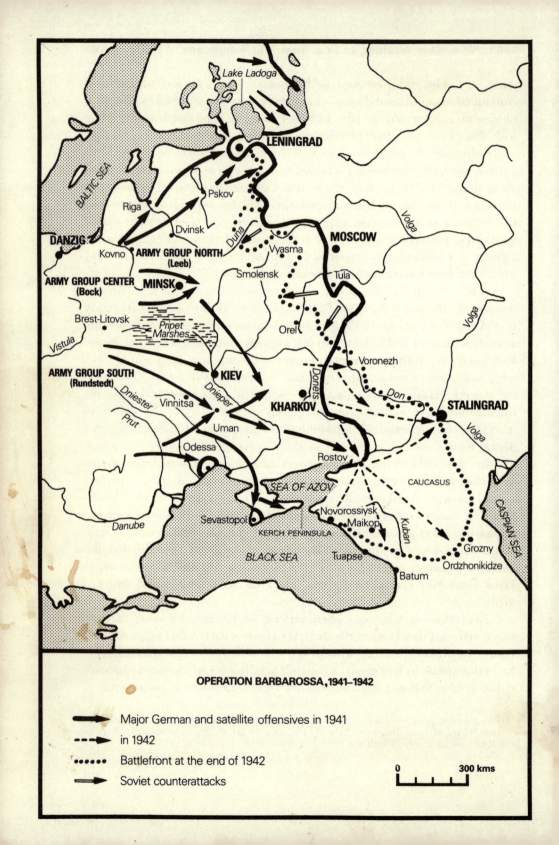

Lake Ladoga

LENINGRAD

BALTIC SEA

Pskov

Riga

Dvinsk

DANZIG

Kovno

ARMY GROUP NORTH
(Leeb)

Duna

Vyasma

MOSCOW

Volga

Smolensk

Tula

ARMY GROUP CENTER
(Bock)

MINSK

Brest-Litovsk

Pripet
Marshes

Orel

Vistula

Voronezh

ARMY GROUP SOUTH
(Rundstedt)

Dniester

KIEV

Dnieper

Donets

Don

STALINGRAD

Vinnitsa

Prut

Uman

KHARKOV

Volga

Odessa

Rostov

CAUCASUS

Volga

SEA OF AZOV

Novorossiysk

Maikop

Kuban

CASPIAN SEA

Sevastopol

KERCH PENINSULA

Grozny

Danube

BLACK SEA

Tuapse

Ordzhonikidze

Batum

OPERATION BARBAROSSA, 1941–1942

→ Major German and satellite offensives in 1941

--→ in 1942

•••••• Battlefront at the end of 1942

→ Soviet counterattacks

0   300 kms

could do a great deal of damage to morale. Then he was struck by a brilliant inspiration—he delivered an address announcing the extraordinary news of Hess's arrival, concluding simply with the words, "This man is insane" (perhaps a slight exaggeration, but certainly an understandable one).

In fact, General Heusinger believes that Hitler was genuinely caught off guard by Hess's disappearance; when Churchill confirmed that Hess had flown to England, Hitler was not only chagrined and disappointed, he was also afraid that Hess's flight, if properly exploited by the British, would have a seriously disturbing and demoralizing effect on the German people.

As for the possibility that the man who parachuted into a field in Scotland in 1941 and is currently serving out a life term in Spandau prison is not Rudolf Hess at all, but a double—a theory that was advanced in a recent book, *The Murder of Rudolf Hess,* by Hugh Thomas, who treated Hess as a surgeon in the British Military Hospital in Berlin—General Heusinger regards this as simply another of the legends that have sprung up around Hitler and his circle over the course of the years. The prisoner in Spandau is not a double, but the original Rudolf Hess.

On May 15 Hitler held a top-secret conclave with his senior generals. He began by declaring angrily that the Russian campaign would not be conducted according to the ordinary laws of war. It would be a racial and ideological struggle, which would have to be waged with unprecedented harshness. His voice rose threateningly as he continued, "All my officers will have to rid themselves of their outmoded ideas of warfare. I know that my way of thinking is beyond the comprehension of my generals—which is what makes me so angry—but my orders must be carried out. My SS men will not be treated as combatants by the Soviets; it follows that the Red Army's political commissars should be liquidated." Hitler stalked out of the conference room, and the generals, outraged and protesting, gathered around Brauchitsch; he assured them that he would do everything in his power to prevent any order of this kind from being carried out.

There were still officers in the German army who had fought in Russia in 1914–17 and had vivid memories of her endless plains, trackless marshes, and Arctic winters. Apart from that, the German military attaché in Moscow had sent reports—making use of the same arguments with which General Caulaincourt had tried to dissuade Napoleon in 1812—outlining the risks and the certain dangers of campaigning in Russia, including the fact that the Red Army was more powerful than the high command had been prepared to admit.

The OKW battle plan evisioned a month of heavy fighting on Russia's borders, after which the Red Army's resistance would gradually collapse. Hitler himself made it clear that he expected the campaign to last several months; that is, the Russians would have to be defeated before the onset of winter, thus avoiding the dangers of waging a two-front war by knocking out one of his adversaries very quickly. He was worried about a possible rapprochement between Great Britain and Soviet Russia, and he believed that it was up to him to prevent it—and this was certainly in keeping with his earlier declaration that it would be criminally irresponsible of any chief of state not to launch a preventative war at the opportune moment.

"I am aware," he told the generals who would carry out Operation Barbarossa, "of the importance of the British Empire to world stability, and of the importance of the Anglo-Saxons to our Nordic race. I have never sought to dispute their preeminence, but if Mr. Churchill in his insane blindness refuses to recognize Germany's critical role in Europe, then he shall have to face the consequences. . . . Before we find ourselves engaged once more in a war on two fronts [as in the First World War], I intend to forestall Mr. Churchill's insane ploy of allying himself with Bolshevism. The English must not think that they can intervene in Europe and dictate the course of European affairs.

"I am embarking on this struggle not for the sake of Germany alone but for all Europe, for the future of the civilized world and for European culture. Destiny has charged us with this mission, and I, the Führer of the German people, cannot and will not shrink from it. And if the gentlemen of the high command suppose that they can warn me off, they are mistaken. On the contrary, the greater the danger of Russia's emerging as a political and economic power, the more promptly that danger must be averted. We will not avoid coming to grips with Russia. What's more, I don't believe these stories about the mighty Red Army— the same sort of thing we heard before the French campaign. . . . Once their armies are beaten in the field, the Soviet state will melt away, and the world will be cured of the Bolshevist contagion. . . ."

Hitler had become increasingly convinced of this, though he could no more prove he was right than Brauchitsch could prove the contrary. But Hitler was also increasingly inclined to treat Brauchitsch as a kind of glorified aide-de-camp. He no longer solicited or accepted advice from any of his generals, and no one could be said to have any influence over this man who thought of himself as both warlord and statesman, who had an unshakable faith in his own infallible "intuition," especially in the realm of politics, and who had an equally deep-seated distrust of everyone around him. At any rate the prospect of the Russian campaign filled the officers of the general staff with the darkest forebodings.

The offensive, scheduled to begin on May 25, was postponed until June 22. The consequences of this delay would be disastrous, but Hitler was eager to secure his southern flank in the Balkans (that is, to rescue the Italian troops). Hitler's ultimate political objective, apart from eradicating world communism, was to dismember the Soviet state, subjugate the Slavic *Untermenschen,* and provide the German people with virtually unlimited *Lebensraum.* Another economic prize, never far from the Führer's thoughts, was the oilfields of the Caucasus.

"When Barbarossa is launched," Hitler announced to the OKH general staff, "the world will simply hold its breath and wait"—this was aimed at Brauchitsch, who had ventured to suggest timidly that certain defensive precautions should be undertaken in the west. It was the Naval High Command, however, which was particularly opposed to Barbarossa, and Grand Admiral Raeder would later pay for his intransigence with the loss of his command. The opposition was still too demoralized to turn the situation to its advantage. On June 16 Canaris got word that the attack order had been passed on to the army commanders; he met with Beck, Goerdeler, Hassell, Oster, and several others to discuss yet another appeal to Brauchitsch and Halder. They quickly agreed that both had acquiesced to Hitler's grand design for the east and were prepared to turn a blind eye to the inevitable cruelties of the SS.

Hitler summoned his army group commanders and the generals who were to take part in Barbarossa to the Chancellery for a final political harangue: "Your armies will shatter the Russian colossus. It will be a hard fight—the Asiatics are cruel and cunning, but you will meet them with a determination as hard and cold as ice. Only one people will come out of this alive—our people. You must make your troops put aside all their notions of restraint and humanity. I expect to annihilate the bulk of the Red Army in the great battles on the frontier. . . . This will be the last campaign of this war, and it will ensure the security of the Reich for many generations. This is a struggle between two antithetical ideologies. We cannot refuse to give battle, and one day the world will thank us for having responded to the call of destiny."

On June 22, 1941—without benefit of crises or political tensions, border incidents or ultimatums—Hitler's troops crossed the Soviet frontier. This was to be the largest military operation in history: 169 divisions (mostly German, of course, with a sprinkling of Hungarians, Finns, and Romanians). The enormous scale of the Barbarossa invasion would be surpassed only by the eventual Soviet counterattack in 1943, though neither Hitler nor his general staff had ever imagined that the Russians could stave off defeat and carry on the struggle for so long by drawing on the resources of vast territories that extended far beyond the Führer's immediate horizons.

At first the Russians, taken by surprise, fell back in disorder. In July Marshal von Bock's Army Group Center took almost 330,000 prisoners, as well as 2,500 tanks and 1,500 guns, in a pocket around Minsk. General Halder asked the Foreign Armies East section of OKH for a report on what the first prisoners who were brought back to the rear thought of their country and of Bolshevism now. "They all love their motherland. The older men have had difficulty in accommodating themselves to Bolshevism, but the younger ones have known nothing else and are proud of their country. They think of us as bandits who have broken into their home, and they will fight ferociously for their 'Little Mother'—Russia. The situation is different in the Ukraine and the Baltic countries, and here our propaganda may be effective in combating Bolshevism if it is conducted in a timely manner and the population is well treated. We will never win them over with our current administrative methods.

"We must do what we can to bring about reform," Halder concluded ruefully, "but we will be beating our heads against a stone wall. Hitler believes himself to be infallible in this respect as well, and he is not open to suggestion." Relations between Hitler and Brauchitsch had deteriorated even further, if possible; the marshal could not hope to have any effect on policy whatsoever, though he continued to churn out memoranda.

Guderian's and General Hermann Hoth's armored divisions, part of Army Group Center, continued to advance; on August 5 they took 310,000 prisoners at Smolensk, 3,200 armored vehicles, and 3,000 guns. At this point Hitler blundered badly: Over Bock's objections, he withdrew these two divisions and an entire army from Army Group Center and sent these troops to reinforce Leeb's Army Group North, whose objective was Leningrad, and Rundstedt's Army Group South, then advancing through the Ukraine toward the Caucasus.

On August 20 General Heusinger reported to General Alfred Jodl—Keitel's deputy, chief of OKW Operations Section—at the Wolf's Lair.

Jodl was an old acquaintance; they had worked together on the army general staff for two years before the war after Jodl took over from Manstein. As General Heusinger recalls, "It took Jodl the Bavarian a week to accomplish what Manstein the Berliner could in a single night. But Jodl was a man of character, and a devil for work as well."

"Marshal von Brauchitsch has asked me to give you an oral report on the data concerning the 'Kiev or Moscow' problem. He has already presented them in a memorandum to the Führer," Heusinger began.

"A memorandum?" Jodl asked uncertainly. "Let's hope that it goes well. Usually nothing much comes of these things."

Heusinger pointed out that this seemed to be the only alternative, since Brauchitsch had not made any headway in his personal discussions with the Führer. "I'm hoping that you'll back me up," Heusinger said, "but to return to the problem—from the very first, the Führer has not really been interested in Moscow. . . . He expects to encircle and annihilate a powerful Russian force to the east of Kiev. More than that, he attaches a great deal of importance to taking the Donets Basin, which would strike a deathblow to Russian industry—"

"Just a moment," Jodl said. "In that respect the Führer is falling back on an earlier campaign plan—to advance on both flanks while keeping the center in place if the Russians continue to hold out. Brauchitsch has known of this plan for some time, which is why the Führer is even less receptive than usual to his objections. There's also the fact that he has an instinctive dread of following in the footsteps of Napoleon. Moscow sends chills down his spine. . . . He is actually afraid of a life-or-death struggle against Bolshevism."

"Which is precisely the reason that we find ourselves in this position," Heusinger replied. "First we must defeat the enemy in the field; we can't begin to concentrate on economic objectives until we have beaten the Red Army, and it is on the road to Moscow that we can be sure of meeting that army. That's where victory is waiting for us, not in the Donets, since the Russians will be forced to take up their positions in front of Moscow, to put together everything they have to throw in our path."

Jodl, continuing to play the role of Hitler's alter ego, returned to the original point: "East of Kiev is where the Russians have their most powerful troop concentrations, since we were unable to destroy them when they were still west of the Dnieper. And finally, what good will all their armies do them if we take away the Donets Basin, and thus most of their armaments production, and if we threaten their lines of communications and their oil reserves in the Caucasus? We'll take Moscow later . . . when it will be easier.''

Heusinger countered with the logical objection: "Clearly we'll be feeling the effects of the Russian winter in the north and the center first. We'll have to break off operations earlier than in the south. Our priorities should be reversed—first the center, then the south. Moreover, the industrial belt around Moscow is at least as valuable as the Donets, to say nothing of the Urals, where the dismantled Kirovograd industrial plants have been relocated.

"What is more, the Russians will be diverting a great many of their forces from Kiev to Moscow as soon as they realize the extreme gravity of the situation. And finally, we should cut their lines of communication. All the major north-south routes pass through Moscow. It's astonishing that the Russians have been able to solve their transportation problems up to now, but after the fall of Moscow they'll be faced with catastrophe. . . . All these ideas are contained in Brauchitsch's memorandum, and he would be grateful for your support."

"I'll do what I can." Jodl spoke sincerely, as if the scales had finally fallen from his eyes. "But the Führer's reasons are also the result of sober reflection. We cannot just flatly deny the force of his arguments. If he refuses to abandon his original plan, there'll be no point in your giving yourself gray hairs worrying about it. We can't compel him to act against his innermost convictions. His intuition has been infallible in the majority of cases. . . ."

"But not always," Heusinger shot back. "Remember Dunkirk . . . England. Here again we may let the decisive moment pass us by."

The battle for the Ukraine was a tremendous success. Kiev fell on September 20, and Marshal Budënny's [2] army group, under attack from both north and south, had disintegrated by the twenty-fifth. With the help of Guderian's panzers, Army Group South took 665,000 prisoners in the Kiev pocket, many thousands of whom would later die of starvation. In the north Leeb's army group began the siege of Leningrad in October. Rundstedt reached the Don on October 15, threatening Rostov and Kharkov. It was only then that Hitler ordered a resumption of the advance toward Moscow. It seemed as if the fall of the enemy's capital would be simply the next in the continuous string of victories since

2. A distinguished cavalry commander in the Russian civil war, but woefully unable to cope with German blitzkrieg tactics. He was immediately recalled by Stalin and only reinstated (in a largely ceremonial post) after the end of the war.

June 22. Once again Hitler would be able to tell his generals, "You were wrong, and I was right."

A deputy chief of the general staff who had just returned from leave described the prevailing mood in Berlin to General Heusinger: "You'd think the war was over. What with our victories at the front, Keitel's rosy-hued communiqués, the propaganda, plus the cutbacks in munitions production—the Berliners are in ecstasy. People were astonished when I told them how worried I was about resupplying the troops this winter.

"I spent an hour at Beck's. He's depressed, the state of his health leaves much to be desired. . . . His arguments are clear, logical, and irrefutable. He has concluded that the war is lost, since the thing that he's been most afraid of since 1938 has come to pass—a world war in which, sooner or later, we will go under. In his opinion we will be stopped in Russia, then the Americans will intervene, and our fate will be sealed."

The autumn rains had begun, and with them the *rasputitsa*, "season of bad roads," which occurred twice a year when the rain of autumn or the melting snow in spring turned the roads of central Russia into muddy torrents. Guderian and his panzers were bogged down, unable to rejoin their army group. Some units had been in the line, fighting without respite, since the beginning, and the Russians stood to profit from every delay.

At OKH two things had become painfully clear—that the Russians would hold out much longer than anyone had expected, and that Marshal Brauchitsch was nearing the end of his tether.

"It's difficult to get down to it with the Russians," an army commander explained, "because they don't follow the ordinary rules of warfare. Everything they do surprises us—they attack where no one expects them, and hold out to the death when the situation is clearly hopeless. If the attack on Moscow succeeds, then perhaps things will take a turn for the better. . . . What do you make of it all, Heusinger?"

"You've already heard all of the main objections to our last offensive—the troops are worn out, our lines of communication dangerously extended, and winter is almost upon us. That's the price we paid for Kiev. If this offensive is successful, we'll have secured a number of decisive advantages, but I don't believe that there will be a total rout. The risk we're taking is enormous. In Bock's army group they feel the same way. Will Guderian get his troops moving again? And after the roads are clear, will we have some reasonable weather before winter sets in? It all depends on that.

"It's true that Brauchitsch is in a bad way, morally and physically exhausted. The briefing sessions at Rastenburg are torture for him now, and he rarely attends them anymore. Halder should be trying to encourage him, otherwise we'll gradually lose all of our influence at OKW. . . . His departure may have unforeseeable consequences: He has not named his successor, and the natural choice would be Reichenau. The Führer thinks that Rundstedt is too old. It would be better to avoid such a change of leadership altogether—after all, hasn't Himmler been encouraging certain people's expectations [i.e., of Reichenau and other pro-Nazi generals]? Brauchitsch at least has done as much as could be expected to protect the army from the worst crimes and outrages of the Party.

"Nowadays Hitler only puts his trust in ruthless fanatics, in monsters like Himmler, who says, 'Let the Russian people bleed to death on the battlefield.' At the beginning of the campaign Hitler told the commanders of the armies before he sent them into battle, 'Blood doesn't matter to the builders of an empire. Genghis Khan deliberately massacred millions of women and children, but who remembers that now?' He has nothing but praise for Stalin—he regrets that he didn't carry out a purge of the generals himself. 'There are only two statesmen in our time who are masters of their own destinies,' he says, 'Stalin and myself.' "

Marshal von Bock was ordered to take Moscow at all costs. All the troops originally under his command were restored to him, and by October 20 they had advanced to within forty miles of Moscow, though most of the units in Army Group Center had already lost half their men and matériel. The news that they were finally going to take the enemy's capital gave a powerful boost to their morale; many of them were singing as they marched off to the "last battle." The central plains were still in the grip of the *rasputitsa,* and their martial ardor was quenched soon enough. Men and machines began to falter.

On November 12 General Halder passed on the orders for what the high command was pleased to call the fall offensive. Their objectives would be Moscow and Gorki, on the Volga, which meant the armies would be advancing over a hundred miles through almost impassable terrain. Logistics would be precarious, since the gauge of the railroads would have to be changed, and each of the three army groups was supplied by a single railroad line. These were especially vulnerable to partisan attacks; during the campaign the lines would be cut in as many as seventy places in a single night. The winter uniforms had also not arrived at the supply depots, for the simple reason that there were none. "In 1940," General Heusinger explains, "after the fall of France, Hitler thought the war was won. To think about ordering winter uniforms for the troops [a year and a half later] would have smacked of defeatism, and to ask the public to donate warm clothes would have made a deplorable impression."

Winter came early and abruptly on November 3; the temperature had already dropped to −20°F., and this was to be a particularly hard winter.

In their thin cloth parkas and knitted sweaters the dauntless warriors of the SS were transformed into shivering, shambling apparitions. The regular army troops had spent all their energies in advancing this far; now they were on the verge of collapse. Their commanders were horrified; Guderian sought out Bock, Bock appealed to Brauchitsch, and all three agreed that the advance could not continue, but there was no possibility that their objections would receive a hearing at supreme headquarters.

At 11:00 PM on November 30 Heusinger burst into Halder's command post. "General, we have just received a telegram from Marshal von Rundstedt—he requests that the Führer rescind the order to hold the line beyond the Mius.[3] If not, he begs to be relieved of his command."

"I expected Rundstedt to take this attitude," Halder said.

"This telegram," Heusinger went on, "is addressed to the Führer personally. Jodl has already gone off to give him a full report. Shouldn't we tell Brauchitsch about this immediately so that he can intercede on Rundstedt's behalf?"

"I'd like to very much," Halder replied, "but it would be better to spare him another pointless emotional scene." (Brauchitsch had suffered a heart attack some three weeks earlier.)

In any case, Heusinger did not feel that Hitler would replace Rundstedt: "He thinks too highly of him. . . . I've asked Jodl to telephone me as soon as he's delivered his report." But when it was almost one o'clock and Heusinger had still not had any word on Hitler's reaction to Rundstedt's telegram, he called the OKW operations chief himself.

"The matter is settled," Jodl announced shortly.

"How? Was the order canceled?"

3. River in southern Russia, some eighty miles to the west of Rostov-on-Don, which Rundstedt's panzers had taken on November 21 but could not hold. By November 30 the Russians had recaptured Rostov, and the entire army group was in full retreat. [Tr.]

"By no means," Jodl replied. "Rundstedt has been relieved of his command; Reichenau will be replacing him. The telegrams have already gone out to both of them."

"Not possible!" Heusinger shouted, "It's not possible," and he slammed down the receiver.

The next afternoon, December 1, at three o'clock in the afternoon, Brauchitsch and Hitler met face to face in the Wolf's Lair.

"Now," Hitler told him, "it's Reichenau who says he can't hold out beyond the Mius for long."

"There are no defensive positions for them to take up," Brauchitsch pointed out. "We should believe what they tell us at the front and fall back twenty kilometers."

Hitler finally gave in. "Very well then, you may authorize Reichenau to withdraw—but it's absolutely essential that he hold the line on the Mius."

"And Rundstedt?" the commander in chief asked uneasily.

"I shall adhere to my original decision. Rundstedt has no one to blame for this but himself. In any case it will do him good to step down for a while. His nerves didn't seem to be holding up too well."

And the worse the situation grew, the more the generals were made to bear the blame personally. "They were sent packing one after another," Heusinger said, "without any consideration for their rank. The senior commanders of that generation saw more than their share of tragedy."

The assault on Moscow was scheduled to begin on December 2. The Soviet high command had hurriedly brought up their crack Siberian reserves [4]—the famous Sibiryak divisions from the Far East. Originally formed and trained by Marshal Tukhachevsky, they were well equipped for winter campaigning, dressed in white, fur-lined uniforms with their weapons and equipment specially treated to withstand the cold. (The temperature had now dropped to thirty below.)

The German troops suffered terribly. They had no felt boots or fur hats; they had wool mittens instead of fur-lined gloves. Their automatic weapons seized up when the lubricating oil froze; in the rear the locomotives were immobilized, at the front the tanks' engines had to be warmed up with bonfires for twelve hours before they would turn over. A more distressing effect of the cold: Many men died after their

4. Richard Sorge, the Soviet master spy in Tokyo, had already informed Moscow that the Japanese had no intention of attacking the Soviet Union from the east.

rectums froze when they stopped to relieve themselves by the side of the road.

The extreme cold and the difficulties of the terrain prevented the Germans from getting their troops into position for the attack until December 4; the temperature had dropped another ten degrees in those two days, to −40°. A former noncom in the Tsarist cavalry, General Georgi Zhukov, had been entrusted with the defense of Moscow on October 9 by Marshal Shaposhnikov, chief of the Soviet general staff. On December 6 Zhukov went over to the offensive: Seventeen Russian armies, spearheaded by the fresh Siberian reserves, were thrown against the German lines. Less than a week earlier mechanized reconnaissance patrols of the German 62d engineers' battalion (2d Armored Division) had reached Khimki, a small port on the Moskva River some five miles away from Moscow—and inspired a brief outbreak of panic in the capital. Another advance party of the 2d Armored, under the command of Lieutenant Colonel Decker, had reached Ozeresskoye, the western terminus of the Moscow streetcar system. At Gorki units of the 2d battalion of the 304th Rifle Regiment were less than twenty miles from the Kremlin, fifteen miles from the outskirts of the city. At Lobnaya shock troops of the 38th engineers' battalion were less than ten miles from Moscow itself.

The German troops seemed to be determined to fight their way through at all costs. At night they could see the Russian antiaircraft shells bursting over the capital, which made their objective—and shelter from the frigid Russian winter—seem tantalizingly close at hand. When they took Moscow, they assured themselves, they would blow up the Kremlin first of all—"to mark the grave of Bolshevism." But then, on December 11, huddled over the map table in his field HQ at Tolstoy's family estate at Yasnaya Polyana, Guderian took stock of the situation and finally gave the order to withdraw. The armies fell back forty miles, in spite of the desperate resistance of three Waffen SS divisions, who refused to deviate from Hitler's standing order that there would be no retreat.

On December 12 Guderian visited Brauchitsch at his home. The commander in chief appeared to be exhausted and completely overwhelmed. Guderian begged him to try to make Hitler understand how the troops were suffering. Brauchitsch promised to do what he could, but Guderian left convinced that the old marshal was in complete disgrace and that there was no chance that he would be allowed to speak to Hitler.

On December 15, in a thatched peasant isba that served as an army corps command post, General Halder was unburdening himself to one of his adjutants: There was nowhere left to turn. On the right wing the Russians had opened up a breach six miles wide; contact with the left wing might be broken off at any moment. They could do nothing to fill the breach; the entire corps had stopped dead in its tracks. The troops were not fit to give battle in open country. The frozen grease on the shell casings had to be laboriously scraped off before the guns could be loaded. Frozen synthetic rubber would crumble at a touch or turn as hard as stone. The tanks' engines had to be kept running all night to keep them from freezing up; there was no antifreeze. Every day more men and matériel were lost to the cold, the most hardened veterans were overwhelmed by all these horrors, and the troops felt the specter of 1812 drawing down on them. The reserves were reduced to a single battalion and two companies of motorized scouts. Ammunition was running out. . . . The Russian troops were battle tested, they could bear the cold, and their morale was considerably stiffened by the presence of political commissars in their ranks. The Germans and their allies had reached the critical point where their losses could no longer be replaced.

Here General Halder's jeremiad was interrupted by the arrival of the army corps commander, frostbitten and shivering with the cold; he had just returned from a tour of the front. "What a day! We had to dig ourselves out five times. I couldn't even reach the left wing; all hell's broken loose over there. The Russian ski troops have broken through our lines, and they're just about to cut our supply line to the north. I've brought up the reserves, but I don't know if they can push them back. . . . And when will we get our rations, our ammunition, our replacements?"

Halder shrugged helplessly. Hundreds of locomotives were stalled on the tracks.

"And what about the Christmas mail? That at least would bring some comfort to the troops in the midst of this terrible shambles—and I've seen enough of those in the course of two wars, but never anything like this. . . . We should also evacuate the frostbite cases and the wounded. We can't leave them up here in the front lines—we owe them at least that much. . . ."

The army was so disorganized by the effects of the cold that Hitler's orders could no longer be carried out. The fighting broke off of its own accord, in spite of the best efforts of the commanders. On December

18 a second army group commander—Bock—was relieved of his command; he was to be replaced by Marshal von Kluge. The following day, at OKH headquarters near Angersburg in the Mauerwald, Marshal Brauchitsch's adjutant, on his own initiative, urged his chief that it would be far better for him to resign than to linger on while the situation deteriorated even further. Shortly afterward the adjutant sought out General Heusinger.

"You've done nothing to be sorry for," Heusinger assured him. "Brauchitsch would have broken under the strain sooner or later. He can't take any more. I realized that myself ten days ago when he returned from a briefing with the Führer. He seemed to be completely at a loss; he didn't even have the strength to tell Halder what had happened. He actually passed out not long ago, which only shows how much he's come up against it lately. At any rate, he's lost whatever influence he once had over Hitler, and through no fault of his own at all. That must have become intolerable. He'll thank you one day for having spared him from the worst." Brauchitsch had asked to be relieved of his command on December 7, and again on December 17; it was announced that his resignation had been accepted on December 19.

The succession was left open. Goering and Himmler were not considered acceptable; Hitler had patched up his differences with Rundstedt, but Rundstedt was still too old. Hitler was least likely to go searching through the ranks of the old-school staff officers for another commander of Brauchitsch's caliber; he needed a simpler personality, someone more easily led. "But who would be the scapegoat for the recent reverses in the east?" Heusinger asked himself. "I'm afraid it will have to be Brauchitsch, but one day the truth will have to come out. . . . Our failure to take Moscow has put an end to our hopes of striking a decisive blow in the east. The American military capability will shortly be brought to bear on the western front, and we have saddled ourselves with the odious burden of another declaration of war. Even having the Japanese on our side will not make up for that."

Hitler was continually finding fault with his commanders, and he would seize on the slightest misstep as a pretext for summary dismissal. He made them pay for his own mistakes as well, as he freely and cynically admitted: "The generals must take the blame for our military setbacks—they can all be replaced, but my prestige is an irreplaceable resource that must on no account be diminished."

The generals would serve out the war with this sword hanging over their heads, always vulnerable to the despotic vagaries of the supreme commander. The army was kept under constant Party surveillance, not by political commissars, but far worse than that, by Himmler's spies and informers.

On the day before Christmas Marshal Brauchitsch was discharged. Halder would stay on as OKH chief of staff, and Hitler announced that he would personally exercise the functions of commander in chief for the eastern front—the special province of OKH; in future generals would be forbidden to submit their resignations. The process that had begun in 1938 with the creation of OKW and Hitler's assumption of the title of supreme commander of the armed forces was now formally complete, and after 1941 Hitler's attempts to assume personal command of the army would become the single most crucial factor in determining both the future course of the war and the political attitudes of the generals.

During the first phase of the campaign the Russians suffered 3,000,000 casualties, the Germans 800,000 (200,000 killed); the losses of the Waffen SS were disproportionately high—43,000 killed or seriously wounded. The idea that the Red Army was about to disintegrate had proved to be a delusion. Far from being cut off, the Soviet capital was still connected by a network of highways and railroads to the vast unconquered territories in the east. The German armies, often short of ammunition, were waging a bitter defensive struggle against a numerically superior adversary on most sectors of the front. In Marshal Zhukov, Stalin had found a commander who was fully capable of carrying out his policy of relentless counterattack.

On December 31 an officer attached to the general staff of the army reserve received a letter from a comrade at the front which has been preserved by General Heusinger:

There is an ill wind blowing out here. Bock has had to give up his army group because Hitler's decided he isn't stern enough. The role of his successor, Kluge, in all this is far from clear. And now Guderian has been sent back to the rear— quite vexed, they tell me, at having been so unjustly treated. General von Leeb [5] is also going to be replaced, along with thirty-five divisional commanders. . . . All these changes of command certainly haven't helped the situation. It's not possible for Hitler to do everything himself. . . .

General Count Hans von Sponeck was accused of having evacuated his positions on the Kerch Peninsula in response to an amphibious assault

---

5. Commander of Army Group North, who favored a vigorous assault on Leningrad. Hitler favored a more cautious and deliberate siege, and Leeb was replaced by General von Küchler in January 1942.

by "a handful of Russians" behind the German lines. Brought up before
a military tribunal presided over by Goering, he was sentenced to death
on Hitler's orders. The sentence was commuted, and he was confined
in a fortress until a few days after July 20, 1944, when he was dispatched
in his cell by an SS execution squad. Sponeck's most unforgivable offense
was to have been born a Prussian—most of his compatriots, unlike the
Bavarians and the Rhinelanders, never had much use for Hitler—and
a nobleman, which only compounded the felony.

9.

1942: "The Russians Are Done For"

General Erich Hoepner, commander of the 4th Armored Group of Kluge's Army Group Center, had become convinced that the armies should execute a strategic withdrawal. But as the German author Paul Carell has observed, "The Wehrmacht never learned the principles or the techniques of carrying out a retreat. The German soldier did not think of this as a particular maneuver that was intended to achieve a precise objective but rather as a disaster that had been thrust upon him by the enemy. Even during the Reichswehr era, training the troops to carry out a retreat was regarded with suspicion; they said rather contemptuously, 'It's just a way of teaching the men to run away.' Later, after 1936, even the doctrine of the 'elastic defense' was eliminated from the training manual; the German soldier was taught only to attack and to hold his position."

On January 8 Hoepner tried desperately to get through to General Halder. He was assured by a junior officer that Halder would call him back; he never did. On his own initiative Hoepner ordered the XX Corps to fall back. Kluge learned of this that evening; he was then presented with the choice of ordering the troops back to their original positions of that morning or confirming the withdrawal order and backing up Hoepner's decision. Characteristically "Clever Hans" managed to avoid both these unpalatable alternatives. He spoke with Hoepner, gave him a thorough dressing-down, and reminded him of the consequences of disobeying an order of the Führer. In fact, he is reported to have given his approval of the withdrawal order, and then, mindful of the reaction at OKW, covered himself by telephoning Hitler at Rastenburg and repeating certain acerbic remarks of Hoepner's about "civilians running the army." Whatever the truth of it was, it is clear that Kluge's report to GHQ touched off another of Hitler's monumental tantrums, the consequences of which we shall examine shortly.

After the bloody "last battle" for Moscow, the first massive German retreat of the war, and the terrible hardship endured by the troops at

the front—all reflected in the long casualty lists in the newspapers—
the mood of the German people was beginning to turn sour, and the
conspirators had begun to think of reviving their long dormant conspiracy. The question was whether Hitler's ritual sacrifice of his commanders
would inspire the senior generals with a new sense of their patriotic
duty (or of self-preservation), and whether the officer corps could be enticed away from the straight path of duty and into the ranks of the
opposition. Halder was still passing on his orders, fully aware of the
tragic consequences they would have for the armies. He was still willing
to receive Colonel von Voss, an envoy who had arrived from France,
with the backing of General von Stülpnagel, to present a plan for a
military operation against the regime. Halder let it be known that he
had no objection to such a plan, though of course there was nothing
that he could do personally.

Hitler was increasingly inclined to regard his generals as a pack
of untrustworthy servants and to treat them with insolent disdain. Guderian's and Hoepner's panzer groups—which had crushed the Polish army
in eight days and the French army in a month—had just been sacrificed
to Hitler's obstinacy, his arrogance, and his uncomprehending disregard
for human suffering. The loss of trained manpower was more critical
than the loss of matériel, and in the following year, when Hitler urgently
needed his elite Corps of Immortals, he discovered that most of them
had perished on the road to Moscow.

The generals gradually began to lose any sense of strategic coordination in the orders they were required to carry out. They were no longer
instructed to surprise, or overwhelm, or outflank, or destroy the enemy;
instead they were simply told, "You will hold the line between here
and there," or "You will advance as far as these coordinates," with
the inevitable postscript, "or you will be relieved of your command."

There were fresh injustices, further examples of Hitler's bad faith,
almost every day. When Marshal von List, who had conducted the brilliant campaign in the Balkans, was abruptly cashiered in August 1942,
even Keitel was moved to demand an explanation. Hitler replied, "I
can't have one of my commanders reporting to me from the front without
bringing back a map that will give me some idea of his army's progress."
(In fact, Hitler had long since forbidden his officers to take military
documents with them on flights over Russian territory, enormous tracts
of which were in the hands of the partisans.) The generals were deeply
affected by these humiliations, these deliberate exercises in cruelty; still,
neither their anger and resentment nor their disapproval of the orders

that they were obliged to carry out seems to have affected their sense of duty. In the meantime Hitler was raising new Waffen SS units, and he came to value and to act on their commanders' advice more and more.

On January 8, 1942, at Rastenburg Hitler was poring over the map tables, surrounded by Keitel, Jodl, Heusinger, Fellgiebel, the chief communications officer, and the Luftwaffe, naval, and SS liaison officers. Halder was the first to speak; he announced that the enemy had been exerting relentless pressure on Army Group Center, repeatedly throwing fresh and almost untrained divisions against the German lines. Hitler was exultant: "Haven't I always told you, Halder? The enemy is desperate—they're attacking us with untrained hordes, whatever troops they can scrape together. My officers are always telling me about the Russians' allegedly far-ranging strategic designs, but all that is nonsense! The Russians know only one way of fighting—they send out their human-wave attacks in whichever sector the danger seems greatest. If it weren't for this accursed winter—the cruelest winter in over a century—we'd be able to exploit these blundering tactics and sweep them from our path. But all that we can do now is hold our positions and not give an inch. There can be no war of movement in this cold, and in any case everything we do—except fall back—only makes me feel stronger!"

Halder ventured to suggest that it was essential to preserve the continuity of the front, since otherwise the Russians would infiltrate in force through the gaps in the German lines and wreak havoc in the rear. Clearly they would have to adopt an elastic defense, which would mean a strategic withdrawal—at least at certain points along the front.

"By no means, Halder!" the Führer thundered back. "If a breach opens up, then the reserves on the left and right wings of the adjacent units will plug it up. The infiltrating enemy forces will be cut off from their own lines and annihilated. . . . With your 'elastic defense,' " he said sardonically, "the breach would never be closed up, and the enemy would continue to exploit his advance until finally the entire front would collapse. In this cold any kind of mobile defense would be pure madness . . . it would just be sacrificing the troops needlessly. This is absolutely out of the question! They must dig in and hold their ground. I don't want to hear any more of your so-called scientific tactics—every man at the front must know what my orders are, and he must know what's at stake."

Halder tried to placate the Führer with assurances that his orders had already been passed on to the troops several days before. "The men know where their duty lies, but they can't break up the frozen ground, so they find billets in the villages to protect themselves from the cold—which is how these gaps in the line are created in the first place."

"In that case," Hitler retorted, "our artillery should blast dugouts out of the ground *between* the villages. Even in the last war the troops could always find refuge in a shell hole."

"The ground is too hard," Halder replied, "and we're short of ammunition. Such a plan could be carried out only on a very small scale. For that matter, even shell craters would not provide enough protection against the cold. The number of frostbite cases has reached critical proportions."

Hitler stiffened, then snapped back angrily, "Evidently the Russians can do anything, isn't that right, Halder? They roam around wherever they please, so they must not be bothered by the cold! No, they can't do everything, any more than we can . . . so don't come running to me with any of these preposterous stories!"

"It's not a question of that, my Führer, but the Russian lines of communications are shorter than our own, and their troops are better outfitted for this weather."

This remark provided a timely diversion, and Halder was off the hook for the moment. The question now was, where were the winter uniforms? A deputy chief of the general staff assured Hitler that they had already been dispatched and should have reached the front by now; the men in the trenches had also been provided with portable charcoal heaters. The chief of the military transport service pointed out that deliveries of supplies were increasingly in arrears, since the Russians had been destroying the locomotives and water towers along the route.

"Very well then," Hitler said, "listen to me. We are going to face this situation with iron resolution. The locomotives that we've been building wear out quickly and run at impractically high speeds; they have splendid brass fittings and tubes running all over the outside of the boilers—which apparently freeze up as soon as it gets cold. We'll have to scrap them all and change over to a totally different design."

The chief of the transport service replied that he had spoken to his minister and that preparations were already under way.

"Keitel! I want to hear what the minister has to say for himself."

"Certainly, my Führer, he'll be here tomorrow."

Hitler turned toward the others in a theatrical gesture of supplication: "So, gentlemen, you must do everything that is humanly possible to resolve all these transport problems. Take every locomotive you can get your hands on—the French have hundreds of them, scattered all over the country. They have to realize that we are waging this struggle on behalf of all Europe, and they'll have to make more of a contribution. Keitel! I'll be telling that to Laval very shortly. . . . And now, Halder, I want a detailed report on the current situation."

Halder presented his report: To the southwest of Moscow the breach had widened between the 2d Armored Group and the 4th Army. Marshal von Kluge was trying to prevent the envelopment of his panzer group, but this would take time. To the west of Moscow the 4th Army was stubbornly contesting every inch of ground. To the northwest of the city the situation was more critical—isolated units were still holding out, but a major breakthrough appeared to be imminent. Consequently "General Hoepner felt compelled to withdraw his troops in order to shorten his defensive lines and preserve the continuity of the front."

This was too much for Hitler: "Has he gone mad?" he shouted. "Does this fellow really expect to save his troops by moving them out of their positions in this weather? And how dare he countermand my standing orders?"

"There was nothing else he could do," Halder replied. "And it is only a *limited* withdrawal, in response to strong enemy pressure. . . . A limited withdrawal," Halder repeated soothingly.

But Hitler was not to be reassured; he was already pacing around the room, his anger mounting with every step: "That is a criminal betrayal of the men under his command! I'll show this fellow what it means to defy one of my strict orders. He has no idea what an ordeal he's inflicting on his men. . . . If this general had half as much courage as they do, he would never have caved in like that. . . . In fact I've had a word or two from Kluge about this already."

The corporal who had lived through all the miseries of the soldier's life in the trenches during the last war was finally about to have his revenge, to settle an old score with "the epaulets," as he called them, who went tearing by in their staff cars, splattering mud on his humble field-gray. The supreme commander, the conqueror of Europe, still harbored a streak of old-fashioned antimilitarianism, the simple soldier's hatred of the brass hats. Hitler continued his diatribe:

"This retreat is a filthy business, and I have no intention of putting up with it. The generals are obliged to obey me, just as much as the rank-and-file soldiers, and this general's idiotic decision will be on his head. What a sham! I'm the one who's in command, and all the others are supposed to carry out my orders without questioning them. Where would we be if all our officers behaved like that? It's cowardice in the face of the enemy, and I'll make an example of this fellow so that he won't ever feel like doing this sort of thing again."

Halder tried to excuse Hoepner's action, explaining that if he thought it best to order a withdrawal, it was only to safeguard his troops, but this only provoked another angry outburst: "I am the one, Halder, I am the one who must bear the final responsibility, and no one else, do you understand? I cannot have it any other way. . . . Keitel!"

"My Führer?"

"General Hoepner is relieved of his duties, effective immediately. He is to be discharged from the Wehrmacht for cowardice and insubordination. I want him brought before a court-martial! Gentlemen, let that be the end of it."

At this point General Heusinger approached Hitler and tried to point out to him that the front was overextended and could not be held. "We held fronts of thirty kilometers in 1914–18," Hitler replied, and that appeared to settle the matter. But shortly afterward, when Heusinger made inquiries at the army historical office, he was told that the longest front during the First World War had been from seven to eight kilometers. Heusinger mentioned this to Hitler; the Führer had been caught out in a contradiction, but he simply blustered his way out: "What right did they have to give out that information? That office isn't authorized to reveal military secrets to the first person who asks!"

Hoepner was sent home in disgrace, deprived of the right to wear his uniform and his decorations, to draw his pension, even to live in the house that the Wehrmacht had provided for him.

On January 20 General von Reichenau died suddenly of a heart attack. Reichenau was an ardent supporter of the Nazi regime, and Hitler had been very attached to him. "He didn't look after himself properly," Hitler remarked to his chief adjutant, General Schmundt. "After you reach fifty, you shouldn't ignore your doctor's advice. In my own case, if I didn't have Dr. Morell, would I still be alive?"

Palmists and astrologers had predicted that Hitler would enjoy a brilliantly successful career that would be interrupted prematurely, which he took to mean that he would meet with an early death. This became an obsession with him, and long before the war he had forbidden the practice of "divination" in Germany; crystal gazers and card readers who persisted in plying their trades were packed off to the concentration camps, along with the Communists, intellectuals, homosexuals, and Jews. As for Dr. Morell, General Heusinger recalls that one day when he complained that he had been feeling tired and worn out, the Führer sent for his miracle doctor immediately. Morell took Heusinger into a bathroom, produced a syringe, and gave Heusinger a shot in the buttocks. "I immediately felt as if my blood was boiling. My head was on fire. For several hours, in fact, I felt particularly energetic, but this was followed by a bout of depression that lasted for several days. I took care never to say anything more about my health in front of Hitler, but I had realized how much harm this regime of almost daily injections had done him."

But Hitler clearly felt quite differently, and he went on to develop a related theme: "You know, Schmundt, I should have liked to prohibit alcohol and tobacco in Germany—smoking is particularly unhealthy— but you can't deprive a man of his so-called pleasures. Still, a great deal of misfortune could be avoided that way. Think of all the crimes that people commit when they're drunk."

Schmundt felt obliged to point out that alcohol, taken in moderation, was a source of pleasure that he, for one, would not wish to deprive himself of.

"I realize, Schmundt," said Hitler, "that you are not altogether normal."

Schmundt brought up the subject of General von Reichenau's successor; he proposed Bock, who had presumably recovered his health since he had left the front a month earlier.

"If he has recovered his sense of judgment as well, I would agree strongly," Hitler said, "but we must be sure. And then, these gentlemen should not imagine that being relieved of their command necessarily means dismissal. In a long campaign it's better to take time off occasionally. We must be certain to keep those generals on who responded well in the last crisis.[1] Rommel, for example, takes it very badly when he has met with a reverse. Hoepner and Sponeck didn't hold up well at all. That sort of thing has a bad effect on the troops. I feel an instinctive sympathy for the front-line soldier, but if you know when to be firm with him, you are sparing him from even greater suffering. . . .

"Our staff officers spend too much time thinking; they make everything too complicated, even Halder. Fortunately I have relieved the

---

1. In fact Bock did replace Rundstedt as commander of Army Group South on January 18, 1942. [Tr.]

high command of the entire burden of responsibility—they were starting to turn our staff conferences into parliamentary debates. . . . Men like Fritsch, Beck, and Brauchitsch only followed me because I gave them no other choice, and instead of rejoicing in the wealth of possibilities that I held out to them—that I am still holding out—they insisted on meddling in things that didn't concern them, and they only had doubts and criticism to offer in return. . . ."

An aide had arrived with a message from General Halder: The Russians had just launched an attack to the south of Kharkov, in the Ukraine. "Get Halder on the telephone," Hitler ordered. "He has to make sure that no one tries any 'maneuvers' of his own. We must hold firm. We should follow the Russians' example: They attack us with untrained levies that they call divisions, and the worst of it is that our generals are completely taken in. These are disorganized hordes, not divisions! If I hadn't stepped in at the beginning, we might have been pushed back to our own borders by now. . . . We'll send them reeling back in disorder, and you'll see how their resistance collapses completely as soon as this weather improves. I know the generals don't understand me, but that's quite beside the point. All they have to do now is obey my orders and look after the men under their command."

For the conspirators the entrance of the Americans into the war had the instantly revitalizing effect of one of Dr. Morell's injections. They began to seek out new contacts, and Beck located an extremely encouraging prospect in General Olbricht, chief of the Army General Services Office, and, more important, adjutant to General Fromm, the commander of the territorial reserve, and Fromm's permanent representative at OKH. Olbricht would devote much of his time to the preparations of a military plan of operations for the conspiracy. Earlier contacts were still kept up with General von Stülpnagel, now commander of the German army of occupation in northern France,[2] and General Alexander von Falkenhausen, military governor of Belgium and northern France. Falkenhausen had served as Chiang Kai-shek's military adviser and had presided over the reorganization of the Chinese army, but he was overly fond of cards and women and, some said, too talkative to be a really effective conspirator.

As for Stülpnagel, he was considered to be somewhat passive, and

2. He had recently been chosen to replace his cousin Otto von Stülpnagel, whose brutal attempts at pacification by means of hostage taking and mass reprisals had not proved a success. [Tr.]

he was hard pressed to justify the mass executions of French hostages, for which as military governor he bore the ultimate responsibility. At best he could claim only to have kept such executions to a "minimum."

At the Wolf's Lair toward the end of March, Hitler, with Jodl standing by his side, was about to announce his plans for the summer offensive: "This year the fundamental problem is to defeat the Russians. Once they are beaten, Germany will become an impregnable fortress. The English and the Americans will never dare to attempt an invasion. . . . The Americans have a naval construction program that is fully as preposterous as their claims for aircraft production. After all, they mustn't take us for a pack of idiots. I created the Wehrmacht from nothing, and I know more about production capability than these American gentlemen who are wrestling with the same problems at this very moment. Apart from that, the Americans will have to fight on two fronts—we mustn't forget the Pacific, where they have already had to come to grips with the Japanese. . . .

"I realize that the Russians have been putting up a surprisingly stiff resistance since December, and that this has given rise to doubts in many of your minds about our chances of final victory. No, gentlemen! What has happened, after all? It was not the Russians who stopped our advance by any means, but an enormous natural catastrophe. We were almost destroyed by the fiercest winter in a hundred years, and if the cold hadn't been working against us, the Russian advance would have collapsed like a soap bubble.

"This year we will take the prize that destiny withheld from us last year, but we will not have dealt the enemy a mortal blow until we have cut off his oil reserves in the Caucasus. This, Halder, will be more effective than another offensive against Moscow. What would you expect to gain from such an operation?"

Halder explained that he hoped to engage the bulk of the Russian forces defending Moscow, cut the Russian communications network into two isolated fragments, deprive the enemy of strategic mobility, and finally, overrun the vital industrial belt around Moscow.

Hitler was unimpressed: "The Russians will have to fight for their oil—which we also have an urgent need for ourselves. The production of the Romanian oil fields is not going to satisfy our long-term requirements."

"Certainly not, my Führer," said Keitel.

At that point Hitler launched into one of his grandiose geopolitical reveries: "Think of the strategic and political advantages that we will enjoy when we have carved out a gigantic crescent from Batum to Stalingrad and Voronezh, by way of Baku.[3] That would bring Turkey into our camp, and we could send out expeditionary corps toward the Persian Gulf and the Urals. The consequences would be staggering, not only for Russia but for England as well.

"The entire Arab world is in ferment. Rommel's operations in Egypt have entered into an entirely new phase. The aerial bombardment of Malta has been going very well, so we should encounter no further problems in resupplying Rommel. . . . You may say whatever you like, but I can think of no other operation that offers us comparable rewards."

Halder tried manfully to attract the Führer's attention to the enormous scale of this campaign, relative to the strength of the German and satellite forces they had at their disposal. A two-hundred-fifty-mile stretch of the upper Don, from Voronezh to Stalingrad, would have to be held by Hungarian, Italian, and Romanian divisions to free sufficient German troops for the main striking force. Halder was particularly distressed by the idea of a two-pronged assault on the Caucasus and the Volga. He proposed instead to cut the Russian lines of communications to the lower Volga by means of a massive buildup of the front along the Don, and only then to move into the Caucasus in force. But by then Hitler had already turned his attention to more peripheral matters:

"All of that will be worked out as the operation develops. Our allies will have to be backed up by German strategic reserves, and they should not be required to defend very large sectors of the front. I hope that our allies will participate on as large a scale as possible. The peoples of Europe must realize that it is their fate that is being decided here as well. . . . Keitel, the French and Spanish divisions should be reinforced."

"Yes, my Führer, that will have top priority."

Jodl, who was now acting as the Führer's deputy for all military operations outside Russia—that is, western Europe, North Africa, the Balkans, Norway, and Finland—broached the subject of a provisional peace treaty with France, stressing the point that sizable concessions

---

3. In other words, this crescent would include virtually all of the Caucasus (including the oil fields of Maikop, Grozny, and Baku, and the Black Sea port of Batum) and the south central plain from Voronezh on the upper Don (about 250 miles southeast of Moscow) to Stalingrad on the lower Volga, only a few hundred miles from the Caspian Sea and Central Asia. [Tr.]

could be extracted from Marshal Pétain in return for granting him this prestige success.

"Believe me, Jodl," Hitler replied, "the French will never be able to be totally honest with us. They feel a deep-seated hatred for us, the like of which cannot even be approximated in our feelings toward them. If peace is ever concluded between us, they would immediately seize the opportunity to default on all their obligations toward us. There are those who think we might also profit from such a peace by acquiring the French colonial empire, but this is a fallacy. The French are merely waiting for a sudden shift in the military situation to take up arms again beside our enemies. All the rest is merely an illusion. . . . No, we must not loosen our grip on them—that is the only just policy."

And in the Ukraine and the Baltic countries, Halder asked, was there not also a considerable advantage to be gained in holding out the promise of a certain degree of autonomy?

"Now then, Halder, we must not delude ourselves about this either. I can't be making promises of this sort to a people when I've just requisitioned their last bushel of grain and their last head of livestock! Later on, though, we shall see."

But Hitler's tone was less indulgent when he went on to announce that he had ordered his Reich commissioners to act with the greatest possible rigor in carrying out these requisitions, and in other administrative matters as well: "Most of all, I don't want to hear any talk of humanitarianism where the east is concerned. They are all Asiatics. Stalin, and the tsars before him, knew how to treat such people, and we should adopt the same methods—even if they are repugnant to our German ideals.

"It is for that very reason that I have taken this responsibility out of the hands of the Wehrmacht and entrusted it to certain Party officials who are less fastidious about such matters. The generals should not be meddling with things that they don't understand. I have strictly circumscribed the role of the German judicial system in these occupied territories. All these fellows with their so-called sense of justice have done nothing to advance my interests. If the courts had been truly vigilant, we would never have been able to get back into politics again after 1923. They believe that their mission is to return criminals to society instead of exterminating them. Our entire penal code is a crime against the German people. The people have the right to demand that the state put these criminals out of action, so they can't do anyone any harm, rather than sending them right back into the community after a term in prison, however long or short it may be.

"All this that I've been telling you applies not only to our system of civil justice but to the Wehrmacht as well. . . . Well then, General Halder, when will we be able to launch our offensive? You mustn't delay too long, because of the early snows in the Caucasus."

Halder explained that the objective of the first phase of the operation was Kharkov, which would then become the staging area for Bock's army group, who would carry out the main offensive against Voronezh: "If we start from there, with our troop concentration completed by June 15, then I can predict that List's army group [4] will be ready to attack to the north of the Sea of Azov at the beginning of July."

"At the outside, Halder. They must have reached the Caucasus by the end of August. Keep all delays to a minimum."

"I will do my best," replied Halder. "The Italians, the Hungarians, and the Romanians will have to provide a great many fresh troops— this problem of our exposed flank along the Don has become something of an obsession with me."

"Halder, you must be content with what they can give you. And in any case the Russians' resistance is about to collapse. Your estimates of the Russian order of battle are not entirely reliable—I don't agree with you there at all. Their losses have been much higher, and their men will have to be trained for combat. For that they'll need instructors, which they don't have. You know how many months it takes to train raw recruits, and don't tell me that the Russians can do it any faster. You hear more and more now that Stalin can do everything—ridiculous! To be sure, he has thrown men into battle who have had almost no training, but these were human herds—I will never stop reminding you of that—which they have the insolence to call 'divisions.'"

"Unfortunately, my Führer, the Russians live closer to nature than our men. They don't have to be taught to take advantage of the terrain or to use camouflage, to use an entrenching tool or to go out on patrol. We were struck by how much technical aptitude they seem to have."

"That may be," Hitler admitted. "We have become too complicated. However, we must be careful not to focus exclusively on our own short-comings, or to imagine that the enemy is all powerful." The conference was adjourned. Halder confirmed that in a few days he would submit a plan of operation for the southern offensive that would reflect Hitler's

---

4. Actually the southern wing of Bock's Army Group South, which was later to be detached for the invasion of the Caucasus. [Tr.]

conception of the campaign. His parting words were: "I would be grateful, my Führer, if you would give some thought to the Moscow operation. We still have a month before we have to come to a decision."

"Yes, Halder, but you should realize that you are not going to convince me all the same. . . . I want your plan to be clear and precise, and I don't want you to have too much interference from the army group commanders. We shall exercise our command firmly, and we shall press forward."

With the first winter of the Russian campaign almost at an end, the mood of the German people had shifted in a direction that was hardly encouraging for the conspirators. The people had not lost confidence in Hitler. To be sure, the radio broadcasts announcing fresh U-boat victories in the Atlantic no longer gathered crowds around the public loudspeakers. The war had become an everyday affair, but though people were bemused by its scale and complexity, they still expected that this spring, as in 1940 and 1941, there would be nothing but good news from the front—Goebbels had assured them that this was not only a dead certainty but "an absolute historical necessity."

There were scattered reports of strike movements in the factories, and a scattered handful of small leftist groups had managed to hold out thus far. In Bremen a few dozen surviving Communists and Social Democrats had organized themselves into cells, but these were totally isolated, except from each other, and relentlessly stalked by the Gestapo. For the conspirators the spring's only noteworthy success was the recruitment of General Henning von Tresckow, Bock's chief of staff.

Tresckow was a Pomeranian squire by birth, a man of many talents, energetic, clearheaded, and high-minded to a fault. He had left the army in 1918 for the Berlin stock exchange, worked for several different banks, and in this capacity had traveled widely in Europe and the Americas, then returned to the army when its ranks were opened again by Hitler's rearmament program. Impressed at first by the accomplishments of the new regime, he became an enthusiastic adherent of the Nazi cause at a time when many officers were still reluctant to declare themselves. But then the Party's total domination over the army and the machinery of state left him angry and disillusioned, and, in spite of the first easy victories of the blitzkrieg, the means by which the war was actually carried out filled him with apprehensions about the future. He had brought his young cousin, Count Fabian von Schlabrendorff, onto Bock's staff, and through him Tresckow learned of the existence of a military opposition group. At first his scruples as a Prussian officer inclined him to keep his distance, though at the same time he filled his staff with young Prussian officers of his own circle who shared his misgivings about the Nazi regime: Colonel von Kleist, Count Hans von Hardenberg, and Count Heinrich von Lehndorff.

Marshal von Bock was scarcely a Nazi himself, though he refused to hear a word spoken against Hitler, whom he continued to admire steadfastly. Bock was a brilliant strategist, of the caliber of Manstein and Rundstedt, and regular army through and through; he was happiest when breathing the smoke of battle, and he dreamed of dying a hero's death on some eastern battlefield. Tresckow tried vainly to win him over to the opposition, but as General Heusinger explains, "I must admit that most of the generals took the same attitude as the German people—they slipped their blinkers on and kept their eyes trained on the road ahead of them."

In the middle of May General Heusinger was approached by a group of young officers in his section; they were still the Führer's men, more or less, though they were beginning to entertain certain doubts and were anxious to know if their CO thought that the decisive moment of victory was at hand.

"It matters little what I think, gentlemen," Heusinger told them. "But it must, I repeat, it must come this year. If we fail to beat the Russians in 1942, then we must abandon hope entirely, since from 1943 on the Western powers will be exerting an increasing pressure on us and will hold down more and more of our troops in the west. . . . You're aware of my reservations about a simultaneous operation against the Caucasus and the Volga. There are several things troubling me— the fact that we will be dividing our forces, the nature and the sheer expanse of the terrain, the limited manpower we have at our disposal, and the flagging morale of our allies. The all-important question is whether the Russians' capacity to resist is almost exhausted—as the Führer has declared it to be, and as our recent successes might also lead us to believe. But, strictly between us, gentlemen, we don't want to—we must not—console ourselves with illusions.

"Halder has asked, and rightly so, whether we shouldn't take up a defensive posture in the east, since a new offensive would overtax our present powers. But for one thing, this subject simply cannot be broached with Hitler. He remains quite unassailable and almost impossible to convince. He broke Brauchitsch's spirit and almost destroyed him physically, and now he is doing the same to Halder. Another point— if we give the Russians room to breathe and if the American threat begins to materialize, then we will be surrendering the initiative to the enemy. Also, there is no other way out except by taking risks, in spite of all our reservations. Hitler has already been acquainted with these in any case, and even if he shares these doubts, he will never admit as much—nor will he admit that the Russians have fooled him. Now he claims that the very strength of the Red Army furnishes clear proof of the correctness of his decision to attack Soviet Russia in the first place. . . .

"And then, he has a prophet's faith in his own mission. . . . This is the source of his strength and his force of will. If that faith is shattered, he will lose his self-assurance, and the entire Nazi edifice will crumble, and Germany along with it. He feels this himself, and it is for that reason that he cannot allow himself to be guided by the facts and thus remains faithful to his conception of the way things ought to be. You should bear all this in mind before you judge him too harshly. For example, he never visits the military hospitals, since he will not allow himself to be touched by the suffering of the wounded; he refuses to visit the battlefields on the Russian front. He doesn't care to witness the sort of devastation that may one day be unleashed on Germany, nor has he ever visited a bombed-out city. For the sake of his mission he has encased himself in artificial armor—Jodl and Schmundt have confirmed to me that this is true.

"And what is his relationship with Halder? Progressing from bad to worse. At first they were able to work together quite satisfactorily, but before long they began to wear on each other. I'll say this much for Halder—he can stand his ground until he gets what he wants, but he takes a kind of professorial tone that strikes Hitler as pedantic, though the ground would instantly give way beneath his feet if he behaved in any other way. But Hitler won't listen to lectures, and he detests Halder for his meticulousness and his objectivity. Halder has tried all sorts of tactics to gain some influence over the Führer, but he has only succeeded in driving himself to distraction; and he must also learn to swallow his anger."

"But during the briefing sessions," asked one of the young officers, "don't the other officers take the chief of staff's part?"

"Ah, then, that is the question!" Heusinger cried. "If the others see that their Führer agrees with Halder, then they all join in the chorus. Otherwise—at best—they keep silent, or they take sides with the Führer. Jodl is the only one who often comes to Halder's defense. As for Keitel— but we will say nothing of Keitel, except that he is careful not to get his whiskers singed. You must not imagine, gentlemen, that these sessions are anything like the humble staff conferences that we are accustomed to here. The sheer numbers involved are incredible—a whole claque of irresponsible counselors, platoons of ADCs, Ribbentrop's liaison officers, all with their ears pricked up. Everyone has his own precious opinion to offer, just as often unsolicited, but they provide Hitler with the sort of audience he needs, nodding in agreement at every word. And then there are the backstairs intrigues, most of them directed against the army. Halder has his work cut out for him in the midst of all this. . . .

"But for the moment, as soldiers we must harness all our energies to the service of victory. In a small group like this we can give free rein to our doubts and apprehensions, but they must never be allowed to filter out of this room. Wars have been lost before simply because commanders believed them to be lost."

On May 21 at a divisional command post south of Balaklezha the commanding general and the commander of an armored division were celebrating the victory at Kharkov, the Wehrmacht's first substantial success in nine months, in which a Russian force of fifty thousand men had been totally encircled.

"But we still have some difficult days ahead of us," the infantry general observed, "because the Russians don't give up all that easily. Timoshenko's going to try every trick he knows to fight his way through to them from the east." Kharkov was to be the only battle in which Manstein was given a totally free hand; he allowed the Russians to advance and then enveloped them in a pincers attack from both flanks. By this time, however, the Germans no longer had the strength to follow up on their initial success, and Kharkov proved to be just a local victory, which had little or no effect on the forward momentum of the Red Army.

At the end of June Jodl arrived at the Wolf's Lair; he had had news from North Africa that he wished to discuss with the Führer personally. He began by criticizing Rommel, laying a great deal of emphasis on the fact that he planned to drive straight on toward El Alamein, instead of the prearranged campaign plan—"after the fall of Tobruk, to take Malta, and only then to cross the frontier into Egypt." Rommel stood high in Hitler's esteem, not only as a brilliant tactician and an audacious commander, but also as a loyal officer, a partisan of the Nazi regime, who was not born into the Prussian ruling caste. "We shouldn't put stumbling blocks in the path of a victorious commander," he said to Jodl. "If Rommel thinks the situation is favorable, we mustn't hold him back. I'm not so sure that the Italians will be able to take Malta."

Jodl did not agree; he saw no reason to scrap their original plan: "Rommel's view of the situation is rather optimistic. If we can't secure his supply lines, he'll be stalled in his tracks."

But now Hitler was in the grip of a prophetic vision: "Jodl!" he cried. "Isn't this a portentous moment! In the east our troops are approaching the Caucasus; in the south Rommel is pressing on toward Suez. The hour of victory has arrived—when these two great pincers converge, the Near East will be within our grasp!"

Two weeks later, around July 10, Hitler was installed in his new forward command post ("Werwolf") at Vinnitsa in the Ukraine. The first question of the day was addressed to Jodl: "What is the situation with Rommel?"

"As I feared, Rommel's drive has stalled before reaching El Alamein. He is not strong enough to mount an offensive against Egypt, and our supply convoys have not been able to get through."

(In fact British intelligence had been providing accurate reports— the so-called Ultra documents—on the German convoy routes and the intentions of Rommel and other Axis commanders for some time. The Germans were using the Enigma cipher machine to secure their communications with their commanders in the field, and a Polish refugee who had worked in the factory where thousands of these machines were produced for the Wehrmacht had passed the secrets of the Enigma's construction to the British. The first German transmissions were successfully deciphered by the Ultra group in April 1940, and the Ultra operation was to make a very large contribution to the Allied victory.)

Hitler came automatically to Rommel's defense: "We should not have held him back. We can't expect him to succeed every time. Let him hold his present line, and perhaps soon enough we'll be able to give him the order to advance. But first we should establish what sort of supplies he requires. . . ." Next he turned toward Halder. "Have you finally got your reports on the Russian prisoners and the captured matériel? To the north of Rostov there must have been many units that were cut off completely from the main Russian force."

Halder appeared to have another opinion, although he had very little information himself. Communicating with the front was difficult, and they had rarely taken so few prisoners in the course of a major attack. The "captured matériel" was scarcely worth discussing.

"Believe me, Halder, the Russians are finished—they have nothing else left to throw against us."

Hitler's groundless optimism, as always, was beginning to grate on Halder's nerves. "That would surprise me," he said. "I can't believe it, in fact. The enemy may be carrying out a systematic withdrawal, since the vastness of their territory allows them a much greater depth of maneuver."

Hitler grew agitated, evidently searching for a scapegoat. "If in fact the enemy had succeeded at that, then Marshal von Bock would be responsible. If he hadn't kept his panzers bottled up at Voronezh, but instead had moved along the Don toward the southeast, then the Russians would never have been able to retreat. I was already thinking of replacing him when he announced that he wanted to scrap all his preparations for the battle of Kharkov and start over at the last moment—but I let myself be taken in again. Now you can see how right I was. . . . He's managed to spoil the entire operation for us.[5] It's a complete shambles. Fortunately the Russians are almost done for and in any case we'll stop them soon enough when we overrun their oil fields."

Halder observed that his original analysis of the situation—that the Russians had carried out an orderly withdrawal beyond the Don—was strategically plausible and definitely should not be ruled out. In his opinion the critical phase of the offensive had still not been reached. In any event the personality conflict between Hitler and his chief of staff had come out completely into the open. (It had been remarked on by Hitler's entourage that Halder rarely used the phrase *mein Führer* anymore.)

"I disagree completely, Halder. We are now in full pursuit of the enemy, and now we must send the bulk of our mechanized units southward, toward the Caucasus. The armored contingent of General Paulus' army[6] can be reduced to an absolute minimum; he'll still reach the Volga without them. Also, if the Russians should decide to stand and fight beyond the Don, or at Rostov, or in the south, then we shall cut them off and encircle them before they can dig themselves in on the northern slopes of the Caucasus."

5. Bock was relieved of his command five days later, on July 15, and his army group was split into two independent wings which were to proceed against the Caucasus and Stalingrad on the lower Volga. [Tr.]

6. Paulus' Sixth Army would be the spearhead of the northern wing of Army Group South, so-called Army Group B, commanded by Marshal Baron Maximilian von Weichs, a spry old Junker who was characterized by Guderian as "an officer who could always make the best of a hopeless situation."

Halder was deeply disturbed by this decision, and he urged Hitler to reconsider—in much the same terms as he had done at the May 15 conference. He presented various arguments to support his opinion that it would be preferable to secure the Don Valley and the lower Volga, to take Stalingrad as soon as possible; then the second phase of the offensive—the drive into the Caucasus—could be undertaken in relative security. But Hitler was not to be moved by mere logic. "Look here, Halder, this Russian resistance that worries you so much is simply going to melt away like a mirage."

Halder had heard quite enough of this, but he managed to remain at least outwardly calm. "I would like to direct your attention to the fact that according to your plan—I repeat, *your* plan—our entire stock of fuel will have to be allocated to List's panzer detachments if they are even going to reach the northern slopes of the Caucasus—I have this on the authority of the deputy chief of the general staff. This means that Paulus will have to move on Stalingrad with his infantry alone, which is to say, very slowly."

"That means that something's gone wrong, Halder, and I want you to find out who's responsible. However, that need not concern us at the moment, and in fact this only confirms my decision to transfer my Leibstandarte [7] back to the western front. I have learned that the English are going to attempt an amphibious landing, and I'll need at least one motorized unit in place there. If they can't join the drive toward the east, they'll be of no use to us here. . . . Yes, Halder, you may shake your head now, but you'll see that everything's going to work out very well in the east, even without the Leibstandarte."

During the month of July Fabian von Schlabrendorff returned to Berlin several times, where he made the acquaintance of Carl Friedrich Goerdeler, still the most enterprising of the civilian opposition group. Goerdeler now had even greater cause to hate the Nazis, since two of his sons had recently been killed on the Russian front. One of them had originally been serving as an officer with the occupation forces in France. Sickened by the endless pillaging and the execution of civilian hostages, he was implicated in a plot to distribute anti-Nazi leaflets in his regiment, brought up before a court-martial, and packed off to the eastern front—which proved to be only a brief stay of execution. For

7. Hitler's personal bodyguard, the SS Adolf Hitler Leibstandarte, had been expanded into a full-fledged panzer division under the command of General Sepp Dietrich, who had begun his career as Hitler's chauffeur and the head of his SS goon squad in the twenties.

Goerdeler, the devoted paterfamilias who had actively supervised his children's education and took so much pride in their accomplishments, this was an especially cruel blow.

He fell in enthusiastically with Schlabrendorff's proposal to return to the front with him and visit Army Group Center HQ. There Goerdeler could meet with Tresckow, who had wrestled with his Prussian conscience and was now an ardent supporter of the conspiracy. They also had great hopes for Tresckow's commanding officer, Marshal von Kluge. Goerdeler would ostensibly be traveling to the front to inspect certain timber concessions that the Bosch firm had acquired in the Smolensk forests; Colonel Oster of the Abwehr provided him with a travel authorization for the military occupation zone.

After a week's journey, changing back and forth between troop trains and freight trains, Goerdeler arrived in Smolensk. He was received enthusiastically by Tresckow, and even Kluge was most accommodating, even to the point of discussing a practical plan of action. As soon as Goerdeler arrived back in Berlin, after an equally exhausting journey, he hurried off to report to General Beck on the encouraging results of his interview with Kluge. But Kluge had already sent a messenger, by plane, to Berlin, who had told Beck that the marshal disapproved of the way in which Goerdeler had taken it upon himself to pay this unexpected visit to his headquarters, and that the marshal wished to dissociate himself from any unwarranted conclusions that might be drawn from such a visit.

"Clever Hans" was running true to form, and Goerdeler felt that the generals had betrayed him again. And as he had done in the past—most recently after his contretemps with Brauchitsch—he retired to restore his energies and plot a new campaign by the family hearth in Königsberg, a kind of fortress of the old German virtues that he was able to maintain inviolate until the end of his precarious career. His wife later recalled that when their younger daughter came home from school one afternoon, she gave the Hitler salute as she came in the front door. Her older sister and Frau Goerdeler braced themselves for an explosive scene, but Goerdeler did not say a word. Later he took his wife aside and explained. "If you criticize at home what a child is taught in school, then education becomes impossible. We must explain things to her slowly and patiently. . . . What a nightmare this government has turned out to be!"

Goerdeler was anxious not to involve his family in his political activities, not simply for their own protection—even so, his wife, his two daughters, and his surviving son would be arrested after July 20, 1944, and sent to a concentration camp—but because he believed that it was the particular duty of the men of his generation to resist the Hitler regime, since it was their own weakness and passivity that had brought him to power originally. "This does not concern the young people," he said. "They had absolutely nothing to do with it."

Several weeks after Goerdeler's abortive mission to Smolensk, Schlabrendorff returned to Berlin to see General Beck; the current situation on the Russian front had convinced his cousin Tresckow that the war was irretrievably lost.

"And why are you telling me this now?" Beck replied. "This war was lost before the first shot was fired." He went on to enumerate Hitler's military "follies": the occupation of Norway, which had cost the Wehrmacht dearly, the Balkan campaign, Rommel's adventure in North Africa—all of which, in his opinion, would lead Germany to certain defeat, even if they made the careers and the fortunes of a handful of ambitious generals. Beck went on to give a detailed prediction, not only of the catastrophe that was brewing in the east, but of how the Wehrmacht would be driven out of France in 1944—first the Allies would land in Sicily, then in Italy, the British would regain a foothold in Greece, and finally they would mount a successful amphibious invasion, assisted by naval, air force, and airborne units, on the northwest coast of France.

In August 1942 General Jodl returned to Hitler's GHQ at Vinnitsa to report on his inspection tour of the front. He had flown over the Caucasus and was now convinced that Hitler's plans for an airborne assault on the Black Sea port of Tuapse, opposite the Maikop oil fields, would end in disaster. "The terrain is so difficult along the main highway that runs from Tuapse across the western Caucasus that it seems impossible that we could relieve our paratroops in time." During his stay in the Caucasus the first snows had already started to fall. The army corps commander in that sector had asked for authorization to withdraw his forward outposts; they had already advanced over a mile beyond the pass through the mountains, where it was almost impossible to resupply them. "I believe," Jodl concluded, "that he can only negotiate this terrain along the Tuapse highway in painfully small increments. It seems unlikely that he will get through by the end of the year. Marshal von List shares my opinion."

"No doubt, Jodl—he could hardly have formed any other opinion, since it was his brilliant generalship that got us into this predicament in the first place. If he had concentrated on taking the highway, he would have gotten through a long time ago. Instead, he has scattered his troops all over the mountainsides, and he has gotten nowhere."

"In my opinion he was off to a good start. He should have expected that the highway would be bitterly contested, and so he chose to try to get through the mountain passes instead. He may be criticized for having concentrated too many of his troops on this objective, which complicates our arrangements for resupplying them over the mountains."

"Jodl," Hitler said acidly, "I didn't send you down there because I wanted to listen to a lot of defeatist talk. You were supposed to present my plan for an airborne assault on Tuapse. Instead, you seem to have come back here determined to be the mouthpiece of the generals at the front. It really wasn't worth the trouble of sending you down there. This morning the Alpine troops reported that they have fallen back on the mountain passes—that is the only positive result of your little airplane ride! As soon as one of my senior commanders gets out of my sight, he seems to fall under some sort of alien spell. I can't count on anyone unless I'm standing right next to him at all times."

Jodl stiffened; he did not have Keitel's servile nature and he could not restrain himself from answering: "If you simply want to throw your paratroops away, then drop them on the Tuapse highway. The same goes for your Alpine troops, if you send them through those passes at this time of year. Apart from that, I wasn't sent down there just to hand over your orders but to make a study of the situation. If all you want is an orderly, then you don't need me when you can use any rank-and-file private!"

Hitler's reaction was predictable; he began by accusing Jodl of insubordination: "You should have forced them to accept my orders in spite of all their objections. That was your mission, General Jodl, and you have failed to carry it out. Thank you, you are dismissed." When Jodl had stalked out of the map room, Hitler sent for his chief adjutant. "Schmundt, from now on I wish to take all my meals in private. Make sure in future that a complete stenographic record is made of every military conference—I don't want them to be able to twist the meaning of my words. And finally, until I decide otherwise, all officers on my personal staff are forbidden to fly to the front unless they have been sent on a specific mission. None of them has the firmness or the energy to do what's required of him."

And in fact the Führer no longer set foot in the staff officers' mess; instead he had his meals brought to him in his private railroad car. Jodl had become a nonperson: Hitler never again shook hands with him or even looked directly at him. The daily briefings were now held in the drawing room of Hitler's railroad car instead of the map room. A ranking SS officer was always present, and Jodl's every word was taken down by eight different stenographers (furnished by Party Secretary Martin Bormann). In addition, he had already been told, by Keitel, that the Führer had decided to replace him with General Paulus, as soon as Paulus had taken Stalingrad. (A less obvious irony here is that Paulus had already associated himself, to some degree at least, with the military conspiracy against Hitler.)

After the front had been more or less stabilized, the Russians launched an agitprop campaign to demoralize the German troops. Their lines were bombarded with leaflets and "passports" that would enable German soldiers to cross the Russian lines in perfect safety; the leaflets supplied more practical tips on fraternization. The impact of all this was negligible; the troops were surprised and curious, but not seriously interested. The army, like the German people at home, would remain dutiful soldiers (or subjects) of the Reich; there was absolutely no trace of an insurrection welling up from below.

In one of the daily briefings at the end of August, Halder informed the Führer that the position of Army Group Center was rapidly becoming untenable. By now their supply lines were reduced to a single road—which could be used only by day, and then under heavy escort, because of partisan ambushes—and a single line of track, which was constantly subjected to enemy artillery fire. Some units would soon be completely cut off, after which they could be resupplied only by air. "I would like for us to consider," Halder said, "a timely withdrawal of our forces and a contraction of the front or, if need be, that the unit commanders be provided with this option, to exercise if they see fit."

"I beg your pardon, Halder," the Führer replied, "but you always seem to end up giving ground. You move the troops back from their positions and into a new defensive line—a shorter one, to be sure, but on unprepared and unfamiliar ground. After a little while the enemy puts more pressure on this line, he breaks through, and after this brilliant tactical retreat, we give up a few dozen more kilometers without a fight. With this sort of tactics, Halder, you'll have us slowly but surely evacuating all our troops from Russia. So much for your art of warfare!"

"But I simply want to consolidate the front," Halder protested.

"Then we will be able to use our reserves more sparingly, and our divisions will no longer have to hold such abnormally extended fronts. If we continue with our present policy, we won't be able to hold much longer."

"Enough talk, Halder," Hitler replied threateningly. "I know what that sort of thing leads to. We must stand firm for the good of the men."

Halder faced him squarely; none of his colleagues on the general staff had ever seen him in such an emotional state. "That's all very well, but our brave men and their officers are dying by the thousands out there, senselessly, and simply because their commanders don't have the right to make the only decision that could save them—because their hands are tied."

Halder had clearly gone too far: Hitler simply looked him up and down for a moment, but the counterblast was not long in coming: "How is it, General Halder, that you can allow yourself to take that tone with me? You want to explain the spirit of the front-line soldier to *me*? What do you know about life at the front? Where were you during the last war? And you dare to accuse me of not understanding the front? As your superior, I forbid you to say such things!" Hitler continued to gesticulate wildly, carrying on a wordless harangue, while Halder, who by now had regained his customary poise, replied that he had not intended to attack the Führer personally, but "my heart is bleeding, and my words simply expressed my compassion for the men at the front." Halder left the GHQ—very likely, he thought, for the last time.

10.

1942–1943: Stalingrad

On September 4 a general whose division was fighting not far from Stalingrad received a visit from a war correspondent. "Strange to have callers in this howling wilderness," the general said to himself, and to his visitor: "What fair wind brings you here, sir?"

"General, I want to be with our troops when they take Stalingrad. The prize that we have sought for so long is about to fall into our hands. The effect on our people, and on the entire world, will be incredible. I would like to be able to provide them with an eyewitness account; that is why I am here."

"Then I'm afraid," the general replied, "that you may be with us for some time."

"What?" The correspondent seemed genuinely surprised. "But that's not what they told me in Berlin, at the Propaganda Ministry."

"Perhaps, my dear sir, but the Propaganda Ministry is not the front. Here we have to contend with stiffer resistance every day; the Russians have launched a whole series of violent counterattacks. We've had to send off too many of our panzers to the Caucasus, and now we haven't got them when we need them to break through the Russian defenses. Our infantry divisions are below strength and worn out; they can hardly be expected to take the city by themselves. Don't forget that we've come over five hundred kilometers just to get this far."

Hitler had announced publicly that nothing could prevent his troops from taking the city and holding it. The German people—and the entire world—expected that before long the swastika flag would be flying over the rubble of Stalingrad as it had been flying from the summit of Mt. Elbrus, the highest mountain in Europe, since August 21.

"But, general, aren't you taking an overly pessimistic view of the situation?" asked the war correspondent.

"No, sir. The Soviet high command seems to have decided to defend Stalingrad to the last man. They are constantly bringing up fresh troops. We have seen that before, at Moscow and Leningrad, don't forget. Still,

I think that we'll reach the city in two or three weeks, but the Russians are contesting every meter of ground with desperate energy. Our troops can feel the cold coming on; they know what to expect if they have to camp out on these steppes without heat or shelter, with no railroads to bring them supplies. They are fighting for their winter quarters, and the enemy knows it."

"So I have come too soon then?"

"I don't want you to give up hope altogether. Stay with us for a while—but if you have to fly back to Berlin before you've accomplished your mission, don't start churning out victory communiqués as soon as you get there. Describe the situation as it really is. That won't be very encouraging, but then at least the people back home won't have a totally false picture of what's happening out here. The men will be grateful to you for that much."

At Werwolf GHQ Heusinger was closeted with Hitler's chief adjutant, General Schmundt. Schmundt was explaining to him that the Führer's aversion to General Halder had become so pronounced that Hitler was ready to explode whenever he caught sight of him. The hostile atmosphere of the daily briefings had become unbearable, and the Führer's nerves could not stand that sort of punishment much longer. "Halder should not forget everything the Führer's been through this past year: Our armies in the east are gaining ground, but only with tremendous effort. Rommel's drive toward Suez has failed because more than half of our supply ships have been torpedoed. All the crises at the front, the loss of Brauchitsch, Bock, Leeb . . . and this stifling heat— it's starting to affect the Führer's health."

"First of all, Schmundt, senior generals should not be treated like schoolboys, and he deliberately got rid of most of them himself."

"But, after all, he's the supreme commander!"

"And that is precisely the problem. He suppresses all individual initiative, he is suspicious of anyone whose opinion differs from his own, he tells no one anything more than is absolutely essential for him to know. This is bound to have serious consequences, and the only reason that Halder has stayed on after their last fateful encounter is that he wants to shield the army from further maltreatment, and he believes the situation will only get worse after he's gone."

Schmundt simply repeated that this business with Halder could not go on for much longer, and that the day was not far off when the Führer would send him packing. In that case, Heusinger replied, the final crisis of command could not be much longer in coming, and for his own part he would take that as his cue to request a transfer to the front.

"But you could never do that, General Heusinger: You must admit that the general staff has not dealt fairly with the Führer. Since 1935 they have tried to sabotage his every decision, and they have been wrong on many occasions. Just think of Beck and Brauchitsch. How can you criticize the Führer for trying to take a firm stand against that kind of intransigence?"

"Schmundt, I think you've said enough. Only the future will tell us who was right—Beck's general staff or Hitler. He talked his way into this war, and soon we'll be fighting for our lives. And the army isn't the only place where these differences arise; but the Luftwaffe, the navy, and the SS prefer to wash their dirty linen in private. Goering, Raeder, and Himmler are always there to cover up for them, and it's only occasionally that Hitler finds out what's happened afterward. But since Brauchitsch left us, there's been no one to protect the army. Hitler and the general staff exist in different worlds. His contempt for sustained intellectual effort, his conviction that he can triumph over objective reality by sheer force of will—all of this will never allow him to see the world as we do.

"Convince Hitler to relinquish his command of the army, and restore freedom of action to the general staff and the commanders at the front, and history will call you blessed. Otherwise the struggle will go on, and every field commander and staff officer who is aware of his responsibilities and who has faced the situation clearly will eventually take sides against the Führer. And that, Schmundt, is all I have to say to you."

"But you must accept the Führer as he is. I don't see any other possibility." And that was the end of their conversation.

Several days after this exchange with General Schmundt, Heusinger was summoned to Hitler's private office at GHQ. "I want to have a word with you, Heusinger. I have just dismissed Halder. . . . I have had to relieve him of his duties as chief of the army general staff because he is not as devoted to the principles of National Socialism nor as convinced of the value of our ideas in action as I expect the chief of my general staff to be. In short, he has not defended my ideas as forcibly as the situation required.

"I have appointed Zeitzler as his successor. I am counting on you to remain in your post and under his orders. He is a new man and still not familiar with the workings of the high command."

Heusinger made good on his promise to Schmundt by requesting that he be reassigned to the command of a front-line unit, since he had been serving on the general staff since 1937, and perhaps, he suggested, it was time to bring in some new blood.

"I understand," said Hitler, "but you were in the front lines during the first war, you were wounded . . . and as a matter of fact I can't really spare you just now. I want you to give General Zeitzler the same kind of support that you gave his predecessor, help him to get his bearings."

Heusinger agreed to stay on, but he admitted frankly that this represented a painful sacrifice for him and urged Hitler to consider relieving him as soon as possible.

"We shall see," Hitler replied, "but there are a great many things that I find painful too."

General Kurt Zeitzler was not so much an anti-Nazi as a non-Nazi—apolitical, not particularly intellectual, and (at the age of forty-five) the youngest general in the Wehrmacht. He was a plain-spoken but essentially dutiful officer,[1] though his first official encounter with the Führer was rather stormy. Hitler opened the first round with one of his routine provocations: "Your general staff is nothing but a pack of defeatists," he announced.

"My Führer," said Zeitzler, "as chief of the army general staff, I must request you to retract that remark." And Hitler, impressed by his new chief of staff's audacity and esprit de corps, promptly apologized. And on September 25—his first day on the job—Zeitzler exhorted his officers to have faith in the Führer and in his leadership—"Any officer who fails to do so will be of absolutely no use to me."

The second winter of the war in the east was about to begin; after a month's heavy fighting, Paulus' Sixth Army was poised for the final assault on Stalingrad. In early November General von Tresckow was sent on a mission to Berlin; he stopped off on the way at OKH headquarters in the Mauerwald to acquaint himself with the latest developments. General Heusinger presented him with a gloomy picture: "With Rommel in retreat and the Anglo-American landings [in Morocco and Algeria on November 8], we are about to lose our foothold in North Africa. Our offensive has broken down hopelessly, and there you have the result of splitting our forces between two different objectives. We're now on the defensive in the Caucasus, after failing to take the oil fields. When Jodl announced to Hitler, 'We'll never get through the Caucasus,' Hitler

---

1. Previously, as an officer on Rundstedt's staff, he had introduced the custom of ending all memoranda to army commanders with the phrase "Heil Hitler!"

flew into a rage and there's been bad blood between them ever since. In Stalingrad we're wearing ourselves out, fighting from house to house, advancing a few meters at a time, and taking very heavy casualties in the process. We've encountered bitter resistance in the worst street fighting of the war, and from an adversary who is still far from being beaten. And all this has come to pass because Hitler has misjudged the nature of the enemy. As for Zeitzler, I know him well—they sent for him because they thought he would be easier to manage than Halder. He is said to have gotten high marks from Goering and Himmler . . . but I think they have misjudged their man. Once he gets his teeth into something, he never lets go. But in any case Hitler takes care of the strategy single-handedly now, and he won't listen to advice from anyone. . . .

"The American contribution in matériel has forced us over to the defensive, and their landing in North Africa proves that they're ready to launch a counteroffensive of their own. And what was our instantaneous reaction to this? The occupation of southern France, which meant the end of all our hopes of winning the French over. Not long ago Laval is supposed to have said to Hitler, 'You want to win the war so you can unite Europe; you should unite Europe now so you can win the war.' Unfortunately it's far too late for that. Our occupation policy is a political aberration. At first our military authorities exercised restraint, but now they have been reinforced—or replaced altogether—by SS contingents who seem to have an unslakable thirst for blood. . . . And that, my dear Tresckow, is all I wanted to say to you. Go and see Beck in Berlin; they tell me he's very worried. . . ."

In Berlin the mood was one of total pessimism. The military conspirators had been following the progress of the war on their own situation map, updated and corrected with information gleaned from Allied radio broadcasts. At Stalingrad the troops were beginning to feel the approach of winter. The Russians had strengthened their defenses even further and were about to counterattack in force.

On the morning of November 19 General Zeitzler put through a call from the front to the Wolf's Lair, where the Führer and his staff had returned at the end of October. "As soon as he wakes up, tell him that the Russians have launched a powerful dawn attack against the Romanian Third Army [on the upper Don front, to the northwest of Stalingrad]. Heim's panzer corps is being brought up to support them. . . ."

Zeitzler flew back to Rastenburg to attend the evening briefing session; he brought news of a second Russian attack against the Romanian Fourth Army to the west of Stalingrad. These troops, he observed, could not be expected to hold very long, since they were deployed along a wide front in flat, open country. Hitler announced pathetically, "When you can't have confidence in anyone, how can you be expected to exercise command? And what has happened to the Romanian Third Army?"

Zeitzler replied bluntly that the Russians had opened up two serious gaps in the front. The situation was still too confused to tell whether the rest of the line would hold, and General Heim's corps would have to attend to both Russian breakthroughs. "General Heim has two armored divisions," Hitler remarked. "It would be most unfortunate if they failed to restore the front. I want to know how many troops the Russians have committed to this business. . . . You'll see, it will be Moscow all over again—but if the front doesn't hold . . ."

Zeitzler was obliged to point out that, apart from the fact that the Romanians were dispersed over a very wide front, there was heavy fog along the Don and Heim's reinforcements included one Romanian division that had never been under fire. "As a precaution I have ordered the entire army group put on alert, so we can bring them up if we have to. We should also be prepared to detach certain elements of the Sixth Army, as far as that is possible." (Paulus' Sixth Army was then heavily engaged at Stalingrad. Paulus himself had been in touch with General Beck through one of his adjutants, General Walther von Seydlitz, who had just been dispatched to Berlin to confirm the gravity of the situation.)

"Attention!" Hitler announced. "The Sixth Army must not be weakened too much in the Stalingrad sector. . . . I don't want anyone trying a stupid trick like that on me!"

But Zeitzler was afraid that the Russians would follow up with a second offensive, to the south of Stalingrad, with the threat that both Russian spearheads would converge to the west of the city. This they would have to avoid at all costs—"And so we shall," Hitler replied confidently.

Three days later, at the evening briefing of November 22, Zeitzler reported that the threat had materialized. The Sixth Army was encircled at Stalingrad.

"This is disgraceful!" Hitler shouted. "And what good did it do to hand two panzer divisions over to General Heim? What did they accomplish? Nothing, absolutely nothing! They completely failed to repair either one of the breaches in the front! Keitel! General Heim is relieved of his command, and I want him brought back here to face a court-martial. I want my generals to understand once and for all that they're expected to do their duty like everyone else, and if not, they'll be responsible for the consequences."

"Yes, my Führer," said Keitel, "this must not be allowed to happen again."

"Keitel, there's something else—I want you to inform Marshal Antonescu [the Romanian commander in chief] that Heim will be brought up on charges. He mustn't think that his army is solely responsible. . . . Zeitzler, where is Paulus now?"

"Still to the west of Stalingrad, my Führer, outside the encircled area. He's trying to push back the enemy drive from the north."

"He must return to Stalingrad immediately—I want to know where I am with my subordinates. We'll entrust the northern and eastern sectors to General Seydlitz. He's the toughest officer we already have in place, and he's had some experience of these temporary encirclements in the past.

"In view of the situation I've decided to make certain changes in the command of the army group. Marshal von Weichs can't be expected to take care of the entire front as far as the south of Stalingrad. Consequently, I would like to deploy a fresh army group around the city itself. Manstein's would be the best, since we certainly won't be planning an offensive against Leningrad in the near future. What else could we do, Zeitzler?"

"At present it would be impossible to break through the Russian ring around Stalingrad; we've used up all our reserves. Instead we must do everything in our power to reestablish a front to the west of the encircled area, to prevent any further erosion of our position to the west. I've also made a study of the logistics and the material requirements of the Sixth Army. They will have to be resupplied from the air, and I doubt if the Luftwaffe can keep that up for long. I've also looked into the possibility of a disengaging action. All our future decisions will have to take these two factors into account, and there's no time to be lost; otherwise the Sixth Army will never be able to break out toward the west."

"Break out?" echoed Hitler suspiciously. "And who said anything about their breaking out?" Zeitzler did not press the point, and the conference broke up.

Two days later, on November 24, the general staff informed the Führer that powerful Russian forces were streaming southward through

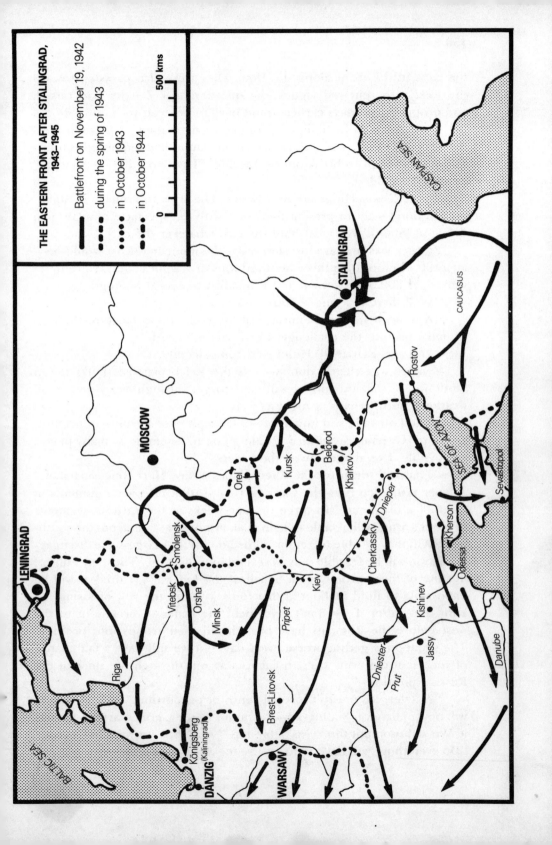

THE EASTERN FRONT AFTER STALINGRAD, 1943–1945

Battlefront on November 19, 1942

during the spring of 1943

in October 1943

in October 1944

500 kms

CASPIAN SEA

CAUCASUS

STALINGRAD

Rostov

MOSCOW

Orel

Kursk

Belgorod

Kharkov

SEA OF AZOV

Sevastopol

LENINGRAD

Smolensk

Vitebsk

Orsha

Minsk

Pripet

Kiev

Cherkassky

Dnieper

Kherson

Odessa

Kishinev

Jassy

Dniester

Prut

Danube

BALTIC SEA

Riga

Königsberg

DANZIG (Kaliningrad)

WARSAW

Brest-Litovsk

the gaps in the front along the Don. They were also pressing toward the west with renewed vigor. The question that Zeitzler had raised, and dropped, two days earlier would have to be dealt with now. Should the Sixth Army hold Stalingrad or try to fight their way out toward the west while there was still time? General Paulus had requested authorization to attempt to break out of the ring. "I see no other alternative," Zeitzler concluded.

"Never!" was Hitler's reply. "Never. The army will remain in Stalingrad! I don't want to present the world with the spectacle of a German defeat at 'Stalin.' We must hold the city, whatever the cost."

Zeitzler was prepared to state what the immediate cost would be—an airlift of more than three hundred tons of supplies a day, since there were over 200,000 German and Romanian troops at Stalingrad.

"Well then, Goering?" Hitler asked.

"A difficult task, my Führer, but given the importance of the city, we must take up the challenge. I give you my word."

"You see, Zeitzler?" Hitler said complacently.

Zeitzler was clearly dubious. "If the Reichsmarshal thinks it can be done . . . but the airlifts will have to get through every day, in all weathers, and perhaps at night as well."

"The Luftwaffe will find a way to triumph over all these difficulties, Zeitzler," Goering responded. "I am going to assemble as many planes as possible; I've already given the orders."

"That will mean two hundred planes a day, Herr Reichsmarshal," Zeitzler reminded him—he was eager to present his own arguments in favor of a breakout. "In three or four weeks at the earliest, elements of Hoth's army will be able to launch an armored assault from the southwest. Will they be able to get through? I doubt it. A large-scale disengaging action will be feasible only in several months' time. Thus, my Führer, in spite of these promises on behalf of the Luftwaffe, I think it will be impossible to hold Stalingrad that long. We run the risk of losing the army altogether if we don't give them the order to break out to the west before the Russians have brought all their troops into position. The situation is getting worse every day, but we still have a fair chance of success if the army tries to cut its way out through the thick of the Russian positions."

"Zeitzler, we mustn't lose all sense of proportion," said Hitler. "I will never abandon Stalingrad—the honor of the German armies forbids it. We will soon put this crisis behind us." And then, turning to Goering: "Do everything you have to to ensure the airlift gets under way immediately at maximum tempo. Zeitzler, use every means at your disposal to stabilize the front to the west of Stalingrad. I am going to send Paulus another telegram to make him fully aware of the importance of his historic mission. But for the rest we can only wait until Manstein takes up his command.''

On the following day, November 25, Heusinger made his report to Zeitzler. He had studied every aspect of the situation and had reached the same conclusion: Paulus would have to fight his way out of Stalingrad, or his army would be annihilated.

''That's my opinion as well,'' Zeitzler told him, ''but I never would have believed that the Führer could be so stubborn. I tried for three days and nights to win him over to our point of view—unsuccessfully. Now he's taken Manstein as his sword—and he claims he can't presume to anticipate Manstein's decision—and Goering, with all his promises, as his buckler.''

Heusinger was equally skeptical about the Stalingrad airlift: ''We've seen it all before, at Dunkirk and during the Battle of Britain . . . the total usurpation of our role by the Luftwaffe. Their chief of operations has assured me that the transport planes that take part in the airlift will have to devote half their carrying capacity to the fuel that they'll need for the return journey.

''And where are these aircraft going to come from? Some of them are currently being used to train our novice pilots, which means we'll be running short of fresh pilots, and God knows how much we need them. And finally there is the crucial question: How long will this airlift have to go on? Paulus can't be relieved until March of next year—at least not if we want to put together an attacking force that will be strong enough to have some chance of success—and it seems unthinkable that the troops could be resupplied from the air in the dead of winter, or that such an effort could be sustained until the spring.''

In Berlin many of the conspirators believed that their own chances of success could only improve as public morale continued to deteriorate, with the collapse of the economy, war weariness, disillusionment, and sheer physical exhaustion, brought on in large part by the success of the Allied bombing raids. Gone were the days when Goering could confidently proclaim, ''If a single British plane gets through to bomb a German city, then you can call me Meyer.''[2]

2. An allusion to the common German expression ''Or you can call me Hans,'' (i.e., ''Joe Zilch,'' ''Mr. Nobody''), which Goering has characteristically given an added anti-Semitic fillip. [Tr.]

At his command post in Stalingrad General Paulus had just finished listening to an extremely pessimistic report from one of his corps commanders. It was the end of November, and soon it would be virtually impossible to continue the airlift; the situation on the ground was scarcely more encouraging.

"Do you think it possible that events could take a turn in our favor?" the general asked.

"I'm not sure," Paulus answered, "that the Führer's ideas can actually be put into practice. But of course I don't have a sufficiently clear command of the overall situation to be able to appreciate the finer points of the Führer's plan."

"In that case," the general suggested, "I think you should definitely try to put yourself in the picture. The fate of some 250,000 German soldiers is at stake here. In a besieged fortress, general, only the fortress commandant can make the final decision. His feelings as an officer as well as a man impel him to act. That's what your men expect of you. You must decide for yourself, without orders, in defiance of your orders if need be. You must strike out to the west at the head of your army— you may lose your own head for it, but at least you'll have saved your troops."

"Naturally it's not a question of my own personal survival, but in the age of the radio does the commandant of a fortress still have the right to act on his own initiative? Won't I simply be interfering with the plans of the high command? Only they can make the decisions and pass on their orders to me. But all of this is still in the embryonic stage; the airlifts have scarcely begun. We shall simply have to wait."

"It will be too late, general. We'll all be dead by then. Hitler will never give the order, or he will give it only after it is too late. General, I implore you to act."

The Sixth Army general staff had put their lives, and the lives of their men, in the hands of General Paulus, and Paulus would do nothing without a direct order from Hitler. The Sixth Army would fight with incredible courage and tenacity, but from that time on their fate was sealed. The shortages of fuel and food, the rigors of another Russian winter would bring enormous losses; some of the wounded could be flown out on the transport planes, but none of them could be replaced in the line.

On November 25 General Baron von Richthofen, commander of the Fourth Air Fleet, wrote in his diary after making a reconnaissance flight over Stalingrad: "The Sixth Army will have to go it alone for at least six weeks. I'll be damned if we can resupply them for that long! Of all the aircraft that took part in the airlift, we have only thirty left. Yesterday we lost twenty-two, and today twenty-nine. And we were able to bring in only seven and a half tons, instead of three hundred. . . .

"It is a disheartening fact that none of our senior commanders, even those who are supposed to have the Führer's confidence, have been able to exert the slightest influence over him. As far as the day-to-day conduct of the war is concerned, we are nothing but vague subalterns, only a little better paid than the rest."

At the beginning of December General Heusinger received a visit from the operations chief of the Foreign Armies East section of OKH.[3] As an intelligence officer, he had his own reasons to be anxious about the fate of Stalingrad. He believed that until now the enemy had been husbanding their forces, but that the Don offensive of November 19 would shortly be followed up by a new offensive against the front held by the Italian and Romanian armies to the west. "And even now," he concluded bitterly, "our general staff still persists in underestimating the Russians."

"You have only confirmed what I've been afraid of all along," replied

---

3. The section chief of Foreign Armies East was himself a former protégé of Heusinger's, Major Reinhard Gehlen, who had originally served with the Fortifications Section and was seconded to the Operations Section in 1941. His first assignment was to assist with the preparations for the Yugoslavian campaign (a military coup that deposed the pro-German regent of Yugoslavia had created an unexpected hitch in Hitler's timetable for the Balkan and Russian campaigns). Gehlen demonstrated a remarkable talent for the delicate craft of intelligence gathering. Although he worked closely with Admiral Canaris, he did not have the advantage of a far-flung network of agents. His specialty (for which he had a technical gift that amounted to real genius) was radio intelligence. He established a network of radio listening posts that enabled him to intercept all Russian radio traffic sent in clear, and this in turn allowed General Heusinger to provide the general staff with updated situation reports on Russian troop movements at the front.

One morning General Halder appeared in Heusinger's office and asked him point-blank, "My intelligence service isn't making much headway. Is there anything you can do to help me, general?"

"All I can do is hand over my most valuable associate, Major Gehlen."

"Thank you," Halder replied, beaming. "That's precisely what I was hoping for, though I didn't dare to ask in so many words."

Gehlen subsequently became the chief of the Foreign Armies East section of OKH, even though Hitler quickly grew to detest him and could never read through one of his reports without losing his temper. Gehlen was an intelligent, scrupulously honest officer who made no attempt to disguise his vision of the coming catastrophe in the east. Hitler decided on several occasions to get rid of him, but Gehlen still managed to finish the war with the rank of major general. He fell into the hands of the Americans (to whom he gave a complete course in the techniques of monitoring Russian radio traffic he had perfected on the eastern front), and afterward—like Heusinger and Speidel, among others—he carved out a new career for himself in the postwar Bundeswehr. He took charge of the reorganization of army intelligence and later achieved a certain international celebrity as the head of the DNB, the West German intelligence service.

Heusinger. Since November 22 he had tried unstintingly to wrench a decision out of Hitler that would allow the Sixth Army to abandon Stalingrad. And from the beginning he encountered opposition from Goering, who had pledged the honor of the Luftwaffe to the success of the airlift. Fifteen days earlier it still might have been possible for the Sixth Army to break through the Russian ring unassisted. But the Russian positions were being constantly reinforced, and the Germans, after weeks on short rations and still waiting for the supplies they had been promised, were no longer in a position to make the attempt.

But Hitler had great hopes for his new Tiger tanks, Heusinger explained, even though they were inadequately equipped for combat as they came off the production lines and were immediately trundled onto flatcars, destined for General Hoth's panzer group on the Don. Hitler had exultantly assured him, "The Tiger tanks will be quite capable of destroying the entire Soviet tank corps."

"As if the war could be won with slogans," Heusinger added contemptuously.

"Then Goebbels would be our greatest general!" the intelligence officer exclaimed.

Heusinger went on with his narrative: "I've gone over all my calculations to demonstrate to Hitler that his conception of the time, the distances, and the forces involved have nothing to do with anything in this world. We must never, under any circumstances, permit Paulus' army to remain in Stalingrad. We might attempt to break through on the left flank, along the Don; that would take ten to fifteen divisions, which could not be in place until February at the earliest. I'd hoped that this study would convince him that his plan is sheer madness, since we don't have those divisions now and by February it will be too late."

During the briefing session of December 15 Hitler asked how the Tiger tanks had fared at the front, and Heusinger gave this scathingly candid report: "A filthy business! Only half of them are moving under their own power; the rest couldn't be driven down off the flatcars because their engines wouldn't start or they broke down shortly afterward. . . . The tanks that were still moving stopped just short of a bridge that will have to be reinforced before it will bear their weight. I should mention nevertheless that the Tiger tanks that have been in action have shown themselves to be superior to their Russian counterparts."

"Ah!" Hitler shouted, slapping his thigh. "If I only had a panzer group like that in Africa! They'd make short work of the English—we'd cure them of their infantile disorders soon enough. . . . But apart from that, Zeitzler, where has Hoth gotten to? His army must open the road to Stalingrad no matter what the cost!"

Zeitzler explained that Hoth had fought his way to within forty miles of Stalingrad, but the attack was almost spent. The moment had come to give Paulus the order to break out toward the west. Even though the failure of the resupply effort had left his troops weak with hunger, they would still be able—knowing what was at stake—to advance that far.

"Just so," Hitler grumbled, "and that means we lose Stalingrad, or deliberately abandon our position. . . . This notion—I'm sure of it—has settled in everyone's mind like a poisonous fog. The report that you've just given me on Hoth's army might even have been intended to coerce me into making this decision."

"The quota for the airlift of three hundred tons per day has never been met, my Führer. For four days I've been living on the same rations that are available to the Sixth Army, and I've discovered for myself how quickly one loses one's strength. You may add to that the cold and the scarcity of firewood. Paulus' army is hurrying to their doom in Stalingrad, and this is our last chance to save them."

"But don't you see, Zeitzler, that if the army makes a sortie to the west and abandons Stalingrad, they will have to leave most of their equipment behind? In this weather they'll die of exposure on the steppes before they've reached Hoth's army."

"Would you like to send me, or perhaps General Heusinger, to consult with Paulus?"

"There's no need for anyone to go there, Zeitzler. I am the only one who knows what has to be done. In any case, what will you do in the Caucasus if Paulus is withdrawn?"

"My point exactly, my Führer. The front will be much more secure. Everything's beginning to give way now. If we could save the Sixth Army, then so much the better—that will allow us to strengthen the rest of the front. Otherwise, there's no point even in discussing the Caucasus."

"There you have it then!" Hitler shouted. "The whole summer offensive would have been in vain! No, these are all idle fantasies, gentlemen. I am going to press Goering to make good on his commitments, but it is essential that Paulus hold Stalingrad until we can relieve him. I'm holding down substantial enemy forces there, and we should be glad that we won't have to face them elsewhere."

"My Führer," said Zeitzler, "let us at least ask Paulus if he thinks he can bring his army out toward the west."

"Very well," Hitler replied after a pause, "but he will not advance to meet Hoth's army and most important, there can be no question of his abandoning Stalingrad. After all, he will have to hold the city to cover his retreat."

Several hours later Zeitzler returned with Paulus' reply: "Possible to advance twenty miles."

"What did I tell you?" Hitler said gloatingly. "It's just that these gentlemen are always urging me to make decisions that can never be carried out. . . . The Sixth Army must hold Stalingrad, Zeitzler, or the Russians will simply fall upon them from the rear. I can do no more than ask Paulus' opinion; he knows what's at stake in this battle. But there is only one possible decision that I can come to: The army must remain in their position until we can relieve them."

"Then the army is lost, my Führer."

"There is no more that I can do. . . . It's beyond human help. I've spoken to Goering—General Milch will be supervising the airlift. Soon everything will be running smoothly again."

On Christmas Day the chief of staff of List's Army Group A called on General Heusinger at OKH headquarters before returning to the Caucasus. "You've arrived just in time," Heusinger told him. "Just take a look at the map. The fall of Stalingrad is only a matter of time. In spite of all our efforts, the airlift isn't working. On most days they're bringing in between twenty-four and a hundred tons of supplies—we've fallen far short of the mark. The troops are on the verge of starvation. We won't be able to disengage them in the foreseeable future, now that the Italians have also been routed on the Don and every available unit has been brought up to keep the front from collapsing. Zeitzler has been fighting desperately to put across his proposal for the evacuation of Stalingrad. He was even beginning to wonder if he shouldn't simply wash his hands of the whole business, but he felt that that would be tantamount to desertion under fire, and it certainly wouldn't have done anything to change Hitler's decision."

On January 1 Paulus received a radio message from Hitler: "Every man of the gallant Sixth Army must greet the New Year in the absolute conviction that the heroes of the Volga will never be forsaken by their Führer, and that the Reich will mobilize all its resources in order to relieve them." On January 8 Paulus rejected a Russian offer of terms.

The Russians had been funneling troops into the Stalingrad sector in enormous concentrations, which relieved some of the pressure on

the Don and gave Manstein a much needed respite in which to repair
the gaps in the front and allowed him to cover the retreat (which Hitler
had finally authorized) of Army Group A in the Caucasus. This was
the greater good, at least as far as Paulus was concerned, for which
his army was about to be sacrificed.

A wounded officer reported the following exchange to General Heusinger after he was evacuated from Stalingrad—a conversation between
two ordinary soldiers that took place during a mid-January blizzard on
the western perimeter of the sector:

"For weeks now all we've got is a spoonful of hot food or coffee.
. . . I can't take it anymore."

"They ought to hang the guy that got us into all this. Karl has all
the luck—a bullet in the head today, a billet at home tomorrow."

"Except he's not going to be waking up. We're the ones who're
going to make it. Adolf isn't going to leave us here to die in this hole,
no matter what. Our lieutenant thinks so too. You should see him, he
looks just like a ghost—nothing but skin and bones. He says there's a
big push going on now, and all we have to do is sit tight. They say
yesterday you could hear shellfire over to the west. They'll get here,
you'll see."

But was it possible that tens of thousands of German soldiers would
be marched off to Russian POW camps in Siberia? The conspirators,
in an agony of suspense, could only wonder what Paulus would decide
to do. Only two solutions seemed possible: Either he would simply shoot
himself, or he would make an appeal to his troops and to the German
people, abandon Stalingrad in defiance of his orders, and give the signal
for a general insurrection against the criminal warlord who was willing
to throw away an entire army for the sake of his personal prestige.

But according to Beck, Paulus would refuse to abandon Stalingrad
until he had received the order to withdraw through the prescribed
channels. And in fact Paulus' last letter to his wife, written at the end
of January, expressed the same sentiment in almost identical terms: "I
am here under orders, and I intend to remain here to the end." During
his stint at Hitler's GHQ Paulus had seen ample evidence of Hitler's
attitude toward his generals: Either they obeyed orders blindly, or they
were treated as deserters.

Heusinger, who first met Friedrich Paulus in 1927, remembers him
as "an intelligent man, an engaging personality, and an officer who
had already embraced the creed of absolute obedience." Paulus was
born in 1890 in Hesse. Most of his family were small farmers and trades-

men; his father was a petty official. Friedrich had prepared for a career as a lawyer, then, in 1910, decided to join the army. He was a handsome young man, tall and thin, with fine, regular features, and he made a distinguished, rather dashing young officer. In 1912 he married a Romanian noblewoman, a great beauty and the daughter of one of the leading princely families; she quickly introduced him into the most exclusive circles of society, and in time bore him three children—two daughters and a son. After serving in the First World War, he was attached to the Defense Ministry staff of the Reichswehr in 1922 and to the general staff in 1931. His health was frail, but he was a tireless worker who kept himself going with coffee and cigarettes. Paulus was modest, almost excessively so, a good comrade, open and congenial, and a gifted staff officer, who carefully weighed the pros and cons of every decision he made.

When Hitler came to power, Paulus felt the self-made aristocrat's disdain for the upstart corporal who deliberately flouted the laws of God, man, and the established social order. However, he remained unswervingly faithful to the dictates of his soldier's conscience: "This is an order from the Führer, and I must obey it."

On January 30 Erich Koch, gauleiter of East Prussia, had invited Goering to join him in hunting the hare on the three districts of Masurian lake country that Goering, in his capacity as master huntsman of the Reich, had allotted to Koch as his private hunting preserve. The day's festivities would end with the coronation of a king of the hunt.

Goering arrived that morning in his private railroad car, *Asia*—truly a movable feast for the eye, with its tapestries, paintings, curios, furs, and silver plate. Gauleiter Koch had provided a robust hunting breakfast—rabbit stew, potted wild goose, a marinade of young boar, venison pie, smoked salmon, Baltic herring, and trout in aspic. Well refreshed, the party set out for the field, which was actually a thousand-acre tract of grassland and fallow fields that included a number of lakes. The line of beaters moved through the covers, and the huntsmen formed a vast semicircle that slowly closed in on itself in a classic enveloping attack. When the circle had drawn in far enough, the huntsman gave a signal—since the hunters were now close enough to do serious damage to each other. They would restrict their fire to the area outside the circle. The startled hares shot off like arrows, but they were deflected in their flight by the animals who had been driven in the opposite direction. The volleys from the circle of hunters only increased their panic.

At the end of the day's shooting the fawn-and-white carcasses of twelve hundred hares were spread out over the field. Goering, with a bag of three hundred to his credit, was acclaimed king of the hunt. He stood alone in the midst of his trophies and struck a pose for the photographers—his paunch protruding regally and his Reichsmarshal's baton held aloft in his right hand.

That same day Paulus was awarded his own marshal's baton in absentia, and on the following day, January 31, Zeitzler reported for the first of the day's briefings at Rastenburg (less than a hundred miles from the site of the Reichsmarshal's recent triumph in the field). Before Hitler had time to say a word, Zeitzler announced: "Here we are then, my Führer—we've lost radio contact with Stalingrad since yesterday. Their last message reads: 'The Russians are outside our bunker. This is our final transmission. Long live Germany.' "

Hitler sat motionless, his face dead white, tears streaming down his cheeks. Then he erupted: "The Russian radio has announced that Stalingrad has fallen and Paulus has been taken prisoner. . . . I can't believe he'd let them take him alive! This is a Soviet propaganda trick! The field marshal was offered the choice between life and immortality; I can't believe he would choose life." He crossed the conference room in long strides. "Keitel! Inform Goebbels immediately—the memory of Stalingrad must become a beacon light for the entire German people. Zeitzler, the divisions of the Sixth Army will be reorganized under their original designations. The army will rise again from the ashes!"

As far as Heusinger was concerned, the real tragedy of Stalingrad was that, when it still would have been possible to save at least part of the army, Paulus had announced in effect: "I've been ordered to hold this position, and here I shall remain." What was needed was a commander who knew when to disobey orders, but there had been only two such cases in the entire history of the German army: In 1812 Marshal Ludwig Yorck von Wartenburg, a Prussian of English Jacobite ancestry who commanded the Prussian contingent in Napoleon's Grande Armée, had prudently taken it upon himself to negotiate an armistice with the Russians. And in 1914 General François, a corps commander in East Prussia, had audaciously pursued a beaten Russian army in defiance of Hindenburg's orders and set the seal on the most decisive German victory of the First World War.

And why did Paulus choose not to kill himself? "Because," Heusinger explains, "he was a man of profound Christian beliefs, incapable of suicide, and because up to the end he wanted to share the fate of his comrades and the men under his command. For both these reasons, he would have looked on suicide as a form of desertion."

The day after the fall of Stalingrad Hitler called the general staff together. "I expect that every one of my officers," he told them, "will prefer death to surrender. The honor of tens of thousands of German soldiers has been tarnished because General Paulus lacked the courage to do what even a weak woman would have done in his place. I regret having raised him to the rank of marshal, and I will never bestow this title on anyone again until the war is over. Paulus could have singled himself out from the mob; he could have found a place for himself in the deathless ranks of our fallen heroes—but he preferred to go to Moscow instead."

11.

1943: Infernal Machines

The first major defeat of the war—which was openly acknowledged as such by a proclamation of national mourning—might have been the signal for a putsch carried out by the generals, almost all of whom had privately blamed Hitler for his refusal to order a withdrawal. Many of them were aware that a military conspiracy—even a shadow civilian government—already existed in Berlin to coordinate their activities. They might even have considered themselves to be released from their oath of allegiance, insofar as they had sworn obedience to Adolf Hitler as chief of state, not as the supreme commander of the armies in the east, as he had been since 1941. At least this was the rationale proposed by Beck, who had offered to take personal command of the insurgent armies. But by now the generals' primary response to every critical situation seems to have become simply to do nothing until it was too late.

Kluge, who was appalled by the Stalingrad debacle and naturally concerned that his own army group might be next, decided to risk a personal appeal to the Führer. But once he was admitted to the innermost recesses of the Wolf's Lair, he could only present his case haltingly and incoherently, and Hitler quickly cut him short by launching into one of his monologues. Finally, however, he was authorized to stabilize the front at certain points, and he withdrew, perfectly prepared to bend to the Führer's will in future.

But it was not only the generals who were haunted by the specter of Stalingrad. In Munich university students took to the streets in response to Hans and Sophie Scholl's leaflets calling on them to avenge their dead. Their "White Rose" network of clandestine propaganda was inspired not by simple war weariness but by a genuine revulsion against the crimes of the Hitler regime. The organizers of this short-lived uprising—both still in their twenties—had emerged from the Catholic student movement of south Germany; they had little contact with the conspirators in Berlin, and even less to do with politics or ideology as such—their program involved little more than passive resistance and sabotage directed against armaments factories and the activities of the Nazi Party.

The conspirators in Berlin were at least agreed that it was time to put an end to the Nazi adventure, but the civilians, Goerdeler among them, still believed that Hitler should be taken alive. Their reasoning was that if Hitler were killed outright, then he might well be resurrected in popular mythology, like the Emperor Barbarossa, which would be embarrassing to the new regime—"If only the Führer had lived, then everything might have come out all right." The new government could be vindicated only if Hitler was physically present in the dock, judged before the world and condemned before the bar of history.

But the military conspirators, who would have to carry out whatever plan was eventually adopted, were not about to lead an insurrection that had no chance of succeeding. They knew that their fellow officers still set great store by their oath of allegiance, and that the majority of the German people were still in the grip of their Führer's charismatic spell. And they were fearful that neither the oath nor the spell could be broken while the Führer still lived. The army would have to be released from the oath of allegiance—this was Beck's conclusion, which Goerdeler finally came to accept—and this meant that Hitler would have to be assassinated. His death would furnish the "initial spark"—this was the code word they would use in future—that would touch off a military uprising, the immediate objective of which would be to seize control of the key points in Berlin and make certain that reliable troops were in complete control of the capital as soon as possible thereafter; this operation would be carried out simultaneously in several other cities as well.

The preparations for this second phase had been entrusted to General Oster (he had been promoted in the interim) and General Olbricht. Oster consulted with Beck on all important questions and did what he could to see that his wishes were carried out. When they had made some progress with their preliminary plan for seizing control of the territory of the Reich, they began the search for a front-line officer who would be capable of organizing the actual attempt on Hitler's life. Their choice fell on General Henning von Tresckow—still serving as chief of staff to the coy Marshal Kluge. For his part, Beck had sounded out Marshal von Manstein and received this reply: "A war is not lost as long as one does not believe it to be lost."

Oster and Tresckow had never spoken to one another directly, however, and it fell to Tresckow's cousin, Major von Schlabrendorff, to organize and maintain a secure line of communication between them.

As Schlabrendorff wrote, long after the event, "You must have lived in Germany during the war to be able to imagine the sort of precautions we had to take, knowing that the Gestapo was lurking everywhere. Even in the most intimate company we could never mention the name of anyone who was indispensable to our enterprise. This obsession with the Gestapo tormented us by day, kept us from sleeping at night, and left us paralyzed with anxiety. To escape from this cycle of terror, one had to have nerves that were far steadier than the average." By the end of 1942 Oster and Tresckow had already met face to face, to discuss the prospects of a military coup in the fairly indefinite future.

At the end of February 1943 Tresckow dispatched his cousin to Berlin for a final meeting with Olbricht. "We're ready," Schlabrendorff announced. "The time has come to kindle the spark. This will be Operation Blitz ['Lightning Flash']." A final joint strategy session was to be held at army group headquarters near Smolensk. Admiral Canaris provided a plane for the Berlin conspirators; he also arranged to be accompanied by a group of officers from his intelligence staff, in order to create the impression that this was nothing more than an ordinary military conference. The conspirators met in a small office that was normally occupied by the editor of the army group newspaper. First they agreed on a cipher with which the leaders of the conspiracy could communicate in future. Then Canaris remarked that he was due back in Berlin on the following day for a meeting with Himmler, which cast something of a chill over the gathering. Canaris could not help smiling—this was the sort of dramatic effect that he found highly gratifying. In fact, he explained, he was going to request Himmler to release a few poor devils who had fallen into the hands of the Gestapo on the pretext that they would make useful informants for the Abwehr.

Tresckow had prepared a plan that required Hitler to be enticed out of his lair on a visit to Kluge's headquarters in the middle of the Smolensk forest.

"For some time," Schlabrendorff's account continues, "my cousin had been cultivating his acquaintance with Hitler's chief adjutant, General Schmundt. The whole point of the operation was to set Hitler down in an unfamiliar environment that was, however, completely familiar to us. Schmundt was not subtle enough to suspect that Tresckow must have had some ulterior motive in asking him to persuade Hitler to visit Marshal Kluge's headquarters at the front."

Hitler finally agreed to such a visit in early March 1943, and, as was his custom, he sent word that he would definitely be arriving at a particular time and then backed out at the last moment. Finally, it was announced that Hitler would be flying to Smolensk on March 13. "If Kluge had made up his mind to act," Schlabrendorff wrote, "then we would have gotten rid of Hitler then and there. We had drawn up a regiment of cavalry around army group headquarters; their commander, Baron von Boeselager, was one of us. Their officers had been hand-picked for this mission, and Boeselager, who was a prudent commander but entirely careless of his own personal safety in combat, would have been in an excellent striking position. Unfortunately, though Kluge admitted that our plan was perfectly feasible, he wanted to have no part of it himself. His support would have been invaluable in galvanizing the other commanders into action, both at the front and in the interior, but he objected that neither the German people nor the rank-and-file soldier could be expected to understand the purpose of our operation. He felt that we should wait until the military situation had deteriorated even further, to a point where everyone would finally have grasped the necessity of eliminating Hitler." In other words, the upshot of Kluge's latest defection was that their plan for overwhelming Hitler's escort by main force would have to be scrapped.

"We decided, Tresckow and I, that we would still make an attempt, in the hope that when we had presented Kluge with the fait accompli, he would then feel free to act and would no longer have to make a secret of his personal convictions. But to appease his tender conscience, we evolved the following plan: not to shoot Hitler but to conceal a bomb on his plane that would explode in mid-flight, so that it would naturally be assumed that his plane had crashed. Colonel Baron Rudolf von Gerstdorff, intelligence chief of the army group general staff, was in a position to procure the explosives for us without arousing suspicion. The bomb and the detonator were of English manufacture, of a type that British pilots dropped over German territory presumably for the benefit of saboteurs. The device itself had the advantage of being compact but still powerful enough to reduce an average-sized room to atoms.

"We successfully tested the explosives several times, and to be sure of the results, we decided to use two bombs, wrapped as a parcel, which looked very much like two bottles of cognac."

In the early morning of March 13 Kluge and Tresckow drove out to the military airfield to welcome the Führer. As always, Hitler was accompanied by a sizable entourage, including his personal cook and his physician, the ubiquitous Dr. Morell. "After meeting in Kluge's office for an hour," Schlabrendorff recalled, "we adjourned for lunch. To be sure, we could have simply left the bomb in the conference room or the staff officers' mess, but that would have meant the death of a number of men whose help would be crucial to our enterprise. As always, Hitler had brought his own food with him, to be prepared by his cook and tasted by Dr. Morell.

"The spectacle of Hitler at table was enough to take anyone's appetite away. With his left hand planted on his thigh, he scooped up his meal of mixed vegetables—he was a strict vegetarian—with the soup spoon he held in his right hand. Never once did he bring the spoon up to his mouth, nor did his right hand ever leave the edge of the table; instead he kept his head hunched over his plate and brought his lips down to meet the spoon—with an occasional pause to sip at one of the nonalcoholic fruit juices that stood by his plate. Naturally it was strictly forbidden to smoke, even after the meal was over.

"During lunch Tresckow asked Colonel Brandt, a member of Hitler's staff, if he would mind taking a package that contained two bottles of cognac back to General Stieff at army supreme headquarters [OKH]. Brandt agreed to take the package.

"I had already telephoned General Oster earlier that morning to give the signal that we were about to proceed with the operation. Olbricht was also notified. After lunch Kluge and Tresckow drove back to the airfield with the Führer. I followed in another car, with the bombs. Hitler and his entourage had arrived in two different planes with a fighter escort. When I saw Hitler shake hands with Kluge and board the plane, I started to arm the bombs. The upper part of the detonators was shaped like the neck of a bottle; I pressed hard against these bottlenecks with a key to make sure that enough pressure had been exerted on the detonating mechanisms. We had calculated that the device would explode half an hour after takeoff. I handed the package over to Colonel Brandt, who we knew would be flying back in Hitler's plane.

"The planes took off toward three o'clock. It seemed that Hitler's fate was sealed. . . . We rushed back to the headquarters compound to send the second code message to Berlin—Operation Blitz was under way.

"We knew that Hitler's plane was provided with a special security system: The fuselage was divided into several independently sealed cabins. The cabin that Hitler would occupy was armor-plated and outfitted with an escape hatch that would permit the occupants to parachute directly out of the plane. But our test firings had indicated that the charge would be sufficient to destroy the entire aircraft, and even if not, we were convinced that the plane would be so severely damaged that it would certainly crash.

"According to our plot of their course, the plane would be brought down in the middle of the afternoon, just before they arrived over Minsk. We expected that the first word of the crash would come to us over the radio from one of the fighter escort.

"Our nerves were raw. The waiting was unbearable, My heart was pounding. . . . The hands of the clock moved, but still there was no word. After two hours we received a staggering piece of news—Hitler's plane had touched down safely at the airstrip at Rastenburg, near his GHQ. Our carefully planned operation had come to nothing.

"I telephoned Berlin and gave the signal that meant that our enterprise had met with failure. Then Tresckow and I began to discuss what to do next. If they were to find the bomb, we would be implicated immediately, which would mean certain death for our entire band of conspirators. Tresckow decided to telephone Brandt and ask him if he still had the package for General Stieff; apparently the real nature of the package had not yet been discovered. We would have to do everything possible to keep it from falling into the hands of General Stieff himself, who was not yet a party to the conspiracy. Tresckow asked Brandt to hold onto the package until the following day, explaining that there had been some confusion about the bottles. 'Fabian von Schlabrendorff,' he added, 'will be reporting to GHQ tomorrow—he'll stop in to see you and exchange the packages.'

"The next day I talked my way on board the regular flight to Rastenburg with a substitute package for General Stieff—which of course contained two bottles of genuine cognac. I still tremble at the recollection of Colonel Brandt's smilingly handing me the package, with a flourish that must have shaken up the contents a good deal. The bombs were still armed, and it would have been entirely possible for them to explode even then. Trying hard to appear as casual as possible, I took the package and made my way to the railroad station at Korschen, not far away, where I could take a sleeping car to Berlin. The moment I got into my compartment, I locked the door, took out a razor blade, and carefully unwrapped the package. Needless to say, the charges were still intact. I disarmed the bombs and removed the detonators. I was astonished to discover that when I had armed the bombs in Smolensk, the capsules had broken, quite according to plan, the acid had eaten its way through the wires, and the firing pins had struck the detonators, but the bombs had not exploded! Only a demolitions expert could have provided me with the true explanation for this anomaly, but at the time all I was concerned with was disposing of these infernal machines, and I threw both charges out the train window into the forest. It was late at night on March 14 when I arrived in Berlin. I went to see Oster to explain what had happened and to show him the detonators, which I had kept with me. Once again a malevolent destiny had brought our efforts to nothing. This was a grievous blow, but it had one positive aspect—it had demonstrated to us that our plans for seizing power in Berlin and the other large cities were still not adequate to the task. . . .

"On my return to the front I immediately sought out Tresckow. He no longer seemed discouraged or crushed; on the contrary, he seemed more firmly resolved than ever to pursue the course that he had chosen, once and for all." And, as Schlabrendorff points out, the failure of Operation Blitz had uncovered two serious flaws—not only in their preparations for the military takeover inside the territory of the Reich, but also in the liaison arrangements between the capital and the officers at the front.

Several similar plots were hatching at the same time in Army Group South. These were largely inspired by confederates of General von Tresckow, who had arranged to be transferred to Manstein's army group, though Manstein himself was not involved in or even aware of their activities. None of these spin-offs of Operation Blitz ever matured beyond the planning stage.

The conspirators on the home front were given another chance a week later, when it was announced that Hitler would attend the opening of an exhibition of Russian battle trophies at the arsenal in Berlin. Colonel von Gerstdorff, who had furnished the explosives for Operation Blitz, was in charge of the opening ceremonies. Hitler's visit was scheduled to last for twenty minutes; the bomb that Gerstdorff intended to use on this occasion had to be armed ten minutes before detonation.

Characteristically the event was postponed several times. On March 23 Hitler finally appeared at the arsenal, accompanied by General Walther Model, with Goering, Himmler, and Keitel following close behind. General Schmundt informed Gerstdorff that Hitler would be inspecting the arsenal for exactly eight minutes. Another near miss for the conspirators—Hitler was enjoying an incredible run of luck (in which he himself was later to detect the hand of Providence).

Within less than a year, Oster and then Canaris would be relieved of their duties after they were betrayed to the Gestapo by one of their own agents. Himmler had long suspected that the Abwehr was a kind of privileged sanctuary for all sorts of activities, but until now he had been unable to come up with any hard evidence. The story that emerged of trafficking in foreign currency and of a "Christian conspiracy" involving the Vatican and Protestant churches in several unfriendly countries furnished him with proof enough. All the functions of the Abwehr were eventually transferred to the various branches of Himmler's Reich Central Security Office, most notably the SD and the Gestapo. Deprived of the resources of the Abwehr and of Canaris' intelligence network, the conspirators were forced to reorganize and retrench severely. The year 1943 had not turned out well for them. They were fortunate, however, in a group of strong-willed young recruits who were not content simply to follow their cautious example. One of the most promising of these was Claus von Stauffenberg.

Count Claus Philip Maria Schenk von Stauffenberg was born on November 15, 1907, in the small town of Lautlingen in what was then the kingdom of Württemberg. He was the third son of Count Alfred Schenk von Stauffenberg, two years younger than his twin brothers, Berthold and Alexander. The Stauffenbergs were of the ancient Swabian nobility; the first recorded bearer of the name, Hugo von Stophenberg, is mentioned in a charter dated August 21, 1262. Claus's father had served for many years as grand marshal of the court of Württemberg, and after the fall of the monarchy in November 1918 he was appointed agent-general, entrusted with the management of the affairs of his abdicated sovereign, Wilhelm II of Württemberg. This distinguished courtier, who had spent his early career in orchestrating the pomp and protocol of the royal court, was a simple, affable man in private life, even something of a nonconformist. A talented craftsman and confirmed tinkerer, he devoted much of his time to restoring the furniture, touching up the decor, and even fixing the plumbing in the family apartments. Claus's mother, born Countess Caroline von Uxküll, was a grandniece of Marshal Count von Gneisenau, the great Prussian military reformer who served as Blücher's chief of staff at Waterloo; she was also distantly related to the insubordinate Marshal Yorck. The countess was a highly cultured woman, a fervent admirer of Goethe and Shakespeare, as well as the contemporary poets. (Imprisoned after the events of July 20, 1944, she made her confinement more bearable by declaiming long passages from *Hamlet* and *Faust* in her cell.)

Claus spent his boyhood in the "old castle," the ancient seat of the counts and dukes of Württemberg, a massive, turreted Renaissance château near Lautlingen, where the grand marshal's family occupied spacious quarters on the second floor. Claus quickly became aware of the influence he exercised over his contemporaries, though he was not so much a leader as a natural organizer—of clubs, literary discussion groups, and musical soirées; he played the cello, Berthold the piano, and Alexander the violin, and the trio gave recitals for their parents and their classmates from the *Gymnasium*. Claus was also an accomplished classicist, and he read both Greek and Latin fluently.

His aristocratic heritage and upbringing were complemented by a more modern and more personal conception of the role of the nobility. He was not concerned with the outward flourishes of the aristocrat's life, and while he was acutely conscious of belonging to a natural elite, he did not feel that this endowed him with any extraordinary rights or privileges. On the contrary, he believed that he was bound to judge himself more severely than other men judged themselves, and that he had an obligation to serve his fellow men; to serve the community, in his eyes, was the highest calling of a nobleman. General Halder was to say many years later that he had "the spirit of a grand seigneur."

Though his health was frail during his adolescence, he belonged to a scout troop and joined them on long hikes through the mountains, scaling rock faces and sleeping around a campfire. The family often stayed in the village of Lautlingen, and they cultivated close ties with villagers, literally so in the case of the three brothers, who worked beside the farmers in their fields like the earnest young aristocrats in Tolstoy's novels. Even today there are still a great many inhabitants of Lautlingen who were christened Alexander, Berthold, or Claus.

In spite of his predilection for music and the arts, he did not hesitate for long in deciding to take up his commission. For him this was a simple matter of genetics—the men on both sides of his family, as far back as they could be traced, had been marshals, staff officers, and ministers of state, and a number of them had been trained for these careers in the elite traditions of the Prussian cavalry. In 1926 he entered the Holzhof Barracks of the Uhlans (light cavalry) at Bamberg, a forbidding red-brick structure on the Nuremberg road on the outskirts of the city. Ensign von Stauffenberg was an avid rider, and he was soon competing in horse shows and even qualified for the German Olympic team. He made second lieutenant by the time he was twenty-two.

Just as he had once been the motive force of the musical soirées and hunting parties of his adolescence, he remained very much in the center of things and was lionized by the city of Bamberg, a sleepy provincial capital, old-fashioned and rather stuffy in its manners, where a Stauffenberg ancestor had once reigned as prince-bishop. Claus's comrades adopted him as their chief, a distinction he seemed to accept as his due, and nicknamed him *der Bamberger Ritter*—the horseman of Bamberg. (The original Bamberg horseman is a masterpiece of thirteenth-century Gothic sculpture which stands against a pillar in the old imperial cathedral—an effigy of an unknown king, or possibly one of the Hohenstaufen emperors, mounted on his charger like a figure from the chivalric epic of *Parzifal*).

Stauffenberg was twenty-three when he met his future wife, Nina von Lenderfeld, who was then barely seventeen. A descendant of Baltic Junkers and the old Bavarian nobility, she was passionately interested in the aristocratic pursuits of heraldry and dressage. She was captivated at her first meeting with this tall (over six feet four), slender, romantic-looking young officer with his unruly shock of thick, black hair. Like his father, Claus was rather disdainful of "what people would say," and he was somewhat negligent of his appearance, at least by Prussian standards. The sculptor Ludwig Thormaelden, a childhood friend of Stauffenberg's, provides this description of him in his memoirs: "At seventeen his character was already fully formed. He embarked on every action he undertook in a spirit of loyalty and frankness." As far as his physical appearance was concerned: "His eyes are a metallic blue. His features are symmetrical, without giving an impression of heaviness. His high, rounded cheekbones suggest the qualities of strength and determination, the prominent ridges over his eyebrows, his powers of concentration and perseverance."

The Bamberger Festsaal stood on a hill above the city, in a square that was surrounded by the battlements, gardens, and courtyards of the old prince-bishop's palace. This was where the young people gathered on Sundays, ostensibly to listen to the public concerts, which in pleasant weather were held outdoors amid the fragrance of the rosebushes, which were carefully tended and pruned by the ancient caretakers of the palace. This was also the objective of the obligatory promenade for the young women of Bamberg, chaperoned by their mothers, who made their way slowly up the narrow winding streets, past the shopstalls and the inns whose customers were protected from indiscreet or reproving glances by cloudy leaded windowpanes that dated back to the Middle Ages. During their betrothal, which lasted for three years, Nina and Claus often walked up, hand in hand, and looked down from the garden parapet over the multicolored, steeply pitched roofs of Bamberg, like a romantic stage set seen from the galleries of an opera house.

They were married in the cathedral church of Sankt Jacob on September 26, 1933, when Stauffenberg was twenty-six; the bride had just turned twenty. She had agreed to a Catholic ceremony, though she was a Protestant, like most of the great families from beyond the Elbe. Claus himself was a convinced but not an observing Catholic. As a child he had attended mass in the village church at Lautlingen, but he had not been to confession since the day of his first communion. He became a regular churchgoer only when the Nazis embarked on their persecution of the clergy, and this was intended as an act of protest and of solidarity with the victims of injustice, rather than as a profession of faith. Then, when Hitler advised the officers of the Wehrmacht not to attend mass in uniform, Claus would become even more steadfast in his devotions, with his cavalry officer's cap tucked under his arm.

Promoted to first lieutenant in 1933, Stauffenberg attended the War College in Berlin from 1936 to 1938. As his wife later recalled, "Claus was passionately concerned with his fellow creatures, with children and animals. Events interested him only insofar as they affected the lives of specific individuals. He was impelled to complete his military training by the thought that this might give him the opportunity to influence young people, to inspire them and to shape their values." As a member of the last generation schooled in the old Prussian tradition, he was torn between his own conception of duty and the exactions of Hitler and the new "revolutionary" chiefs of the Wehrmacht; at this time, in spite of everything, he still believed in National Socialism.

He was profoundly disturbed by the Blomberg-Fritsch crisis of 1938, and as luck would have it, he was serving at that time with Hoepner's 3d Armored Division in the Thüringerwald, which was supposed to intercept the Waffen SS and move on Berlin during the abortive generals' putsch of September. His letters to his wife during the Sudeten crisis were filled with bitterness and uncertainty: He spoke of Germany as "mein Reich," but he knew that Hitler was leading his country to disaster. After the war broke out, he fought bravely at the front, but he continued to maintain close contacts with other like-minded young officers, aristocrats like himself and adversaries of the regime.

In 1942 he began to search for others who shared not only his beliefs but his determination to destroy Hitler as well. He did not hesitate to beard the marshals in their dens, to try to stir them into action, to convince them that "something must be done." That fall when one general announced gravely, "We must tell the Führer the truth!" Stauffenberg replied with brutal candor, "It's not a question of telling him the truth but of killing him, and I'm ready to do it myself."

On January 1, 1943, he was promoted to lieutenant colonel, and two weeks later he was sent to North Africa with the 10th Panzer Division. On his arrival at the front, he joined the staff of the divisional commander, Baron von Broich. They took to each other immediately and soon were discussing philosophy, literature, and politics together late into the night; a perfect sympathy developed between these two gentlemen at arms. Stauffenberg was more and more firmly convinced that the regime would have to be overthrown by force, though he found it difficult to reconcile this with his Christian convictions. But in fact his religious beliefs only intensified his hatred of the Nazi regime and its overlord, though the desperate military situation was also a factor in his calculations. General von Broich felt that the regime could be overthrown only with the help and the leadership of the army. Clearly Hitler and his criminal henchmen would never step down of their own free will, and if Germany were not rid of them in the near future, then everything would be lost.

From the point of view of Hitler and the high command, Germany was clearly in need of a spectacular victory on the Russian front to compensate for the disaster of Stalingrad. Marshal von Manstein felt that he had a workable plan, based essentially on the principles of the war of mobility; at first Hitler turned it down on vague political grounds, though in fact he simply could not bring himself to give up any territory, for whatever reasons. Zeitzler and other members of the general staff pressed for a limited offensive against Kursk, which would not require any initial sacrifice of territory. Kursk made a tempting target for them, since it could be attacked simultaneously from the north and the south, and a large body of Soviet troops would be trapped inside the salient. Marshal Model (who had received his baton on March 30) would lead the 9th Army, which was attached to Army Group Center, southward from Orel while General Hoth's 4th Panzer Army and General Kempf's Panzer Group would move north from Kharkov; they would all meet at Kursk. General Zeitzler was the principal architect of this plan and preparations were already under way in March; there were unforeseen difficulties involved in rounding up sufficient troops for the new offensive, which was codenamed Operation Citadel.

In North Africa the Allies had achieved total air superiority by the spring of 1943, and thus they could allow themselves the luxury of

pursuing a single enemy vehicle with a whole squadron of fighters. Stauffenberg was one of their victims. He had left on a reconnaissance mission
on April 7; his car was found overturned and riddled by machine-gun
fire on a road near Safia in Tunisia. General von Broich, who had set
out after him an hour later, was also attacked by a squadron of twenty
fighters. He managed to evade further pursuit, but when he caught sight
of Stauffenberg's car, he was convinced that his friend could not have
escaped with his life. Stauffenberg himself however was found critically
wounded but still alive. Destiny, the general thought to himself, is saving
him for a different future.

Stauffenberg had lost his right hand, and the surgeons in the military
hospital in Carthage were forced to amputate part of his right arm and
the ring finger and little finger of his left hand. He had been shot through
the right eye—the bullet had exited by his ear—but the doctors hoped
that his left eye could be saved. He was flown out to a hospital in Munich
as soon as he could be moved. His condition was still critical, and he
was in terrible pain, but he refused sedatives, since he was afraid of
becoming a drug addict. When his wife came to visit him she was confronted by a gauze-wrapped apparition with one arm immobilized in
plaster. He could still speak, in a scarcely audible voice: "The time
has come for us to try to pull the Reich out of this morass. We have
to do something."

"And you're in fine shape to do it, too," she replied teasingly, but
Stauffenberg was not to be distracted from his brooding reflections:
"Yes, we're all responsible for this situation we're in, and it's our duty
to do what we must to save our fatherland." Later he told his uncle,
Count von Uxküll, "Since the generals haven't accomplished anything,
then it's up to the colonels now." The count replied that General Olbricht, a friend of Beck's and one of the bitterest enemies of the regime,
would be pleased to find a place for Stauffenberg at his headquarters
in Berlin as soon as he had recovered from his wounds.

Operation Citadel had originally been slated for mid-April. Marshal
Model approved of the plan in principle, but he was concerned that
not enough troops had been committed to the offensive. Guderian—
who had recently been recalled to duty as inspector general of the mechanized forces—did not approve; he expected that the panzer divisions
would be taking heavy losses, and tanks and trained crews could no
longer be spared from the western front. Kluge and Manstein both favored the plan initially, though Manstein was worried that the offensive
had already been delayed too long—weeks had gone by, and Hitler

had still not made up his mind. And as the weeks passed the essential character of the offensive had changed. Instead of a ruthless and decisive surprise attack, the high command was now envisaging an all-out frontal engagement, a supreme test of strength with the Russians. While the Führer temporized, the Red Army had been preparing for the attack with all possible speed; a Soviet agent at OKW headquarters had tipped them off that Kursk would be the objective, and they were willing to let the Wehrmacht make the first move.

In Munich, Stauffenberg's crisis had passed, and he had embarked on a long convalescence. His extraordinary force of will sustained him through even the worst moments of his ordeal. The pain was still almost unendurable, but he managed to teach himself to carry out all the ordinary tasks of life—he even learned to write with just three fingers. When a friend tried to cheer him up with the suggestion of an artificial arm and a glass eye would make him as good as new, he replied, "I'm quite happy the way I am. In fact if I had all my fingers back, I wouldn't know what to do with them."

At the Wolf's Lair in the last days of May, Zeitzler tried to convince Hitler to move against Kursk by the end of June at the latest. "The enemy is bringing up fresh troops, and I don't want to wait until they've brought up their new tanks and assault guns as well."

"You mustn't say such things, Zeitzler. Our Panther tanks are far superior to any of the Russian tanks, and two battalions of Panthers will give a powerful impetus to our attack. . . .

"This has not been an easy time for us, Zeitzler! We've lost Stalingrad and Tunis, the tally of our U-boat sinkings has fallen off alarmingly, and there have been serious errors in the conduct of the war in the air. Add to that the political crises, which I have no right to ignore: Italy is in total disarray. Mussolini has never understood military matters, and since the fall of Tunis, the clique surrounding the royal family has steadily been gaining ground. In Romania Antonescu's power has been shaken by the loss of his armies in Russia—and as for the king, I have no confidence in him whatsoever. In Hungary that old fox Horthy is just waiting for his chance to go over to the English. And of course the Casablanca conference[1] is bound to have had a certain impact on these overly susceptible characters. . . . Also, what I need is a totally decisive military victory, and as soon as possible, but the odds must be heavily in our favor."

1. January 1942, at which Roosevelt first enunciated the Allied demand for the unconditional surrender of the Axis powers. [Tr.]

Zeitzler asked Hitler to take the appropriate steps to ensure that the new Panther tanks would be ready to go into action by June 10 at the latest. "Otherwise," he added, "let us begin the attack without them, or else use them in a counterattack, but only after the Russians have launched their offensive."

"Impossible," said Hitler.

Jodl tried to intercede: "We must be careful, my Führer, not to saddle ourselves with another lost battle. The operation that Zeitzler has suggested, after the Russian attack, is certainly worthy of some consideration."

"Listen to me, Jodl"—Hitler's voice rose—"I can't simply wait for weeks until Herr Stalin is obliging enough to attack. I must seize the initiative from him as quickly as possible. The situation is going to change overnight. No one can tell me that this coalition of the Western powers and Russia is going to last indefinitely—it will last only until problems start to arise. One day it will collapse of its own weight, and the more relentlessly we hammer at the Russians, the sooner that day will come. They are in the process of regrouping right now after their astonishing successes of the last six months. If they meet with a few setbacks now, perhaps their enthusiasm will dissipate completely. . . . That's part of the Slavic character, and that is exactly what Messrs. Roosevelt and Churchill are afraid of. After all, who are these men? One of them is sick, and the other is drinking and smoking himself to death. As for the third, Herr Stalin, I still have some respect for him. He carries out his programs decisively, without wavering—I would have done well to imitate his unscrupulous tactics. But he's ten years older than I am. It would be the very devil if I didn't outlive all three of them. . . . By the way, Jodl, what's been going on with Seydlitz?"

"He's been making propaganda on the Soviet radio, but it's not entirely clear that this isn't some sort of a Russian trick."

"I can't believe," Hitler said, "that a German general would take part in such a thing voluntarily. We'll have to get to the bottom of this immediately, Keitel, with the help of the court-martial's inquiry into his case."

"Absolutely, my Führer."

The fall of Stalingrad had given the Russians a considerably wider field in which to exercise their propaganda—92,000 soldiers of the Wehrmacht, including 2,000 officers and 24 generals, had fallen into their hands. The seventh section of the Red Army General Political

Bureau had adopted a different line from that previously taken by the German Communist émigrés in the Soviet Union, who included Walter Ulbricht, the future "little Stalin" of East Germany, and Wilhelm Pieck, first president of the German Democratic Republic. The official Soviet propaganda campaign carefully avoided the customary evocations of the class struggle; they preferred to appeal to the patriotic sentiments and nationalistic ideals of their captive audience: Even if Germany could no longer win the war, that did not necessarily mean that all was lost. But Hitler would have to be eliminated if the army and the German nation were to be spared from total destruction, since Hitler had sworn that the war could end only in victory, or *Götterdämmerung*. (The Soviets of course never said a word about "unconditional surrender," which had become the unofficial guiding principle of the Allied war effort since January 1942.) The troops themselves, worn out in an unequal struggle, had become increasingly convinced that Hitler was driving them toward the abyss, and they still believed that an "honorable peace" was possible. This was, after all, the ultimate hope of the conspirators themselves.

The German officers were treated favorably by their Russian captors. They rode in comfortable trains instead of cattle cars, and the conditions in the officers' camp were quite acceptable, all things considered—particularly since their troops were held to be responsible for the atrocities committed by the SS behind the German lines. All officers, whatever their rank, were exempt from manual labor. In this atmosphere the idea of forming an organization with the aim of bringing the war to an end, and in general of salvaging what could still be saved from the rubble, quickly took root, and before long even some of the senior officers came around.

The National Committee for a Free Germany was founded on July 12 and 13, 1943, at Krasnogorsk, with an initial membership of thirty-eight, presided over by the émigré Erich Weinert. They set out to publish a manifesto, the wording of which was the cause of some contention between the officers and the representatives of the Communist émigré community. The Russians came down diplomatically on the side of the officers, assuring them, among other things, that their flag would bear the old imperial colors—black, white, and red.

This did not put an end to the dissension between the two factions, however, which resulted in the formation of the Association of German Officers on September 11 and 12; this group would operate along parallel lines with the Free Germany committee, though completely independently. General Walther von Seydlitz agreed to become the president of the association, and he immediately embarked on a campaign to convince the German high command to lead an insurrection against Hitler before the Red Army had reached the borders of the Reich. General Edler von Savich and Colonels Hooven and Steidle were appointed as his vice-presidents. But the Russians intervened once again, and the two groups were reunited, under Communist leadership, with Seydlitz and Savich as vice-presidents. Seydlitz remained active as a propagandist; his letter to Marshal Model, one of many he wrote to various members of the high command, began by invoking the military defeats at Stalingrad and on the Don, in the Caucasus and North Africa. He implored Model to force Hitler to order a general withdrawal: "Withdraw your troops from Russian soil, and lead them back beyond the frontiers of the Reich—this is the only condition under which an honorable peace can be obtained." On the other side of the lines the conspirators were clinging to the same illusion of a separate peace, though after the Tehran Conference in December there could be no doubt that Roosevelt, Churchill, and Stalin were unalterably committed to the principle of unconditional surrender. In any event the collapse of Army Group Center in July 1944 would bring a second major influx of German prisoners into the Soviet camps, where fully half of the officers and three-quarters of the enlisted men joined the Free Germany committee or the Association of German Officers.

Zeitzler reminded the Führer that it was primarily the relatives of soldiers listed as missing at the front who were listening to this Soviet propaganda, since the Russians broadcast the names of every German soldier who had fallen into their hands. Perhaps if the German radio stations could also broadcast an official announcement in such cases . . .

"Out of the question!" Hitler shot back. "Our prisoners will certainly never be coming back from Russia alive. We would only be encouraging our people to delude themselves with false hope. Instead we should be cracking down on everyone who listens to these enemy broadcasts— but the courts have still not grasped this fact yet, nor have your military tribunals, Keitel! I'll be taking all the political cases out of their hands soon enough, so that they can be resolved by more energetic measures."

Zeitzler brought the subject back to military matters: He wanted to establish a secondary defensive line on the Dnieper, Berezina, and Duna rivers, but Hitler interrupted him before he could supply any of the details.

"That way no one would try to hold the front any longer. You must simply banish that idea from your thoughts, Zeitzler. If our troops ever got wind of such a thing, they'd want to fall back immediately. They should have only one objective in mind—to stand fast and hold the front."

"My Führer, it is the duty of the high command to make certain that their decisions do not give rise to such aberrations. You must have confidence in them."

Hitler stiffened and turned to face Zeitzler. "Don't talk to me about confidence! As long as everything's going well, my generals are exultant. Then when the going gets harder, they begin to lose heart. That's something I'm quite familiar with. . . . All this must end in a great victory for us—any other way of looking at or thinking about the situation should be considered a crime."

In mid-June Hitler summoned the commanders of the armies and army groups to Rastenburg. Later that evening they would be meeting with Heusinger at OKH headquarters in the Mauerwald. Before he left Rastenburg, Heusinger took Jodl aside: "Something must be done to stop this headlong progress toward disaster."

Jodl replied, "I agree entirely—we're simply hastening to meet our doom, but the man who is leading us is our destiny, and one does not escape one's destiny."

Later that evening Heusinger was sitting in his office with a group of the front-line generals. "You ask me, gentlemen, why things worked out as they did at Tunis. I can't give you a precise opinion, since OKW tries to keep us at some remove from their theater of operations. Still, it is clear at least that our operation in the Mediterranean could not be sustained with half measures. If we wanted to fight in North Africa, we should have first secured our lines of communications by taking Gibraltar and Malta. But we chose not to, and we have failed—our army in North Africa found themselves caught in a trap, and we could neither evacuate nor reinforce them.

"The decision to abandon North Africa should have been made as soon as the Allies came ashore. We would have saved part of Rommel's armies, but instead we tried to hold out in a hopeless situation, and none of them were able to get out."

Kluge asked if it was not too late—since June 11 had come and gone—to launch the Kursk offensive.

"I'm afraid so," Heusinger replied. "The risk seems to be much greater now. It would be better to prepare a counterattack, but the field marshals didn't raise any serious objections [to the plans for the

Citadel offensive] this evening. Zeitzler warned them. We can't wage these internal struggles by ourselves; at the very least Hitler must appoint a commander in chief for the eastern front. Zeitzler has prepared the ground well, but he hasn't followed through. You must encourage your generals to show some initiative before it's too late."

"But the Führer won't let them say a word! He virtually crushes them under his heel," protested one of the army commanders.

"Yes," Heusinger replied, "since the marshals are perfectly willing to go along with him. It's time indeed that they began to show their mettle, by raising the issue of a genuine war cabinet. I know, you're going to tell me that other, more compliant individuals will simply be found to take their places. And unfortunately you're right. But it is important to make Hitler understand that field marshals are not corporals. As for the general staff, he's despised them all since Beck's time, and he considers them all to be politically unreliable, spineless, and intellectually contaminated. Fortunately Zeitzler is bearing up well under the pressures exerted by Schmundt and the other ADCs. In any case, gentlemen, let us continue to work closely together."

In the meantime *der Tag* for Operation Citadel had been shifted up to the beginning of July. Manstein felt that the moment had passed and the operation was no longer feasible. Model insisted that the entire offensive be scratched, but Hitler had made his decision—even though he had confessed to Guderian the day before that he was sickened by the very thought of Operation Citadel. The attack began on July 4, at two o'clock on a sweltering afternoon with a storm threatening. For several days the issue was in doubt, but on July 10—the same day that the Allies landed in Sicily—Model's army sustained heavy losses in the north: 50,000 men, 400 tanks and guns, and 500 planes. In the south the Russian armor advanced during the night of July 11–12 as far as Prokovka, about eighty miles south of Kursk; they came up against the German panzers on the following afternoon, a day of intense, stifling heat, under low cloud cover that hampered the German air support. This would be the greatest tank battle of the Second World War, and its consequences for the Wehrmacht would be even more disastrous than those of Stalingrad.

A week later Schmundt sought out Hitler in his private office in the Wolf's Lair to inform him that the forward elements of the armored group had been unable to advance any closer to Kursk. The offensive was stalled completely, and the army group had requested that it be called off.

"Apparently," Hitler shouted, "when things don't go quite as well as they'd hoped, they want to throw in the towel immediately. They've never believed this operation could succeed. Send for Zeitzler and Jodl. The trouble with all these generals is that they lack faith—they calculate, they weigh their decisions carefully, they examine every aspect of the problem, but they never take action. They believe everything they hear about the enemy, but they don't have the slightest notion of what can be accomplished by sheer force of will. . . . Zeitzler too is beginning to think too much. I should have reorganized the officer corps much earlier. Blomberg was too soft. Fritsch and Blomberg were never behind me. . . .

"I must have complete confidence in my generals. Goering's as gruff as a bear—and a bear can turn on you, after all—and he's leading the life of a Renaissance grandee, wearing himself out with dissipation. Keitel's as faithful as a spaniel, he does whatever I tell him to, but he doesn't count for much with the others. Jodl and Zeitzler are devoted to me, but even their devotion has its limits. . . . Rundstedt is an able man but too old. I can't trust Kleist or Manstein; they're intelligent, but they're not National Socialists. And what's more, Manstein is a capable commander when he has plenty of troops behind him, but he doesn't know how to get out of a tight corner. . . . Rommel, Model, Schörner— those are the men I want—tactful, energetic, plenty of fighting spirit, and they're all National Socialists. I'm going to need a great many more like them. . . . And what about my other generals? I've always had to push them along ahead of me. I've been battling with their doubts and scruples since 1935. What sort of soldiers are they? They don't have the stomach for a fight. They should make a vocation of warfare, the thrill of combat, of victory, but they are all mere ciphers, the products of a decadent age. I don't understand them, but I intend to show them what it means to be a soldier."

In spite of the heavy rains, Manstein's troops had been making some headway, but Hitler had finally decided, on July 13, that it would be more prudent to order a retreat. The 2d SS Panzer Corps was sent off to try to contain the Allied invasion of Italy, and two panzer divisions were transferred to Army Group Center, to help prop up their collapsing front around Orel, which was finally liberated by the Red Army on August 5.

At about that time Baron Ewald von Kleist's son, Ewald Heinrich, returned to Schmentzin castle on convalescent leave; he had been wounded on the Russian front. He confided to his father—a dedicated opponent of the regime since the days before Munich—that he had joined with other young officers in a conspiracy and that their group was devoted heart and soul to Colonel von Stauffenberg. The baron approved of this decision and gave him every encouragement.

At the end of July, Jodl came to Hitler with the news that Badoglio's new government in Rome was prepared to deal in good faith with Germany and to honor the terms of their alliance.

"We have nothing but political dilettantes in Rome," Hitler exclaimed. "Kesselring doesn't understand any of it either, especially since he chooses not to get involved. Why did Badoglio get rid of Mussolini?"

"The Duce was dismissed by the Fascist grand council," Jodl said.

"You mustn't believe such foolishness, Jodl. I know how these things are done. Zeitzler, what's the situation in the east?"

The chief of staff responded with a pessimistic survey of recent developments; he concluded by saying, "I can see nothing for it but to evacuate the Donets Basin so that we can bring back more divisions to strengthen our positions around Kiev."

Hitler was not pleased by this suggestion. "Obviously—and we should keep evacuating until one fine day we find ourselves back at our own borders again! And the Russians will have reconquered their entire country without losing a man. Zeitzler, you let the Russians worry you too much. If I abandon the Donets Basin, the war will be as good as lost in a few months. We won't have enough coal!"

Zeitzler stood his ground and tried another line of argument: "My Führer, Speer has informed me that the situation is not as serious as all that. In any case, we haven't been able to move any coal out of the Donets for some time because the railroads are in such poor condition."

"And how can Speer give out that information? And to you, Zeitzler! The next thing you know he'll be meddling into the way we're running the war. Not another word about evacuation, Zeitzler. We will hold the Donets."

Zeitzler's next suggestion had the fervent backing of the entire general staff. The conduct of all operations on the eastern front down to the Sea of Azov should be entrusted to Manstein, which would mean a unified command in the east.

"Just so, Zeitzler! So that Herr Manstein can do whatever he chooses, is that it? He'll give up the whole Ukraine for me just to bring off one of his 'maneuvers.' But how I'll feed the German people—that's the least of his worries. Zeitzler, we must keep matters in our own hands instead of letting Manstein have his way with us."

Nevertheless, at the end of August, Manstein found it impossible to hold the front any longer, and this touched off a general retreat. The Germans had scored local tactical successes, but with the collapse of Operation Citadel they had lost the initiative in the east, and they would never regain it. Their panzer reserves were exhausted, and the German withdrawal turned what might have been a Russian defeat into a Russian victory. Captain Jacques Bagnères, a veteran of the Normandie-Neimen Esquadrille (a French volunteer formation in the Soviet air force), told us that "if the Russians had caved in at Kursk and Orel, then Moscow and Leningrad would have fallen quickly enough. They had no reserves to back up the enormous forces they had committed to the counterattack. The fighting was intense. The Soviets threw away an entire air force every day, and our squadron was virtually decimated. But the Red Army, in a positively superhuman effort, managed to withstand the thirty-eight divisions of Kluge's Army Group Center. The Germans broke in July and August; in September they fell back on Vitebsk and Orsha in Byelorussia."

By this time Stauffenberg had returned to Berlin. Before taking up his post at the Ministry of Defense, he moved into his brother Berthold's two-story house in the residential suburb of Wannsee in order to devote the remainder of his leave to the planning of the conspiracy. He was shut up in his room for days on end, studying the rosters of Wehrmacht staff officers in Germany and along the immense front that still stretched from one end of Europe to the other. He sifted through the names of all the sector commanders to see how many of them could be counted on. As during his convalescence, he worked with single-minded intensity, and he had learned to be almost completely self-sufficient—though Berthold's faithful housekeeper, a war widow called Frau Weichbrot, still had to cut his meat for him at mealtimes. He would drop into a deep sleep as soon as his work for the day was over, and not even the air-raid siren, which was mounted on the roof of the house directly overhead, could awaken him.

Stauffenberg was planning the future of a new Germany, a democratic socialist state. He was more optimistic and rather less realistic than Beck—now something of a skeptic—in believing that the Western Allies could not refuse to lend their support to a German government that had voluntarily rid itself of Hitler and his henchmen. Above all he hoped to spare his beloved fatherland the humiliating consequences of an unconditional surrender.

He reported to Olbricht at the end of August to discuss the duties he would be expected to carry out in his new post. But instead Olbricht asked him straight out if he felt himself to be physically and morally prepared to participate in the planning of a coup d'état. His friend Uxküll had already told him what Stauffenberg's answer would be, and when the time came, he agreed enthusiastically. As soon as he left Olbricht, Stauffenberg put off an appointment he had made, at the urging of his friends and family, with Dr. Sauerbruch, to investigate the possibility of fitting him out with an artificial arm. Another operation and a long course of therapy would interfere with his other plans. Stauffenberg felt that he had survived only by a special dispensation from the Almighty, and he concluded from this—as had General von Broich—that he was destined to accomplish some great mission.

In the first week in September a group of engineers, technicians, Party officials, and officers gathered at a site near Rastenburg; the Führer was going to inspect the latest model tanks, light field-guns, and antitank guns just off the production lines. Hitler launched into a discourse on the virtues of the Soviet antitank gun: "It is crudely made but quite well-suited to its purpose. I have the impression that it's more serviceable than ours—as far as the weight and construction are concerned, it seems to have a more rational design."

"It's a question of the alloys," said one of the engineers. "The shortage of rare metals—"

"Now, then," Hitler broke in, "that excuse won't work anymore, since we have the resources of all of Europe at our disposal. No, we always want our weapons to be too sophisticated, and we expect them to have a whole range of virtues that are incompatible with one another. As a result, they're too fragile and difficult to manage. Here, look at the way the trunnions are sticking up on this gun barrel—it will be spotted by an enemy tank and put out of action before it can fire a shot. . . ."

At this point Keitel came trotting up to him, puffing with the exertion: "My Führer, you must excuse me for interrupting you. The Italians have asked for an armistice, and Anglo-American troops have landed at Salerno."

"What have I been telling you all this time, gentlemen?" Hitler appealed to his entire entourage to bear witness. "But you didn't want to believe me! The king and Badoglio must be arrested immediately!"

The Führer had scarcely had time to digest the news of Italy's defection when Zeitzler asked to have a word with him. He had just spoken with Marshal Antonescu and General Heusinger. The Romanian troops in the Crimea were in danger of being cut off and would have to be evacuated.

"They will hold their positions," Hitler replied coldly. "Send Marshal Antonescu to me."

At around five o'clock Hitler closeted himself with Antonescu for over an hour. When the Romanian strongman emerged from Hitler's office, he announced to Heusinger and Zeitzler, "The Führer is right. My troops should remain in the Crimea. A division will be transferred from Norway to reinforce them."

"It will take them two months to get there," Zeitzler pointed out.

"There will also be two armored units which will be available immediately."

"Which ones exactly?" Heusinger asked skeptically.

Antonescu named them. "Why do you ask?"

"They've just returned from the front—they're completely worn out."

Antonescu was still under the Führer's spell, and he stuck by his decision. Two days later, however, OKH headquarters was informed that he had ordered the evacuation of his troops from the Crimea. "This gives you some idea," comments General Heusinger, "of what the atmosphere at GHQ was like. Hitler's arts of persuasion, his ferocious desire to win you over, were virtually limitless. I met with him six or seven hundred times at the daily conferences, and time and time again after I left the room I would allow myself an hour of relaxation and repose to clear my mind, to forget every word he had said, and only then could I arrive at a rational and realistic decision."

By early October Stauffenberg had already taken up his duties as chief of staff of Olbricht's General Army Office, a post from which he could exercise a fair measure of control over various aspects of the army's operations within the territory of the Reich. He was still in a great deal of pain, and though he bore his sufferings uncomplainingly, he had become rather highstrung and his manner was sometimes erratic and imperious, though he seemed to have overcome the feelings of physical inferiority that had been troubling him during his convalescence. In any case, Claus and Berthold were still linked by a bond of total sympathy and understanding; their political opinions were identical, and Claus never undertook anything without his elder brother's approval. Their uncle, Count von Uxküll, was also living in the house at Wannsee with them, and though, at sixty-seven, he was a great deal older than most of the conspirators, he was no less enthusiastic for all that. His daughter, Olga von Saucken, who was also aware of what her cousins were planning, later recalled the old count's saying to her, "For years I did everything in my power to convince the younger people—our cousins Yorck and Hofacker, our friends Schulenburg and Kleist—that we had to take some sort of action against this regime. Now we are finally in a position to do so, but unfortunately I'm afraid that it's too late. The opportune moment has passed. Naturally this will never prevent me from throwing in my lot, finally and irrevocably, with the conspiracy. For even if I no longer believe that there can be any real chance of success, our activities will still have one purpose—to show the world that is watching us that, thanks to the daring of a few courageous Germans, we did try to rid ourselves of that pack of criminals."

The count was equally fervent in his endorsement of Stauffenberg: "If our plot still has any chance of succeeding, it has only been since my nephew has joined us. He has been the driving spark, the catalyst for all our efforts over the last few years. And now his finger is poised on the trigger. . . . I am an old man, my dear Olga, and the critical task for me now is to take care of Claus. Without him, our entire enterprise would be deprived of its heart and its brain. And his injuries have left him so badly handicapped—I feel that if I can look after his health, then I will be of some use at least. His work as a staff officer and his clandestine activities on behalf of the conspiracy require enormous endurance and presence of mind. Fortunately it's not too difficult for him to unwind a bit. When he comes home, he simply needs to lie down for fifteen or twenty minutes, then he gets up refreshed and ready to lead a discussion without the slightest hint of fatigue. Even though we've all been living in an atmosphere of incredible tension, our dear, good Claus's rich, infectious laughter can always bring us back to ourselves."

On November 1 Stauffenberg was appointed to a more important post—chief of staff of the newly organized Replacement Army and adjutant to its commander in chief, General Fromm. This promotion brought with it two important tactical advantages: Now he was in direct contact with the commanders at the front, which would enable him to supervise the sort of coordinated action that would be essential to the planning of the coup, and he was one of the few younger officers who enjoyed access to Hitler's GHQ at Rastenburg—which convinced him that he himself would have to be the assassin as well as the master planner of the conspiracy. There were those who felt that Stauffenberg was hardly suited to the task, since a one-eyed man with only three fingers might not be the best candidate to carry out a mission that required precise physical coordination under the most exacting circumstances. Did they have the right to ask a man who had already suffered so much for his country's sake to risk death a second time? And wasn't he the father of three children besides? (A fourth child, a girl, would be born in January 1945, six months after her father's death.) At any rate the generals and the other senior officers had been brooding for so long on the risks and uncertainties involved that the real possibility of taking any action at all had virtually dwindled into insignificance. Even the best-intentioned among them were overwhelmed with doubts, and Stauffenberg, whatever his deficiencies might have been, was not one to be troubled by second thoughts.

In November 1943 Gehlen's deputy, the operations chief of the Foreign Armies East section, met once again with General Heusinger to discuss the situation at the front, which was even more disheartening now than after Kursk or Stalingrad. The numerical superiority of the Red Army in men and matériel was beginning to tell against the Wehrmacht. The Russians' crop of draft-age men who were fit for service was twice as great as the Germans' each year. The Russian soldier had proved himself to be better suited to heavy labor, and, naturally enough, more able to withstand the punishing extremes of climate on the Russian plains. The Red Army was deployed on interior lines. The Wehrmacht was now fighting on two fronts; its troops were dispersed all over Europe. Russian industrial production was increasing every month, and since the Luftwaffe was no longer in a position to mount a convincing threat, the Russians were able to concentrate almost entirely on their land forces, while the Germans were still waging a desperate struggle in the air over Germany and beneath the waters of the North Atlantic.

"And what's more," the intelligence officer continued, "the Soviet high command has learned a great deal, though we might still have a strategic advantage over them if we were less stubborn."

"You don't have to tell me that!" Heusinger replied ruefully. "But you know only too well that Hitler's conceived a violent dislike for the idea of a war of mobility—'maneuvering,' he calls it—and he thinks all he has to do is hold our present positions. . . . He doesn't allow his commanders the slightest freedom of action. . . . And how is the Vlasov organization coming along?"

"We've been trying to form them up for months now. Himmler seems to have taken an interest in the matter, and he's had more success with them than we have so far. He'll certainly get the credit, and we'll be made to look like fools once again—which fits in very well with the Führer's grand plan to undermine the influence of the army. But we'd have had two or three Vlasov divisions by now if they'd only let us get ahead with it. And Vlasov himself is furious that the SS is taking his precious army away from him, though that's not likely to do him much good."

General Vlasov had been Chiang Kai-shek's chief Soviet military adviser from 1938 to 1940. In 1941 he took part in the defense of Kiev and the battle for Moscow. Later Stalin had ordered him to mount a suicidal counterattack against the German positions on the River Volkhov. His encircled army had held out with incredible tenacity, which made a certain impression on the German high command, as General Heusinger relates:

"At that time the commander of Army Group North was General Küchler—a simple, straightforward, uncomplicated officer who managed to get along comparatively well with Hitler. One day he was summoned to GHQ, and as soon as he arrived, Hitler opened up on him at point-blank range: 'How is it possible, General Küchler, that General Vlasov and his army are completely surrounded, without supplies, and you still haven't taken them prisoner?'

"Küchler expected to be sent packing at any moment, but he kept a cool head. 'That region is very heavily wooded,' he replied, 'and it's not easy to flush them out. Besides—and I tell you this in strictest confidence, my Führer—Vlasov and his men can live off pine-tree bark, and as for the marshes, that doesn't trouble them a bit, since they've all got webbed feet.'

"Hitler burst out laughing and slapped his thigh, and Küchler went on to fight another day."

Vlasov finally surrendered in the spring of 1942, and later made his well-publicized decision to collaborate with the Germans, to help them destroy Stalin by raising a so-called Russian Army of Liberation in the German POW camps. (Major Claus von Stauffenberg had originally been one of the officers assigned to supervise the outfitting and indoctrination of this anti-Bolshevik legion.)

Gehlen's deputy went on with his grim recital: "I'm not allowed to use my best agent on the Russian front, because he's half Jewish—Himmler's orders. I've figured out a way to keep him on, but only at considerable risk to myself, since if the SS ever suspected . . . All the more, since they keep on worming their way into military counterintelligence operations. I also know that they have a score to settle with Halder, and with you too, General Heusinger. You ought to be careful—they're none too fond of OKH Operations."

In December Heusinger received a telephone call from General von Glydenfeld, the chief of staff of Army Group South. He had just sent back a situation report on the Russian breakthrough at Kiev, and he insisted that this information should be brought to the Führer's attention as soon as possible. "I only hope," Heusinger told him, "that you haven't put anything in your report that's likely to bruise the Führer's sensibilities. You know that he's gotten to be suspicious of everything that Manstein suggests to him. Hitler is determined to prove to Manstein that he's more intelligent than Manstein, and all it would take would be for him to find a single phrase that he considered lacking in precision, and that would be the end of the entire report. He just did the same thing with a general who had told him that such-and-such a mission was impossible. Hitler asked him for a precise estimate of his unit's fuel reserves—the sort of detail that a staff officer normally takes care of. Hitler rattled off the exact figure from memory—you know what a phenomenal memory he has—and then apparently he told the general that he wasn't fit to hold his command. . . . And you know what Himmler said to him about Manstein not too long ago—'He's a devout Christian, and as such, incapable of genuine loyalty.' "

"Incredible! You see how they're destroying our best men. And if everything is prescribed from on high, down to the last detail, then there's no point in being a field marshal at all—you might just as well be a corporal."

The armies were fighting desperately to hold along the entire Russian front. In the north the last German forces outside Leningrad, besieged since October 1941, were finally driven off.

Berlin had been transformed into a ruinous nightmare landscape. The latest night bombing raid had totally leveled the block that housed the Ministry of Defense in the Bendlerstrasse, though the ministerial offices had been put back into service with surprising speed. The Luftwaffe was totally outclassed, overwhelmed in fact, but Goering seemed to be immune from all reprisal. He was solely to blame for the devastation of the city, but Hitler chose to keep him on in recognition of his past services. The Luftwaffe and the Reichsmarshal had both been resting on the laurels they had won in 1939–41, and now they were experiencing a terrible awakening. But Hitler also chose to blame most of this on fate. Though he cried out in agony, and tears welled up in his eyes while he listened to the reports of another city's destruction, he unaccountably did not tap Goering as the obvious scapegoat, but simply remarked, "In war you can do anything you like, except lose."

Stauffenberg was convinced that the corps commanders and the other officers in key positions would march on his orders if he promised them Iron Crosses all around and threatened them with the firing squad if they refused. As for the civilian population, exhausted by the forced-labor drafts, the night bombing raids, and the mounting difficulties of simply keeping themselves and their families fed, they would doubtless remain as they were—brave but unresisting. It was true that in certain quarters discontent had given way to overt hostility, but these were isolated cases. The majority of the German people did not blame Hitler or the regime; like their Führer, they attributed all their trials and privations to the workings of an inscrutable fate. Goebbels, the most faithful of Hitler's servants, was concerned about cowardice and desertion, but not about treason as such; he complacently ignored the tiny minority of Germans who actively opposed his master, and left it to Himmler and the Gestapo to sniff them out.

12.

1944: "When the Oxcart Gets Stuck in the Mud"

On January 30, 1944, Jodl, whose relationship with the Führer had lately grown increasingly cordial, was awarded the Gold Party Cross. Other, less fortunate commanders were becoming demoralized by Hitler's violent and capricious outbursts, though at the same time the supreme commander was less and less inclined to tolerate any personal caprices on the part of his deputies. Hitler did not subscribe to the truism that great talent often goes hand in hand with an independent spirit, except possibly in his own case.

At the end of February Ewald Heinrich von Kleist, who was spending another leave at Schmentzin castle, received an urgent phone call summoning him to the Bendlerstrasse in Berlin. There he was informed by one of the conspirators that Hitler would be inspecting the new uniforms for the Replacement Army on February 11, either in Berlin or at Rastenburg. The chief of the Administrative Section of OKH, General Helmuth Stieff—who had been recruited into the conspiracy since the episode with the cognac bottles—would be organizing the event in either case. It had been decided that one of the officers who was modeling the new uniforms would be provided with a bomb, which he would detonate as soon as Hitler came near him. "We're looking for a volunteer," Kleist was told, "and of course he must be willing to sacrifice his life."

Kleist asked to think this over for twenty-four hours. In fact he wanted to consult with his father, and the next morning at breakfast in the baronial dining hall at Schmentzin, Kleist outlined the details of the latest plot. The old man's face was grave and impassive. "My son, you must accept. The man who refused such an honor could never know another day's happiness." Ewald Heinrich returned to Berlin immediately, sought out his friend Stauffenberg at the Bendlerstrasse, and told him that he had decided to accept. But Kleist was never given the chance to prove his bravery in this spectacular manner, since the barracks in which the uniforms were stored was destroyed by Allied incendiaries a few days before the demonstration was scheduled to take place.

In the Ukraine the battle was still raging. At the end of February an officer who had survived the breakout from the Cherkassky region, a hundred miles southeast of Kiev, reported to General Heusinger: "We could see it coming from a long way off. The Russians had virtually no choice but to encircle us. Seydlitz and his National Committee for a Free Germany had explained it all to us very clearly. Their propaganda leaflets had become very disturbing. At first they were appealing to us to collaborate with the Russians; now they were calling on our troops to turn against their officers, not just against Hitler. The men were still unmoved by this propaganda, but the fear of encirclement was a more serious matter. Since Stalingrad this had become a kind of mass psychosis; our men had absolutely no confidence in any kind of disengaging action. But as it turned out, they derived a great deal of comfort from the fact that a Waffen SS division was trapped in the pocket along with us, since they thought that Hitler would never let *them* down! In fact, the men don't want to believe that Hitler alone is to blame, and they did a great deal of grumbling among themselves to the effect that 'the generals are the real culprits in all this.'

"The breakout—or rather, the mass flight to the west—succeeded. Our units formed up in wide columns and crushed everything that tried to stand up against them. . . . So much the worse for the men who fell by the wayside. . . . There were five divisions in all. Probably half the men got through, but we had to abandon almost all our equipment. It was impossible to get it out through the snow."

Heusinger interrupted him. "Have you made a detailed report to Hitler?"

"General, it was impossible. I could barely get a word in before he started in about reforming the divisions that had been wiped out. Then he announced that the submarine and the air war were shortly going to turn in our favor, and as soon as we had pushed back the invader [in Italy], then the worst would be over."

"It's always the same old story. Instead of listening to what the front-line soldiers have to say—since he never gets up to the front anymore himself—he prefers to deluge them with propaganda à la Goebbels. Did you speak to him about Seydlitz?"

"Yes, general. That was when he really got excited. He would abandon all restraint, he said. He'd have all their families arrested. . . . A very painful scene to have to witness."

The majority of the commanders at the front confirmed this officer's account of the troops' unshakable faith in the Führer. "He'll see us through this one," they assured one another, and when things were going badly, it was, "If the Führer only knew!" Goebbels' program had succeeded—not to allow any of the front-line commanders to share the limelight with the Führer, nor to allow any of the marshals to acquire a popular following (Rommel was the only exception to this, since he had never served on the general staff, he was a National Socialist, and Hitler did not regard him as a potential rival). Others felt that this attitude was not simply the result of Goebbels' propaganda but of a more profound characteristic of the German soldier—his adherence to the *Führerprinzip*. The soldier kept his eyes fixed on the leader he had chosen; his entire consciousness as a soldier was bounded by his desire to believe in him. Thus any who were disturbed by the course of events could only conclude, "He's succeeded so far, and he's certain to find the best way out of it this time." Those few individuals who were still capable of forming their own judgments and drawing their own conclusions could not help wondering how it was all going to turn out. It would be death for them to speak their thoughts out loud, but they were secretly hoping that the generals would intervene.

"The eternal drama," Heusinger noted. "When everything's going well, we're roundly condemned if we have anything to do with politics. But then, when the oxcart gets stuck in the mud, everyone's clamoring for us to take the matter in hand—even though just a short while ago they were all at such pains to keep it *out* of our hands. In '14–'18 the German soldier paid with his blood for the mistakes of his political leaders. The American army is better treated: They're brought into play only when the political conditions are ripe for the rational conduct of a war. Then if events take a different turn, the government takes their appropriation away from them. It's just the opposite with us: We're always having to step in and save a situation that's already been spoiled by the politicians. The worst of it is that our successes are never exploited politically—not in Poland or in France or in the Balkans. Hitler was intoxicated by these early victories and he neither wanted nor was able to hold himself in check. And since everything's started going so badly, he doesn't dare try to negotiate with his enemies."

When would there be an Allied landing in the west—and could it be repulsed? This was a question that a great many Germans were asking themselves just then. "I am disturbed by the weakness of our position in the west," Heusinger observed. "That is where we will pay the price for our adventures in the east, and the Atlantic Wall is just an enormous bluff. The enemy is far superior to us in matériel, particularly in airpower."

Stauffenberg was convinced that there was no more room for delay. Olbricht had arranged that all important orders that affected the Replacement Army would be reported orally to the Führer, which would provide Stauffenberg with many opportunities of visiting the Wolf's Lair in the months to come. Hitler left Rastenburg now only for an occasional foray to the Eagle's Nest in his beloved Berchtesgaden. Stauffenberg had also decided that he would have to destroy Hitler, Goering, and Himmler at a single stroke.

In March General Heusinger suffered a nervous collapse and was admitted to the military hospital at Gastein. He was more a victim of war weariness than of any specific physical or emotional malady. He was overwhelmed by his manifold responsibilities, he had gone without leave for several years, and he was simply exhausted by the atmosphere of febrile bickering and mindless sloganeering at Hitler's GHQ. Hitler's own doctors were extremely anxious about the Führer's mental state at this time, and he certainly manifested a wealth of alarming symptoms—his delusions, his morbid suspiciousness, bordering on paranoia, his near-hysterical outbursts, his megalomaniacal self-assurance, even his wild, flailing gestures, all suggested that his grasp on reality was intermittent at best. But in Hitler's case Dr. Morell was always hovering in the shadows with his miraculous bag full of pills and hypodermics, ready to soothe and sedate his patient and lull him into a dreamless sleep.

Two weeks after his arrival at the hospital Heusinger received a telephone call from his adjutant asking him to return to GHQ as soon as possible. He did not explain the reason for this, except to say that Zeitzler had to see him urgently and that "Marshals Manstein and von Kleist [1] are about to leave us." At the end of April Heusinger secured his doctor's reluctant permission to return to duty and presented himself at OKH headquarters at Berchtesgaden. Zeitzler was there to welcome him. "Thanks for coming, Heusinger. It's impossible for me to avoid a total break with Hitler, so you'll be filling in for me at the briefings until further notice."

"What's happened then?"

---

1. Ewald von Kleist (the baron's cousin) had replaced List as commander of Army Group A in August 1942, after the ill-fated assault on Tuapse (see pp. 138–139). [Tr.]

"It's because Manstein and Kleist have been relieved. When I found out, I told Schmundt to tell the Führer that I was leaving too. I sent in my resignation, which didn't change anything except that Manstein and Kleist have had swords added to their Knight's Crosses as a consolation prize. . . . I got a royal chewing-out. Generals have been forbidden to resign their commissions during wartime. He alone, the Führer, will decide how long I'm to remain at my post. Manstein and Kleist, he said, are only going to take a brief rest; he'll find something else for them to do soon enough. As for me, I should look after myself better—my nerves are stretched to the breaking point. Then, changing the subject, he began to hold forth on our military reverses, and by that point he had become quite cordial toward me.

"And speaking of military reverses, he started in, once again, on the iniquities of the high command . . . generals' wavering in the face of difficulties . . . the men are too soft. Then our allies—the Italians, and the Hungarians, who almost managed to slip through his fingers two weeks ago.[2] Then came the Luftwaffe's turn—totally incapable of protecting us against the enemy's bombers. And when I tried to discuss some of his latest decisions with him, he trailed off into one of his interminable political and economic monologues."

What can I possibly hope to accomplish in the midst of all this? Heusinger asked himself ruefully. Several hours later he arrived at the Eagle's Nest; Keitel was waiting for him in his office, and he immediately began to rake Zeitzler over the coals. "He's sent in his papers! How could he do such a thing to the Führer?"

"It's fortunate, Keitel, that he's finally decided to do it, which has made him all that much more independent. If others had only done the same!"

Keitel sighed heavily. "Yes, you're right, Heusinger. Unfortunately, I let the moment slip by long ago. If someday I'm called to account for every piece of paper I've signed my name to, they're going to hang me for sure. . . . I'm the real sacrificial lamb around here."

General Schmundt came into Keitel's office. "A good thing you've come back, Heusinger. Zeitzler and the Führer have had an irreparable falling-out. The Führer's nerves are in such a state that he must avoid all unnecessary emotional stress—and this is the moment that Zeitzler

2. Admiral Horthy's government in Hungary had been negotiating secretly with the Allies for almost a year. In mid-March, after Hitler presented him with an ultimatum, Horthy was forced to install a new, pro-Nazi cabinet and submit to what amounted to a German protectorate over his country. [Tr.]

picks for this monumental dereliction of duty! I bitterly regret the day that I proposed him as Halder's successor."

"It was inevitable, Schmundt. For some time now Zeitzler has been forced to choose—either cooperate blindly, as Keitel has done, or break with Hitler altogether."

"Be reasonable, Heusinger! Does that mean that he has to destroy our Führer?"

"It's not just the Führer's health that's at stake, but a great deal more than that, Schmundt. If Hitler refuses to give in—to face the consequences of all our military setbacks and to listen to what his advisers have to tell him—then this is simply the logical, in fact the desirable, outcome. Not only do I understand completely what Zeitzler has done, but I am delighted that he has finally decided to do it."

"The time has come to look around for a successor," suggested Schmundt, "and who else could it be but you, Heusinger?"

"Not I, gentlemen, if you please. You know that I've been trying to leave for some time now. As far as I'm concerned, this system of command is both exhausting and infuriating. I'll never be able to get Hitler to agree to anything. . . . He wants his chief of staff to be obedient to a fault, with no personal opinions of his own, someone who will be occupied exclusively with the technical workings of the machinery of command—while he continues to take care of everything else himself. With Zeitzler gone, you will not find another chief of staff, in the traditional sense, to replace him. You will have to look elsewhere, Schmundt, and you can imagine what the result is going to be. I can only think of one solution: Abolish the dual command [OKH and OKW], put both of them under the direction of a single individual, and take the responsibility for the daily conduct of operations out of Hitler's hands."

"To be sure," said Schmundt, "the high command does lack unity. But that's because Beck put up such a fight when the Führer wanted to organize the Wehrmacht supreme command. The Führer isn't the only one who's responsible."

"Not true, Schmundt. Beck wanted a unified command for the Wehrmacht, but he believed—and with good reason—that it should be provided by the army, which, considering Germany's geographical situation, comprises the greater part of the Wehrmacht."

"Tell me, Heusinger—suppose there were someone more capable than the Führer. How could he ever hope to work his will on the likes of Goering, Himmler, and Admiral Doenitz?"

"Listen to me, Schmundt. Himmler is the only one who has to be put in his place. Hitler will have to take care of that himself sooner or later. The others would cave in if Hitler deputized all his authority to this new man. For that matter, Goering doesn't do much of anything anymore."

"The Führer has too much mistrust for the generals as a class. You know that, Heusinger. And it's primarily their fault—they've never offered him their full cooperation. . . ."

"That's quite enough, Schmundt. We'll never be able to agree on this, and only the future can tell which one of us was right. I'm going to leave now, and it's essential that we reach a decision about the Crimea. It would be unpardonable for us to sacrifice any more divisions."

"Talking of that," said Schmundt, "did they manage to fly Marshal Keitel's son out of Sevastopol? We certainly can't allow him to fall into enemy hands."

"They've been pestering me to death about that business for days now," Heusinger replied sharply. "That's your department, not mine. I think that he got out—but there are a hundred thousand men who are still there."

By the end of May the staff officers could talk of nothing but the anticipated Allied landing in the west. Some wondered whether the whole thing might not be an enormous bluff (as Heusinger had said of the Atlantic Wall that was designed to contain the enemy on the beaches). Heusinger's adjutant did not share this opinion; he was merely surprised that the suspense had been kept up for so long, since there was no doubt that the invasion would not be too long in coming. It was said that Hitler was convinced that the Allies' primary objective would be the Cotentin Peninsula—the tip of Normandy that juts into the English Channel. Others thought that it would be farther east, at the mouth of the Seine—or possibly the Mediterranean coast. But that, at least, was a possibility that the high command had effectively ruled out.

General Heusinger's own belief was that, no matter where or when the landing came, everything would depend on whether the invasion force could be driven back into the sea within forty-eight hours; if not, then it would be too late. "In short, everything depends on our meager armored reserves, on their initial deployment, or if it comes to that, on how quickly they can be brought up to oppose the landing. This uncertainty will be sure to weigh heavily against us, and let's not forget that the enemy's air superiority will make all troop movements very difficult." More to the point, General Heusinger felt—though he con-

Hitler confers with (left to right) Heusinger, Paulus, and Marshal von Weichs in 1942. *(Archives of General Heusinger).*

OKH conference in 1941: Brauchitsch, Heusinger, and an unidentified aide consult a situation map. Facing them is General Halder, OKH chief of staff. *(Archives of General Heusinger)*

Stauffenberg (left) and his friend and fellow conspirator Colonel Albrecht Mertz von Quirnheim at "Werwolf" GHQ in the Ukraine, 1942.

Marshal Hans Gunther von Kluge, who succeeded Rommel as commander in chief in the West in July 1944 and sealed the fate of the Paris conspiracy three days later.

General Adolf Heusinger in June 1944. Apart from Stauffenberg, the only officer at the July 20 conference who had certain knowledge of the plot against Hitler.

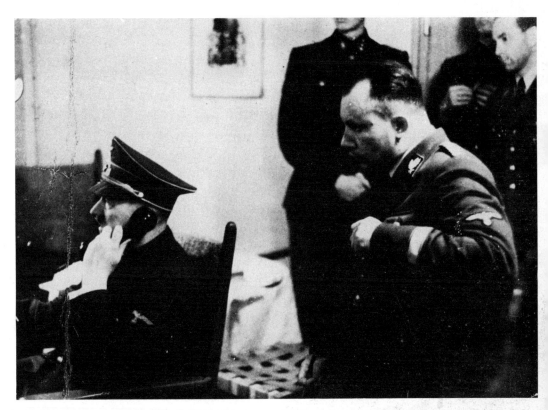

July 20. A few hours after the explosion Hitler assures his front-line commanders that the plot has failed. (The conspirators in Berlin had already let it be known that Hitler was dead and that the Valkyrie directive was in effect.)

Hitler and Mussolini inspect the wreckage of the situation barracks. *(Keystone)*

Aftermath of the explosion: A bemused SS man exhibits Hitler's trousers for the camera—they were later sent to Eva Braun as a momento of his providential escape.

The reprisals. General Erich Hoepner and Marshal Erwin von Witzleben, dressed in shabby civilian clothes, appear before the People's Court in Berlin. No effort has been spared to humiliate the defendants—Witzleben has even been deprived of his belt.

Adolf Heusinger in 1957, Inspector General of the
Bundeswehr. *(Archives of General Heusinger)*

Countess von Stauffenberg with some of her grandchildren. *(Private collection of Countess Nina von
Stauffenberg)*

fided this opinion only to his most trusted friends—that the war was lost. Only a radical change in the military and political leadership could possibly stave off the worst . . . but he was unwilling to say any more on this subject. Heusinger had already learned from Tresckow, Wagner, and Fellgiebel that preparations to assassinate Hitler were under way. In May he had asked Tresckow, "Would Churchill be prepared to make peace with Germany if Hitler were out of the picture?" A few weeks later Tresckow returned with the answer—no. "But," he added, "we intend to proceed with our mission." He also told Heusinger that Stauffenberg had undertaken to plan and carry out the assassination. "We'll let you know when." (But in fact when the day came, Tresckow was at his post on the Russian front and was unable to get word to Heusinger in time.)

General Zeitzler returned from his self-imposed exile after several weeks in order to resume the struggle for control of the high command. D-day had finally arrived. On June 6, 1944, the Allies came ashore on the beaches of Normandy, and Zeitzler returned disheartened from the midday briefing session to commiserate with General Heusinger. "Anglo-American troops have set foot on French soil. A few hours could make all the difference, and once again, instead of flying a group of officers out to the front, instead of reaching a decision or just giving a free hand to the commander in chief in the west, the Führer holds endless discussions, temporizes, and simply sits and waits. It's as if this were no more than a theoretical exercise, a *kriegspiel*. The whole day's going to slip by as if nothing had happened. We're losing the perfect opportunity for a counterattack. Jodl's calmness is enough to drive you to despair. Keitel is simply floating with the current, as usual, refusing to take sides. Instead of taking immediate action, they're carrying out a witchhunt. I've had enough of this, Heusinger! Do you think I should propose you as my successor?"

"Under no circumstances. That would be a useless experiment, doomed to failure. Our high command has gotten so lethargic, I doubt that anyone will be able to revive them."

General Fellgiebel, OKH communications chief, came into Heusinger's office. "If they can mount a successful offensive in the west, Heusinger, what do you think will be the upshot?"

"We should simply make an all-out attempt to push the enemy back into the sea, and then follow up on this success by opening negotiations. We must end the war before all of this crumbles into nothing."

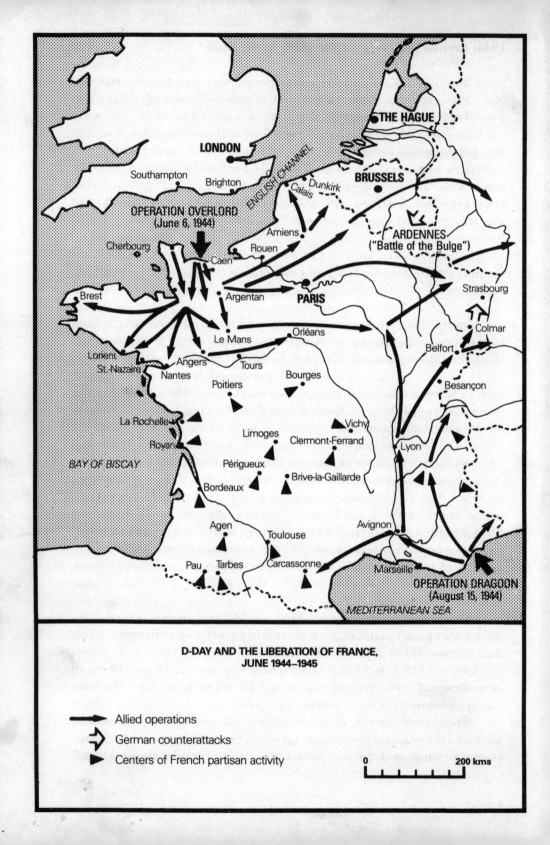

THE HAGUE

LONDON

Southampton
Brighton

Dunkirk
Calais

BRUSSELS

ENGLISH CHANNEL

OPERATION OVERLORD
(June 6, 1944)

Amiens

Rouen

ARDENNES
("Battle of the Bulge")

Cherbourg

Caen

Strasbourg

Brest

Argentan

PARIS

Colmar

Le Mans

Orléans

Belfort

Lorient
St. Nazaire

Angers

Tours

Besançon

Nantes

Poitiers

Bourges

La Rochelle

Limoges

Vichy

Lyon

Royan

Clermont-Ferrand

Périgueux

Brive-la-Gaillarde

BAY OF BISCAY

Bordeaux

Agen

Avignon

Toulouse

Pau   Tarbes

Carcassonne

Marseille

OPERATION DRAGOON
(August 15, 1944)

MEDITERRANEAN SEA

D-DAY AND THE LIBERATION OF FRANCE,
JUNE 1944–1945

→ Allied operations

⇨ German counterattacks

▶ Centers of French partisan activity

0   200 kms

"And our oath of allegiance, Heusinger? With or without Hitler?"

"The future of our people transcends every other consideration. I've wrestled with my conscience far too long."

"And that's enough for me, my dear fellow." (Fellgiebel was to play a central role in the conspiracy of July 20.)

At the end of June Marshal von Rundstedt announced that he could not exercise his command any longer unless he was allowed complete freedom of action. He was relieved immediately and replaced by Marshal von Kluge, who became the new commander in chief of the western theater of operations on July 7.

Since the first days of July the Stauffenberg household on the Tristanstrasse in Wannsee had been filled with unaccustomed activity. On the third floor, behind the blackout curtains, Claus and Berthold sat on a pair of old garden chairs—the same ones on which they had once held their after-dinner discussions on the family estate at Lautlingen—and spent long hours planning the attempt on Hitler's life. Everything of value had been removed from the house; the full-length portrait of their father in his marshal's regalia had been taken down from the wall in Berthold's bedroom. Claus occupied an adjoining room, but in fact the brothers rarely left the third-floor study, where Frau Weichbrodt served them dinner every night. They received no visitors except for Lieutenant von Haeften and a young woman whom Frau Weichbrodt referred to with diffident and slightly uneasy respect as *die Fliegerin,* "the aviatrix." She was the wife of the third of the Stauffenberg brothers, Alexander, the only one of the three who had not rallied to the conspiracy, since he had been sent off on a special mission in France, Greece, or Lithuania—no one was quite certain. "The aviatrix" was a remarkable personality: As fearless as her brother-in-law Claus, she had been the only woman test pilot to fly a Stuka, the shrieking dive bomber that had sown such panic during the French campaign in 1940. But she had fallen from grace quickly and tarnished her heroine's halo when the rumor spread that her loyalty to the Hitler regime left much to be desired. Now she had joined her husband's brothers in their conspiracy; she felt particularly drawn to Claus, whose courage she greatly admired. At this point he was still convinced that Hitler, Goering, and Himmler would all have to be done away with—the latter in particular, whom the conspirators knew to be quite capable of seizing this opportunity to set himself up in the Führer's place and thwarting all their plans for establishing an anti-Nazi provisional government. Stauffenberg's own state of mind at this time is best revealed by these remarks, quoted by the historian Joachim Kramarz: "Whoever hesitates to act will go down in history as a traitor to his fatherland. Whoever refuses to act will be a traitor to his own conscience."

At about the same time, the beginning of July, General Heusinger was filling in for General Zeitzler, who had been taken ill, at the daily briefing at Hitler's GHQ at the Berghof, near Berchtesgaden.

"Make it brief today, please," Keitel suggested.

"I'll confine myself to the essentials," Heusinger answered crisply as Hitler came into the conference room and cast a rapid, worried glance over the situation map, which showed the position of the army groups on the southern Russian front.

"Anything special today, Heusinger?"

At this point Heusinger requested that arrangements be made for the defense of East Prussia and the General Government—that part of Poland which lay directly to the south, and thus was critical to the strategic integrity of the Reich.

"Not a single Russian soldier will set foot on our soil!" Hitler shouted. "We will never allow that to happen!"

Heusinger suggested then that, as a precaution, defensive positions should be constructed and the civilian population evacuated, especially the refugees who had already been driven from the bombed-out cities of western Germany.

"You're going to drive the people to rebellion! That's completely out of the question, Heusinger. The population should be able to take themselves in hand if it should come to that."

Heusinger reminded Hitler that there were still a number of gaps to be plugged up in the front, and he went on to sketch a concise and objective picture of a situation that was rapidly taking on the proportions of a major catastrophe. For the first time the Russians had demonstrated a great deal of skill and flexibility in the use of their artillery; they had also assembled a major aerial striking force. The vast distances involved, the scarcity of reserves, and these new tactics on the part of the Russians seemed likely to have already taken the decision out of their hands.

But Hitler refused to admit it. "Come on, then—if everyone stuck to his post and did his duty, this could never have happened in the first place. But I'm going to look into the situation closely—things simply can't go on like this."

"I've already ordered an investigation, my Führer," Keitel chimed in, and Goering prudently added, "So have I—for the Luftwaffe."

"It's more important and certainly more urgent to decide how to stabilize the front," Heusinger broke in sternly.

"What do you mean 'more important'? It seems to me that it's important for the generals to do their duty—or that they be compelled to do so," Hitler repeated ominously. "Tell me, Keitel, how many troops can be mobilized in Germany?"

"In fifteen days, my Führer, the divisions that are now being raised will be ready to go into combat."

"Then send them to the front right away."

"We had intended to send them to the western front," Jodl pointed out. "Extremely heavy fighting is about to begin around the enemy beachheads. Perhaps they could play a more decisive role there, as far as the overall situation is concerned."

"But first I have to stop up these holes," Hitler said. "Then we shall see what we can do for them in the west."

Heusinger observed that these fresh divisions could not be brought up to engage the enemy for at least three weeks, because of the transport problems involved, when in fact they were needed right away.

"Can we withdraw any troops from Norway?" Hitler asked.

"No more than a division," Jodl replied.

"Then issue the order for them to set out immediately for the front."

"I'll telephone right away, my Führer," said Keitel.

Jodl observed that these were garrison troops who would have to be equipped with transport vehicles before they could be sent into combat, and Heusinger repeated pessimistically that it would still take at least three weeks before this single division could be brought to the front by sea and railroad. Goering explained apologetically that the Luftwaffe's landing strips were constantly being overrun as the Russians advanced, and consequently he was unable to offer any assistance in this matter.

Then Heusinger was handed an urgent telegram from Marshal Model,[3] now commander of Army Group Center, asking that two panzer divisions be detached from the northern Ukraine army group and sent off to him immediately.

"Give Model one panzer division from the northern Ukraine, and they can have one of the new divisions in exchange. . . . At least we'll

---

3. "A very capable officer," General Heusinger says of him. "He did his job well without asking too many questions, and he was always sent wherever things had just taken a turn for the worse."

finally be able to keep the Russian armor from advancing any farther!'' Hitler exulted.

Heusinger turned to Keitel and said, "There isn't enough fuel on hand to move even a single panzer division from the northern Ukraine up to Model's front. I must ask you, Herr Feldmarschall, to dip down into your reserves. If they have to go by railroad, they'll arrive too late.''

Keitel threw up his arms in a gesture of supplication. "Since this has the highest priority, I'll do everything in my power to get the fuel for them. But I implore you—it must be used sparingly, since I really have no idea where I'll be able to get hold of any more.''

Heusinger then proposed that it was time for the high command to return to Rastenburg to be closer to the eastern front.

"I've been thinking about that myself,'' said Hitler. "Jodl, do you think that anything's going to happen in the west over the next few days?''

"I hope not.''

"In any case,'' Hitler went on, "the first thing is to get that panzer division on the march. Who should command them at Vilna [the capital of Lithuania]? I need a man of towering energy there, since Vilna must be held at all costs.''

Keitel proposed General Stahel. "He has a very distinguished record, my Führer.''

"The most energetic of my officers,'' added Goering, "and I will gladly put him at your disposal.''

"A good idea,'' said Hitler. "Send for him at once. I want to see him before he goes.''

Heusinger left the room, accompanied by General Schmundt. "It's incredible how the Führer manages to cope with every situation that arises, don't you think, Heusinger?''

"But it will take more than this inspired tinkering to resolve the crisis that we're faced with now. Has Kluge already taken up his new command in the west?''

"He's on his way now. Rundstedt can take no more, and the Führer didn't want Rommel. General Zeitzler's recent collapse has made a very strong impression on him. It's extraordinary how much the man has had to put up with!''

"You know very well, Schmundt, that if he wants to keep making all the decisions himself, he can't expect it to be otherwise.''

By this time Hitler had also left the conference room. He walked with a stoop and he looked worn out and harassed as he made his way back to his private quarters and the first of the day's sessions with Dr. Morell.

Stauffenberg, who had attended this last conference at Berchtesgaden, now returned to Berlin with the bomb that General Stieff had given him still in his briefcase, since he had discovered that Himmler would not be joining them. However, as time wore on there would be less and less justification for the coup; it was too late to alter the destiny of the Third Reich. The only alternative to absolute annihilation—since the Allies still refused to negotiate—was unconditional surrender.

On July 14 General Fromm ordered Stauffenberg to attend the next day's session at the Wolf's Lair to report on their progress in forging a territorial reserve out of the unpromising collection of worn-out veterans and raw recruits that they had at their disposal. Before he took off for Rastenburg the next morning, Stauffenberg ordered the troops in the garrisons outside Berlin who were to be the striking force of Operation Valkyrie to be put on full alert at 11:00 AM.

But when he came into the conference room, he realized that Himmler had failed to show up again. He decided to telephone General Olbricht for last-minute instructions. Lieutenant von Haeften answered the phone, and Stauffenberg asked him if he should set off the bomb in any case. Haeften told him to go ahead and went to inform Generals Olbricht and Hoepner in the neighboring office. Both generals were furious with Haeften, a mere lieutenant in the army reserve, for having taken such a responsibility on himself without consulting them. But there was nothing for them to do but sit in Olbricht's office and wait for further news from Rastenburg. Finally Stauffenberg's call came through—by the time he had gotten back to the conference after his conversation with Haeften, Hitler had already left the room.

A number of the conspirators had begun to question the firmness of Stauffenberg's resolve and suggested resurrecting an earlier plan for a coup d'état that would be touched off among the armies of the west. Beck was opposed to this; Stauffenberg had given him his word of honor that he would detonate the bomb on his next visit to GHQ, no matter what the circumstances. "It would be better to have a putsch that is only partly successful with Hitler dead than a putsch that succeeds totally in Berlin and in the west with Hitler still alive." Moreover Beck was also opposed to the suggestion of a final appeal to Marshal von Kluge. "Who could possibly have any confidence left in Kluge after he's deserted us so many times?"

On July 16 Hitler visited OKH headquarters in the Mauerwald; the daily briefing was held in the office of the chief of staff. First Heusinger handed the Führer a telegram from General Stahel in Vilna, which he read impatiently and flung down on the map table. "What a piece of insolence! I didn't send Stahel to Vilna so that he could simply turn around and clear out! He must hold the city. He must stand by his post to the bitter end! That's no more than what's expected of the captain of a warship. What cowardice . . . ridiculous . . . this fellow must do his duty—get on the radio and tell him that."

Heusinger did not reply.

"Don't you understand what I'm saying to you?"

"Stahel isn't asking this for his own sake but for his men. There are eight hundred men trapped in a terribly cramped space, with no heavy guns. They can't hold out any longer."

"What nonsense!" Hitler rumbled. "How can Stahel expect to make a sortie with so few men? None of them will get through. How can you even suggest such a thing to me? There's a general for you—always retreat at the first sign of trouble!"

"There have been quite a few generals who have stayed at their posts until the end. They are responsible for their men—"

"Don't talk to me about responsibility. They are supposed to obey orders. I'll assume full responsibility and no one else. To send me a filthy scrap of paper like that—has he no shame?"

After this exchange an uneasy silence fell over the room. All the officers stood frozen as Hitler bent down to peer at the maps, while Heusinger leaned over his shoulder and spoke to him in a low voice, like a doctor trying to soothe a feverish patient.

"The only choice that's left to them is death or capture. They can hold out no longer. Shouldn't we do what we can to ease their burden?"

"All this has happened because Army Group North is not attacking, because they will not attack. It's all very well to give them the orders, but these generals always find some way of wriggling out of it. You don't actually suppose that a single one of those men will get out of Vilna alive?"

"It's hardly a question of that. But we might at least give them a chance. It's easier for men to face death when they are the masters of their own fate, when they can strike out for themselves rather than waging a hopeless defense. At least let them have that illusion, make it easier for them to die if death is inevitable."

Hitler straightened up and stared balefully at Heusinger. "Do what you like, but you won't save a single one of them."

On July 17 word came that Rommel had been seriously wounded when his staff car was strafed by enemy fighters in Normandy. For several months he had been sympathetic to the aims of the conspiracy, but he had always refused to declare himself until Hitler's death was an actual certainty. On the same day the conspirators learned from their police contacts that Goerdeler was about to be arrested. Julius Leber, a former Social Democratic deputy in the Reichstag and a friend of Stauffenberg's, had already been picked up, and it seemed entirely possible that he would break under torture. The conspirators could feel the net drawing in all around them. They warned Goerdeler that a warrant had been issued for his arrest. He was about to leave for a meeting at General Beck's, and they had enormous difficulty in persuading him not to go, since Beck was still under close surveillance and there was no point in his simply throwing himself into the hands of his pursuers. That evening Goerdeler hurried back to his own house, let himself in by a back entrance, went straight to his office, burned all his compromising papers, and turned over his keys to his wife. The next day, the eighteenth, he said his farewells to his family, as he had done so many times in the past before setting off on his travels. This time Frau Goerdeler was convinced she would never see her husband again.

On July 19 Heusinger presented himself at the Wolf's Lair for the midday briefing. The northern Ukraine army group was in desperate straits—the Russian breakthrough in the south could not be contained; in the north their advance had ripped an enormous gash in the German lines, and the troops in the center who had still managed to hold their postions would have to be withdrawn. "It's essential," Heusinger's report concluded, "for us to ascertain how many troops can be diverted from the resources of the General Government. I don't know what we can expect the Replacement Army to provide."

"I suggest that Colonel von Stauffenberg come tomorrow to give us the facts and figures," said Keitel.

"I had the same thought," added Heusinger.

"Good, send for Stauffenberg tomorrow." With that, Hitler got to his feet; the briefing was at an end.

"One more thing," said Heusinger. "They've just brought me this dispatch. General Stahel has made a successful sortie from Vilna and fought his way through to our lines with five hundred of his men."

Hitler picked up the dispatch and read it through without saying a word; there were tears in his eyes. "Hitler," General Heusinger told us, "always refused to visit the bombed-out cities and the hospitals. He was afraid that the sight of the wounded might make him weaken, give in to pity. For that matter, the sight of so much human suffering, wretchedness, and unhappiness would have forced him to confront his own overwhelming responsibility for all of this."

For Claus von Stauffenberg, the nineteenth began like any other day. When he arrived at his office in the Bendlerstrasse, he still had no idea that tomorrow would be his last chance to strike. The day was taken up with routine business; at three o'clock he met with an officer from the front to discuss the details of the latest order of the day. The high command had finally, reluctantly drawn up a contingency plan in case of a Soviet invasion of the Reich. Bialystok, on the Russo-Polish border, had fallen on the previous day; the Russians were threatening another breakthrough in the Ukraine while in France and Italy the Wehrmacht had given up hope of containing the Allied invasion of "Fortress Europe."

Stauffenberg was certainly aware of what all this portended, and by the time he returned to Berthold's house in Wannsee, he had already had word from Rastenburg that he was expected to report to Hitler the next day on the state of readiness of the Replacement Army. If anything, he was even more determined to go through with his mission than he had been on the previous occasions in the past week. In the early morning, before setting out, he told Berthold, "No other choice is possible now. We have crossed the Rubicon."

13.

July 20, 1944: Exercise Completed

Berlin, 5 PM

Stauffenburg had finally arrived at the Bendlerstrasse, and Beck—who was wearing his uniform today for the first time since 1938—decided that it was now or never. At his urging, Olbricht had his staff send out the orders proclaiming a state of emergency; the first phase of Operation Valkyrie was launched. The conspirators had drafted a series of instructions authorizing the Wehrmacht to assume full civil powers, to disarm the SS, to subject all Party organizations to military jurisdiction, and, if necessary, to arrest the chiefs of the Nazi administration. The Defense Ministry exchange, with its eight hundred telephone and telegraph lines, transmitted the Valkyrie orders with its customary brisk efficiency. Stauffenburg's old comrade Colonel Albrecht Mertz von Quirnheim saw to it that this phase of the operation, at any rate, was carried out exactly as planned.

The arrival of Stauffenberg himself, radiating energy and determination, had done a great deal to restore the spirits of the Replacement Army officers gathered at the Bendlerstrasse. He had gone without sleep for days, had just returned from a harrowing adventure, and he had emerged from the beast's lair unscathed and still seemed to be in complete mastery of himself and of the situation. Amid the clatter of the teleprinters he sought out all the generals whom he believed to be trustworthy and told them the same thing he had told Olbricht when he first arrived: "Hitler is dead. Keitel is lying when he claims that our enterprise has failed." And to those who were already privy to the conspiracy he added in less forbidding tones: "I'm counting on you, and I hope that you won't desert us now."

A more prudent summary of the day's events was offered by General Beck, who suggested, "Perhaps it would be more accurate to say that we've received certain reports that leave the question of Hitler's death somewhat in doubt." But no one paid much attention to Beck, who was the only officer present not wearing any decorations from the present war. And in fact the entire conduct of the Valkyrie operation so far had suffered from an excess of prudence. The conspirators had already squandered the best part of the afternoon, since even with Hitler still alive it might have been possible to ward off his inevitable counterstroke if the Valkyrie orders had gone out a few hours earlier. Was Stauffenberg himself beginning to suspect that Hitler might still be alive? In either case, dead or alive, the only course that was open to him now was to proceed with the operation as planned.

Even so, the conspirators' attempts to paralyze the nerve centers of the Nazi regime in Berlin—the radio transmitters and the telephone exchange, the Ministry of the Interior—were undertaken more or less haphazardly, by troops whose loyalty the conspirators had no very good reason to count on. They had even neglected to draw up a cordon of troops around their own headquarters in the Bendlerstrasse, and it was only when the Valkyrie orders had actually gone out over the wires that they thought of securing the government buildings in downtown Berlin, including the SS barracks on the Prinz Albrechtstrasse.

General von Hase, the commander of the Berlin garrison and one of the ringleaders of the conspiracy, entrusted this mission to a young officer, Major Remer, who commanded the Grossdeutschland guards battalion. Remer was not a party to the conspiracy, nor had General von Hase taken the trouble to sound him out before assigning him to occupy part of the center of the city with three companies of his guards. Hase simply showed Remer a map with the objectives circled in red and told him, "The Führer has met with an accident—we don't know whether he's been killed or not."

Remer raised no objections, even though several of the buildings that Hase had told him to secure were not under military jurisdiction. Before he left the general's office, he asked, "You don't know what the Führer's condition is, then?"

"No," General von Hase replied, "we'll tell you as soon as we find out."

The general's apparently cavalier approach to this vital mission may seem incredible, but in fact it can be explained in terms of the old-school Prussian officer's unshakable faith in military discipline. The idea that a young officer like Remer could possibly disobey a direct order from a superior seems never to have crossed the general's mind. Remer returned to the battalion's barracks, assembled his three companies in the courtyard, and repeated Hase's instructions to his officers. A certain

Lieutenant Hagen, a "political education" officer who happened to be on the scene, sensed there was something distinctly odd about all this. Since he had worked in the Propaganda Ministry before the war and was acquainted with Goebbels personally, he suggested that he might arrange for Remer to confer with his former chief. Remer agreed, and the troops were deployed around the grounds of the Propaganda Ministry while Remer and Hagen went in to confront Goebbels.

Goebbels had already spoken with Hitler on the telephone, and he saw immediately how to deal with the situation. He told Remer that the Führer was still very much alive, that he had just met with Mussolini as planned, and that he himself had just spoken with him. Remer appeared to be completely stunned by this piece of news. Goebbels put through a call to Rastenburg and handed Remer the telephone. He recognized the Führer's voice and came to attention as Hitler briefly explained to him what had happened; he finished by saying, "A clique of lawless, faithless officers have made an attempt on my life, but I am unharmed. I order you to crush this rebellion by any means necessary. You will take your orders from no one but me—your authority is absolute. Do you understand?"

"Yes, my Führer." Remer was both astounded and intoxicated by this unexpected promotion. His first official act as the Führer's deputy in Berlin was to order his troops to cordon off the Bendlerstrasse.

Meanwhile the conspirators had met with still another setback. Witzleben, the only one of the marshals who was totally committed to Valkyrie, had arrived at the Bendlerstrasse, firmly clutching his baton. He had undertaken to rally his troops and lend the considerable weight of his prestige to the conspiracy, but after meeting for an hour with Beck and Stauffenberg, he stalked out. "I'm going back home," he announced to the group of young officers who were waiting expectantly in the anteroom. Witzleben was appalled by the slipshod preparations that had been made for the occupation of Berlin and the unpardonable lapses in the execution of Valkyrie so far. The disappointment was too much for him to bear, and in fact he did go home after he left the Bendlerstrasse, though he later went out to his headquarters at Zossen to await developments.

At about 9:00 PM General Olbricht realized that troops were moving through the streets outside the ministry. He felt, if only for a moment, that all was not lost after all, that the army was finally taking control of the capital. Shortly before seven his wife had telephoned him to ask if there was any news. "It's just a matter of time," he told her, but in fact he had already given up hope. He called together the officers in the building—some forty in all—and instructed them to secure the building against attack. He appointed his aide, Lieutenant von der Saucken, to take charge of this improvised guard detail. Ewald Heinrich von Kleist was sent off to find General von Hase and round up enough reliable troops from the garrison to defend the ministry. Hase was not to be found; Goebbels had already summoned him to the Propaganda Ministry, where he had promptly been arrested. At nine fifteen Major Remer appeared in the Bendlerstrasse at the head of his detachment. After a brief skirmish the ministry was surrounded; the conspirators were trapped. (One of the few shots fired grazed Stauffenberg's right arm.)

In the meantime the radio had been broadcasting Hitler's official account of the day's events—the work of a tiny group of ambitious army officers, an unconscionable act of criminal lunacy. . . .

The final act of the tragedy began at about 10:00 PM. The officers in the ministry gathered around General Olbricht, who told them, "We are going to remain here and defend ourselves. We will hold out for a night or two, or it is equally possible that we will be crushed within the hour. I intend to die a soldier's death."

Olbricht made this declaration simply and unaffectedly as he stood with one hand resting on the shoulder of his young son-in-law, Major Friedrich Georgi. A few minutes before ten thirty Georgi managed to slip out of the ministry and past Remer's men; it was he who would convey the general's farewell message to Frau Olbricht. At 10:30 PM exactly, Remer's guards battalion, who had made no attempt to occupy the ministry, were relieved by the SS; the pace of events was about to accelerate sharply.

The ministry was now in total chaos. A great many of the officers present, who had been at least partially won over to the conspiracy, were now beginning to waver. The fatal irresolution of the chief conspirators, the defection of Witzleben and Fromm, the broadcasts on the radio, and the ominous presence of Remer's troops outside had naturally caused considerable alarm; the arrival of the SS made up their minds for them. They decided to save themselves by turning their coats while there was still time.

One of them, Lieutenant Colonel Bodo von der Heyden, burst in on Stauffenberg, pistol in hand, shouting "Treason! Treason!" He fired, and Stauffenberg was wounded in the back. He staggered, then straightened up and made his way into the room where Beck and a group of loyal officers had gathered. Heyden and his comrades released General Fromm, whom the conspirators had been holding under guard in a nearby office. Now that the tide had finally turned, Fromm decided that it was time for him to regain control of his command. He went in to confront General Beck and the others, brandishing a pistol: "Gentlemen, I'm going to treat you just as you've treated me. You are all guilty of treason and you deserve to die. Put down your weapons."

Beck refused. "You're not about to give such an order to your former superior officer. I shall face the consequences of this situation myself."

"Very well, make it quick then."

Beck picked up a pistol that was lying on the table, walked over in front of an armchair, raised the pistol to his head, and pulled the trigger. The bullet only creased the top of his skull. He collapsed into the armchair, and the pistol slipped from his fingers. Stauffenberg rushed over and helped him up—as Beck murmured softly, "I'm thinking of old times. . . ." Fromm announced to the others that he would give them a few minutes to write their farewell letters. Several of the conspirators sat down at a round table in the office and began to write.

Five minutes later Fromm returned and intoned solemnly that he had convened a court-martial in the name of the Führer: Olbricht, Stauffenberg, Haeften, and Quirnheim had been condemned to death. He ordered a lieutenant to take the prisoners down into the courtyard and carry out the sentence immediately. Then he turned to Beck: "How are you feeling now?" Beck asked for a pistol, and his request was granted.

"Take your time," said Fromm. Beck fired but once again failed to kill himself. Fromm ordered one of his officers to put an end to his suffering.

In the courtyard the four condemned conspirators were brought before a hastily assembled firing squad. "Long live our holy eternal Germany!" Stauffenberg cried out, which was answered by a cry of *"Unser Führer Adolf Hitler! Sieg Heil!"* from General Kortzfleisch [1] and the SS men as the shots died away. The bodies of Beck, Olbricht, Stauffenberg, Quirnheim, and Haeften were loaded onto a truck and driven out to the nearest cemetery. The SS burial squad roused the caretaker and

1. Commander of the Berlin military district, a Nazi loyalist who had been arrested by the conspirators and released a few minutes earlier by General Fromm.

dug a mass grave by lantern light. At dawn they would return to photograph the bodies before burning them.

Paris, Shortly Before Midnight

In the Hôtel Raphaël five or six members of Stülpnagel's staff—most of them administrators rather than troop commanders—were preparing to carry out their assigned missions. They had assembled in the small Empire-style drawing room of Suite 703 where they had often held their secret conclaves; they were apprehensive but still hopeful that Stülpnagel, reinforced by the mandate of Marshal von Kluge, would shortly be ordering them into action. The door opened, and Colonel von Linstow walked into the room, looking ill and haggard—he was experiencing a flareup of the heart condition that had kept him from active service at the front. He beckoned for Baron von Teuchert to come closer. "The struggle in Berlin is almost over. All is lost." He stretched out on a sofa and said weakly, "It was Stauffenberg who called just now. He gave the news himself and told us that his assassins were at the door."

Teuchert tried to comfort him. "Even if the coup in Berlin has failed, we must still succeed in Paris. Our organization here is solid."

Linstow gradually recovered his composure. He did not mention another conversation he had had, with General Blumentritt. Blumentritt had been ordered by Kluge to suspend operations against the Gestapo, but he had demurred, claiming that it was already too late; by midnight the arrests had already been carried out. Stülpnagel's intention had been to cut off all channels of communication with the Reich, making it impossible for any orders countermanding the Valkyrie directive to get through. Thanks to the perfect understanding between Stülpnagel and Boineburg, both gentlemen soldiers of the same vintage, the first phase of the operation in Paris had been an unqualified success.

At 12:30 AM Admiral Krancke, commander in chief of the Western Naval Group, called Kluge from his headquarters near the Bois de Boulogne and gave him an indignant account of the events in Paris. Kluge thanked the admiral for his trouble and told him, "There's no cause for alarm—all appropriate measures have been taken." Krancke still took the precaution of alerting all naval units in Paris, in case these measures should prove to be insufficient. About fifteen minutes later—quite unaware of the drama that had just been played out at La Roche–Guyon—

he tried Kluge again, but could not get through. His suspicions aroused, he muttered to himself, "You never know where you are with these reactionary army commanders."

Between 1:00 and 1:10 AM the German radio stations broadcast speeches by Hitler, Goering, and Admiral Doenitz, all exulting that the criminal plot against the Führer had been foiled. By now Krancke was champing at the bit. Blumentritt called from his headquarters at Saint-Germain to tell him that he had personally received the order to relieve Stülpnagel of his command and to release SS Generals Oberg and Knochen and the captive SD men. But Krancke, still skeptical, insisted on calling Blumentritt's adjutant, Colonel Unger: "Release General Oberg and the SD personnel immediately, or I'll turn the job over to my own men."

Unger was not about to be intimidated, however. "Admiral, there is nothing I can do about it at the moment, and for that matter I can only carry out the orders of my superiors. These may only be countermanded by the military governor, and I have not been informed that he has seen fit to do so." This sent Krancke into a paroxysm that would have been worthy of the Führer himself.

At 1:40 AM Krancke called Colonel von Linstow, but Linstow was equally adamant. The admiral was just about to call out his sailors and marines when the crisis was dispelled by a final phone call from Colonel von Linstow: "Lieutenant Colonel von Kraewell has been ordered to release Oberg and the SD men."

At 1:56 AM Krancke canceled the alert, but his rage against the treacherous General von Stülpnagel was unabated.

About ten minutes earlier Kluge had received a telegram from Berlin: "The ringleaders have been executed." It was signed by General Fromm, who had apparently managed to hang on as commander in chief of the Replacement Army. This Kluge found very puzzling, since he was under the impression that Fromm himself had had extensive dealings with the conspirators, and yet he had presumably given the order for their execution. Kluge was unaware that Fromm was already on Hitler's blacklist and would shortly be replaced by Himmler, but he already had reason enough to feel panic. Apart from his ordinary anxieties about the latest Allied offensive in Normandy, he now had to reckon with the indiscriminate thirst for vengeance of the Führer in Berlin.

It was past midnight when Stülpnagel and his companions returned to Paris. Boineburg had just arrived at the Hôtel Raphaël to announce that the operation against the SS and the Gestapo had been completed. He noticed that there were crimson patches on Stülpnagel's face; the general smiled sadly and gave him a lifeless handshake. Boineburg asked what Kluge's decision had been.

"He needs more time to think—until nine o'clock this morning."

It was clear that this was not true, that Stülpnagel himself was playing for time, and only moments later the radio announced that the Führer was about to address the German people. Stülpnagel, Boineburg, Linstow, Hofacker, and the other officers present crowded around the radio set. Stülpnagel felt as if he were listening to his death sentence, but he stood firm and erect and heard the ravings of the Nazi triumvirate— Hitler, Goering, and Doenitz—through to the end: "A small clique of generals afflicted with delusions of grandeur have plotted this crime. . . . We are going to put an end to all such traitorous machinations."

But help was about to arrive from a most unexpected quarter. Otto Abetz, a former professor at the University of Karlsruhe, now German ambassador in Paris, had always been a partisan of détente between France and Germany. He had met with Stülpnagel some time before July 20, and neither attempted to conceal from the other his opinion that Hitler was leading Germany down the road to catastrophe. Serious differences of opinion on other subjects arose between them and their talks ended inconclusively, but Abetz was still essentially well disposed toward Stülpnagel.

At the moment, however, Stülpnagel was finally forced to bow to the inevitable. He turned to Boineberg and said to him in a toneless voice, "We must avoid a confrontation with the navy. You have your orders to release the prisoners. Show them the orders, and bring Oberg back here to the Raphaël."

Boineburg went off to the Hôtel Continental on the rue de Castiglione, not far from command headquarters in the Hôtel Meurice. He was smiling when he strode into the hotel ballroom, where the senior SS officers had been detained. "Good evening, gentlemen," he said as he snapped out a Hitler salute. Then he went up to find Oberg and Knochen, who had been sequestered in a separate suite for the last few hours, drinking cognac and listening to the radio while an army officer stood guard in the outer room. They leapt to their feet as Boineburg came in. "Gentlemen, I have good news for you—you are free to go."

"What's the meaning of this filthy business, Boineburg?" Oberg thundered back.

"You'll have to ask the military governor. I've been asked to accompany you back to the Hôtel Raphaël."

Oberg collected both his revolvers and followed Boineburg into the hall. When they arrived at the Raphaël, Boineburg made directly for the table where Stülpnagel, Linstow, and the others were sitting. "Here is the prisoner," Boineburg announced, half seriously, half ironically. Oberg and Stülpnagel simply stared at each other, and it was at this point that Ambassador Abetz made a timely intervention, trying at once to pacify General Oberg and to shake Stülpnagel's mood of cold determination, which by now was mingled with a certain mental confusion.

"No matter what's been going on in Berlin," he told them, "here in France—with the battle for Normandy raging—all Germans should be standing shoulder to shoulder." Then he turned toward Oberg. "You want to know why the military governor had you arrested? Very well— he had received information on the highest level that Himmler was trying to seize power and that it was none other than the SS who were responsible for the attempt on the Führer's life."

"But how could Stülpnagel have doubted the loyalty of the SS?" Oberg cried indignantly. "That's totally unacceptable!"

Abetz was prepared for this objection. "You mustn't bear him any ill will on that account. He was acting in good faith and in accordance with the orders he had received."

Oberg said nothing and Stülpnagel made no attempt to elaborate on Abetz's explanation. The tension had abated slightly, however, and Abetz called for champagne all round. It was up to him now to work out a diplomatic formula that both the SS and the Wehrmacht could accept—the SS would certainly not want to publicize their inglorious role in the night's events, and the army would welcome any plausible explanation for their conduct, since they were eager to avoid an investigation and all that would entail. Both parties would have to protect themselves from the inquisitors of Himmler's Reich Central Security Office, and, finally, both would want to avoid losing face with the French people. Blumentritt was vastly relieved by the unexpected course events had taken; by sunrise Boineburg and Oberg had sat down together to draft a communiqué that could be read to the troops later that morning.

But Stülpnagel could not extricate himself so easily from all this; he could scarcely pretend that he had been conducting a routine military exercise. Blumentritt advised him to return to his quarters and await instructions—in other words, to put himself under house arrest. Stülpnagel remained erect and impassive, but he made no attempt to delude himself. In spite of his friends' best efforts, he was done for.

Earlier that night Kluge—an officer who was not without courage in the face of the enemy—had picked up the telephone to denounce Stülpnagel to the Wehrmacht high command, even as Boineburg and Blumentritt were trying to hammer out a compromise with the aggrieved SS generals in Paris. When Blumentritt returned to his headquarters at Saint-Germain in the early morning, a message from OKW was waiting on his desk. Keitel had called to inform him that Stülpnagel had been ordered to Berlin immediately to give an account of the previous night's events. When Blumentritt called Kluge to tell him about this latest development, the marshal simply remarked, "Well, it's starting then," and hung up. But Kluge's attempts to cover his tracks—since his contacts with Beck and Olbricht would certainly touch off an investigation—would be so much effort wasted. On July 21 Hitler told Guderian, "Kluge knew all about the plot," even though he had just received an effusive telegram from Kluge congratulating him on his providential escape.

14.

After July 20, 1944: The Last Knights

Baron Ewald von Kleist-Schmentzin and his son Ewald Heinrich, who had been arrested at the Bendlerstrasse the night before, were brought to the same prison in Berlin. Ewald Heinrich saw his father standing with his face to the wall, but he made no attempt to attract his attention, for fear of provoking some sort of violent reprisal on the part of his Gestapo escort. He sought out an acquaintance among the military guards, who arranged for him to meet with his father that night in an unoccupied cell.

"So, my son, what kind of fate do they have in store for you?"

"I shall probably be hanged. And you?"

"There can be no doubt of it. They've beaten and tortured me, an SS officer struck me across the face. 'You can kill me,' I shouted at them, 'but I shall never talk!' "

The baron would be executed on April 9, 1945; he never confessed, even though a detailed account of his mission to London in August 1938 was found tucked away in a safe at OKH headquarters in Zossen.

On July 21 the Gestapo went to search Goerdeler's house, but Goerdeler himself had already gone to ground at Duchener Heide. Shortly after, however, he would return to Berlin, wearing makeup and a disguise; he was convinced that even a failed attempt on Hitler's life was certain to unleash a general insurrection. This time Goerdeler's incorrigible optimism would cost him dearly, since he might have fled the country on July 19, with two days' head start on the Gestapo.

That morning in Paris Stülpnagel ran into a close friend of his in the lobby of the Hôtel Raphaël. He took him aside and told him, "I have no intention of trying to evade the consequences of my actions. We have done nothing to reproach ourselves for. Get yourself to a safe place—you run the risk of implicating yourself simply by standing here and talking to me." He shook hands warmly with his friend and headed to his office. When he got to there, he exchanged the usual pleasantries with his secretary, Countess Podewils, and was told that he had been called back to Berlin. His premonition of a few hours earlier had been borne out soon enough, since this summons could have only one meaning. After all, Stülpnagel and his colleagues had had similar plans for the heads of the SD in Paris. A court-martial was to have convened at dawn, and by midnight sandbags were already being stacked up in the courtyard of the École Militaire, where the 1st Guards Regiment was billeted, for the convenience of the firing squad.

Stülpnagel decided to leave Paris at 11:30 AM, and he sent word to OKH that he planned to report to them in Berlin at nine o'clock the next morning. He would be making the journey by car, but he refused to allow his orderly officer, Dr. Baumgart, to accompany him. He took his leave of Countess Podewils and Baumgart with his usual soft-spoken cordiality—he had led them to believe that he had been reassigned to a new command. As he was about to step out the door, he remembered that he was to have dinner with Ernst Jünger that evening. "I'm sorry to have to break our engagement," he said to the countess. "Give him my best regards and explain to him that I've been called back to Berlin unexpectedly."

The car headed eastward out of Paris; the general had chosen to return to Germany by way of Metz and Verdun in Alsace-Lorraine. At Meaux on the River Marne the car broke down, and while they were waiting for another to be sent on from Paris, Stülpnagel stretched out on a folding cot in the garage and went to sleep, for the first time in many hours. The second car arrived at about three o'clock, and they drove on past the great battlefields of the First World War—Château-Thierry, the valley of the Marne, the western slopes of the Argonne, and the statue of Sainte Geneviève, near Sainte-Menehould, where the last German offensive of the war was turned back. Then they were in the Argonne Forest, whose thick stands of beech trees made an ideal refuge for the Maquis; a number of German vehicles had already been ambushed along this route. Stülpnagel ordered the driver, Sergeant Major Schauf, to stop the car so that he could check the weapons that had been provided in case of just such an eventuality. That at least was what Schauf and the general's personal orderly, Corporal Fischer, assumed that the general had in mind. There were no untoward incidents on the road through the Argonne, though Schauf kept driving at a fairly rapid clip, from fifty to sixty miles per hour.

At dusk they were crossing the plains of Alsace, and then the hills that sloped down to the valley of the Meuse, and beyond the grassy, overgrown fortifications, the gray outline of a city dominated by ruined spires. This was Verdun. After they had crossed the bridge over the Meuse, Stülpnagel asked the driver to turn off onto the road that led north toward Sedan. There, on both banks of the Meuse, had been the bloodiest battleground of the First World War, where Staff Captain von Stülpnagel had seen the heaviest fighting of his career. Hundreds of his old comrades of the Darmstadt Grenadier Guards had fallen in the woods of Caures and near Beaumont in February 1916. They followed a road that wound up the slopes above Charny, to the north of Verdun, and as soon as they reached the top, the car slowed down. Stülpnagel could see the old fort—now the ossuary—of Douaumont, and far away to the north, the outlines of Hill 304 and the Mort-Homme, all bitterly contested strongpoints during the Battle of Verdun. As Stülpnagel pointed out these landmarks to his young companions he seemed to be lost in a kind of reverie.

After they had passed through a small village in the Meuse Valley, Stülpnagel told Schauf to turn off the Sedan road and onto a side road that followed the river to the west. Then he ordered the car to stop; he got out and told Schauf to wait for him in Champs, the next village. "I need to stretch my legs," he explained.

They drove off slowly. Schauf and Fischer were uneasy about leaving the general to fend for himself in uninhabited countryside that was also the hunting ground of the Maquis. They decided to stop the car after the next bend in the road and wait for him.

Then they heard a gunshot. They piled back into the car, made a U-turn, and drove back to the spot where they had left the general ten minutes earlier. There was no one to be seen. They jumped out and hurried down the towpath of the canal that ran alongside the road. Suddenly they caught sight of a body floating with the current in the shallow water of the canal; they could make out the green tunic with red piping on the cuffs and collar. "The general!" cried Schauf, and he hurled himself into the canal.

A few moments later Stülpnagel was lying on the bank. "What's happened, general?" cried Schauf, but Stülpnagel could not answer him. His hands twitched spasmodically. He had been shot through the right temple. Clearly they would have to get him to the German military hospital in Verdun as quickly as possible. Immediately afterward Schauf called the Hôtel Majestic in Paris to inform his staff that "General Stülpnagel has been critically wounded by terrorists." Colonel von Linstow was staggered by this piece of news, which he duly passed on to Blumentritt, who in turn called Kluge, who listened but said nothing. General Oberg of the SS was also notified.

Stülpnagel was operated on that night and was soon out of danger, though he would never regain his eyesight. All the physical evidence suggested a suicide attempt rather than a partisan ambush. As the examining physician explained it, "Apparently the general set out with the firm intention of putting an end to his life in the very place where he fought during the last war, on his old battlegrounds."

Ernst Jünger wrote in his journal, "Another harvest of victims! Drawn this time from among that small knightly band, the last of the knights, the free spirits, whose thoughts and feelings went beyond those of the common herd."

By this time the Gestapo had traced Goerdeler back to Berlin. With the help of a Protestant pastor, he had attempted to escape to Sweden, and when this proved impossible, he set out on foot for Königsberg—with a price of a million marks on his head, dead or alive. At the end of August he was recognized in a village tavern in his native East Prussia by a woman who had once worked for his family, and was immediately picked up by the police. (After the war she explained that since the Führer was always right, then Goerdeler must have been a monstrous criminal indeed; the ten million marks was still in her possession—she had not spent a pfennig of it.) Goerdeler boldly faced his captors, who would shortly be handing him over to his executioners; his entire family was forced to run the gauntlet of Himmler's various police forces—the Kripo (criminal police), the SD, finally the Gestapo. His younger daughter, Nina, who was not yet fourteen, and his two grandchildren were dispatched to an SS "children's village" to be brought up under a different name, just as was done with Stauffenberg's children. The rest of the family was dispersed, to Dachau, Buchenwald, and several other camps. They were eventually liberated by the Allies, but Goerdeler himself was executed on February 2, 1945, along with Johannes Popitz, former Prussian Minister of Finance, a distinguished member of Beck's Wednesday Club, and Father Delp, a Jesuit who was associated with the Moltke group.

On July 24 Reichsmarshal Goering decided, as a token of his affection for the Führer and as a means of strengthening the ties between the army and the Party, that in future the traditional army salute would be replaced by the Hitler salute in all branches of the Wehrmacht.

On July 25 General Oberg arrived at the military hospital in Verdun; he had decided to take charge of Stülpnagel's interrogation personally.

It was Oberg's wish that Stülpnagel, now blind and helpless, might be induced to speak freely without being tortured. For once, Oberg was acting in the character of an old-school army officer rather than as the grand master of the Gestapo when he came to sit by Stülpnagel's bedside. Stülpnagel was willing to assume the entire burden of guilt, and he made no attempt to exonerate himself. He only asked one favor of Oberg, that his family be spared any reprisal. This promise would not be kept. Stülpnagel was allowed to remain in Verdun until his wounds had healed; then the SS brought him to Berlin and the People's Court, and then to the gallows.

In Paris a notably efficient Gestapo agent called Maulaz succeeded in arresting Hofacker on July 25. On the twenty-third Baron von Teuchert had visited him in his hiding place. Hofacker hoped to get his family to safety, and then to make his own way to Switzerland or to join the French Resistance. But there would not be time enough for that.

The Gestapo was counting on Hofacker to be a treasure trove of information for them, but he kept silent until the very end. Through five months of captivity he faced death with the same tranquil courage, and finally, when it became clear that he would admit nothing, he was hanged on December 20, 1944, the last victim of the July 20 uprising in Paris.

Ewald Heinrich von Kleist was to have better luck. He was set free by the Gestapo in the hope that he would put them on the track of a close friend, General Hammerstein's son, who had been a fugitive since the night of the coup. The ruse was unsuccessful, since both young officers sought the protection of their old CO, the commander of the Potsdam Regiment, who provided them with special travel orders for the front. In the confusion that followed in the wake of Valkyrie the regimental staff was apparently unaware they had both been summarily expelled from the army, and at the war's end they found themselves in the relative safety of the Italian front.

In the last days of July little encouraging news reached Marshal von Kluge at his headquarters at La Roche–Guyon. The SD was off the leash, and there were more suicides every day. General Henning von Tresckow, now commanding the Second Army in the east, crept out into no-man's land and blew his head off with a rifle grenade. General Wagner, the quartermaster-general, shot himself, as did Lieutenant Colonel von Voss, who had served under Witzleben on the western front. (Prompted by Stülpnagel's unfortunate example, General Wagner held a pistol to each temple to make certain he would be killed outright.) Colonel von Linstow, his health broken, might have been easy prey for the Gestapo, but he died heroically, without revealing a single name.

In August, on the other side of the lines, Marshal Paulus was finally stirred to action. He had been reluctant to lend his support to the Committee for a Free Germany, since he did not feel that it was appropriate for officers who had been taken prisoner to engage in political activity. But at the end of July and in early August, when he gradually learned the details of the abortive military uprising, he began to reexamine his decision. Then came the news that his old comrades Witzleben and Hoepner had been in the front rank of the insurgents. He was well acquainted with Stauffenberg, who had served under him in the Organizational Section of OKH, and when he learned of his courageous attempt to destroy Hitler, all of Paulus' earlier reservations vanished; his oath of allegiance had become a dead letter.

On August 8 Witzleben and Hoepner were condemned to death by the People's Court, after a vicious and degrading show trial, and hanged. On the same day Marshal Paulus broadcast an appeal to the German armies in the east over the Soviet radio. His entire family was immediately picked up by the Gestapo.

At the daily conference on August 15 General Jodl asked brusquely, "Has Marshal von Kluge returned to his headquarters yet, or has he gone over to the enemy?" This question was clearly prompted by Hitler's own suspicions; Kluge had left on an inspection tour of his forward outposts several days before, and since then there had been no word of him.

On the morning of August 17 Marshal Model, whom Hitler had just appointed to replace Kluge, arrived in Paris with the order relieving Kluge of his command. The Führer had not thought it worthwhile to inform Kluge himself of his demotion, though this was confirmed by a telegram, signed by Keitel, which arrived at La Roche–Guyon at seven o'clock that evening: "Marshal von Kluge, commander in chief on the western front and commander of Army Group B, is relieved from active duty. He will be succeeded by Marshal Model." By then Kluge had returned to La Roche–Guyon, and this brutal dismissal struck a bitter blow to his pride; the sequel would be even less agreeable—an investigation, arrest by the Gestapo, quickly followed by the verdict of a court-martial. "It's all over," he told Blumentritt. "Say good-by to your wife and children for me." Then, drawing himself up, he added, "It won't be as difficult as all that, Blumentritt."

He planned to leave La Roche–Guyon the day after Model's arrival. He wrote a letter to his wife, which he entrusted to his orderly officer— much to the surprise of the latter, since presumably the marshal would be seeing his family again in a day or two. A short while later Kluge gave him another for his son, a lieutenant in the army, and a third addressed to the Führer.

He left at dawn on the nineteenth, accompanied by his orderly officer and a small armed escort. The Americans had crossed the Seine and had advanced as far as Vernon and Maintes-la-Jolie, almost due east of them, so they were obliged to make a wide detour to the north. When they reached the forest of Compiègne, Kluge ordered a brief halt, got out of the car, and began to pace.

They set off again, heading east now, along the same route through the battlegrounds of the First World War that Stülpnagel had followed a few weeks earlier. At noon Kluge asked the driver to stop again. With the sun directly overhead, the August heat was stifling. They spread out a blanket on the ground in the shade of a small grove of trees, and Kluge sat down, a little apart from the others. They brought him something to eat, and then he asked his orderly officer for some stationery, since he wanted to write to his brother (who was a lieutenant general). About fifteen minutes later he handed his orderly officer an envelope, asked him to make sure that it reached his brother as soon as possible, and added, "Get ready to set off again immediately." His orderly officer had scarcely turned around when Kluge took out a cyanide capsule, broke it open, and held it up to his face. He died within seconds—he had chosen the same way out that Rommel would be coerced into taking several months later, on October 14.

The last lines of Kluge's letter to Hitler read: "I am taking my leave of you, my Führer, as one who has been closer to you than you may realize, and firm in the conviction that I have always done my duty to the utmost of my powers. Heil, my Führer!"

In Paris meanwhile the devotees of total collaboration and "the new European order" were determined to hold out to the end—and even still cherished hopes of an eventual German victory. "I have always been at some pains," wrote Jacques de Lesdain in *L'Illustration*, "to implant in the minds of my readers the conviction, nay the certainty, that the armies of the Reich will be quite capable of throwing back the enemy on the day the supreme command decides to unleash their reserves." He added that ". . . the fact that the Führer has emerged unscathed from a frightful ordeal that was actuated by the blackest treachery and perfidy cannot be explained as mere happenstance. The sort of chance which on several widely separated occasions has preserved the life of a man whose death had been envisaged by a meticulously planned conspiracy deserves the name of Providence or Destiny.

"This attempt on the life of the founder of the new Europe, the inaugurator of this magnificent and supremely rational design, represents the culmination of the most dangerous of all the intrigues that have been hatched by the adversaries of a new order that will sweep away all false preconceptions and lead the struggle against the disgraceful, self-serving machinations of certain sectors of society.

"The creation of a new Europe, united, stable, and secure, must seem (in the eyes of everyone who is not blinded by hatred) to be the only practicable and equitable solution to the problems that have been created by the inevitable participation of the masses in our political life. The removal of the Führer under the present circumstances might very well have discouraged many of those who have contributed their labors to the building of this new Europe. . . . Destiny has shown us once again that the founder of National Socialism has been chosen to bring this great European enterprise to fruition. . . . The only tangible result of the activities of his enemies has been to harden the will of the faithful, to inspire them with an unshakable determination to conquer. . . . The creation of a new Europe is even more of a certainty today than it was before the tragic events of the twentieth of July."

And while the ideologues of collaboration dreamed of a united Europe under the National Socialist banner, the captive press observed that "Paris and her gifted creative artists have given evidence of their serenity and their faith that France is about to take wing again, which is the highest aspiration of the French people." Advertisements inserted by Balenciaga, Lanvin, Lelong, Patou, Rochas, and Maggy-Rouff (haute couture); Mauboussin, Van Cleef et Arpels (jewelry); Leroy, Max (furs); and Hermès (deluxe leather goods) furnished a more pragmatic demonstration of the assertion that "Paris is still very much alive."

General Heusinger had been taken directly to the Rastenburg district hospital immediately after the explosion; his arms, legs, and face were badly burned and both his eardrums had been pierced. He was arrested by two Gestapo agents on July 23, acting on Himmler's orders. After his release from the hospital, he was conveyed by three uniformed Gestapo men to the Prinz Albrechtstrasse prison in Berlin, where he was lodged in an underground cell pending interrogation. The cell door was left unlocked, though there were two SS men standing guard in the corridor. During his first night in prison, the air-raid sirens sent everyone scuttling down to the shelters, and Heusinger found himself standing next to Ernst Kaltenbrunner, head of the SD, who asked him point-blank, "How long had you known about it, general?"

Although Heusinger had still not completely recovered from the shock of being blown off his feet by a bomb just a week or so earlier, he still had the presence of mind to reply unhesitatingly, "I find that question unacceptable, and I will not answer it."

Simply having been aware of the plot was worth a death sentence, but Heusinger's defense was rock-solid: After all, he himself had been severely burned and had sustained other injuries as well, for which he was still being treated in the prison infirmary.

His first interrogation began with a Kripo inspector reading him a series of statements he was alleged to have made between 1941 and 1944. "This is taken from the testimony of one of the conspirators, General Heusinger. You have always spoken very harshly of the Führer. You advocated a wholesale reorganization of the command structure, and you insisted that our Führer should be set aside. Do you admit that you made these statements, and do you have anything else to say?"

"I can't tell you if I expressed these sentiments in the precise terms and under the precise circumstances you have described. But I don't deny that I did make certain statements to that effect, if not in those identical words."

"Do you admit that you have been in overt opposition to the Führer for years?"

"I didn't approve of his military decisions. There were a great many of them that I believed to be extremely ill advised, and I did everything in my power to mitigate their effects at least, for the good of the men at the front."

"And when did you begin to take this attitude?"

"At first during the Russian campaign, and then increasingly so after Stalingrad."

"And in spite of these opinions, you still chose to remain at your post?"

"I made no attempt to conceal my opinions, as far as was consistent with military discipline."

"But you still expressed the wish that the Führer should be forcibly removed from power."

"Excuse me, but I don't believe that the words 'forcibly removed from power' appear anywhere in the statements I'm accused of having made. I wanted the Führer to step down as supreme commander in favor of a professional soldier, and I particularly wanted Marshal Keitel to be replaced by someone more competent. Ask your witnesses if, apart from that, I have ever said one word—either to them directly or in their presence—in behalf of a violent solution."

"But didn't the spirit of your remarks still encompass such a solution?"

"I leave you to rule on whatever insinuations you might care to make about the intent of these statements—after the fact. I demand to be confronted with my accusers."

Forty-eight hours later Heusinger was brought face to face with the state's principal witness against him, in the presence of the Kripo inspector who had questioned him earlier. "I have only one thing to ask you," Heusinger said. "In the conversations that you've described, did I ever say anything about removing the Führer by force?"

"I've never claimed that you did. In my deposition I simply wanted to clarify the underlying causes that resulted in the attempt on the Führer's life."

"And that was still the construction that you put on General Heusinger's remarks?" the inspector asked.

"From all that I have heard, that is the only possible construction."

The witness was asked to set down a written declaration of everything he had told his interrogators so far.

Three weeks later Heusinger was questioned again, this time by a different police inspector.

"Did you know General von Tresckow?"

"Yes, before the war he was one of my staff officers."

"Had you had much contact with him since the beginning of the war?"

"Yes, as head of the Operations Section, I often met with the various chiefs of staff and other officers from the army groups, including Tresckow."

"Did he come to see you often?"

"Several times."

"Do you know what's become of him?"

"He's been killed, as far as I know."

"Really? Then you don't think he's with the Russians?"

"I can't imagine what he'd be doing there."

"And what did the two of you talk about?"

"Urgent military matters."

"Didn't you feel that he tended to be very skeptical?"

"He was an especially intelligent staff officer, a man of wide-ranging views. He and I were both disturbed by the way in which the war was being conducted."

"He never told you anything of his plans?"

"What plans do you mean? I don't follow."

"His plans for removing the Führer as supreme commander."

"I spoke to him about the structure of the high command. We were looking for men who would be more capable than Keitel and the current roster of generals in facing up to the gigantic problems that we were confronted with."

"Did he broach any other subjects with you?"

"He often asked for my opinion of the military situation."

"And who else was present during these conversations?"

"We were alone, for the most part."

"Do you know Fabian von Schlabrendorff, Tresckow's orderly officer?"

"Yes, but only by sight."

"And since he accompanied Tresckow, he must have taken part in these conversations."

"No, he used to wait outside."

"But he still brought you a letter from Tresckow on one occasion?"

"Possibly. When?"

"During the winter of '43–'44. What was in that letter?"

"I only have a vague memory of it—something to do with some personnel problem."

"Ah! And Schlabrendorff discussed the contents of this letter with you?"

"I don't believe that I spoke to him at all, since I scarcely knew him."

"Why did Tresckow send you this letter by messenger instead of through the mails?"

"As far as I know, Schlabrendorff happened to be going to Berlin already, and he dropped off the letter on his way. That's common practice."

"And what was the personnel problem that he wanted to bring to your attention?"

"It had to do with filling certain vacant positions on the general staff."

"We are in possession of that letter, general."

"Then why are you asking me all these questions? You know better than I do what that letter is about."

"You discussed the plot against the Führer with Tresckow, and on more than one occasion. We have concrete evidence of this." The Kripo man assumed a threatening air, as if he were about to produce the incriminating documents on the spot, but Heusinger was not intimidated, since he had already had some experience of this sort of ploy.

"I would be very interested to see how you would go about proving such an allegation—why don't you show me now?" With this the session came abruptly to an end, and Heusinger was led back to his cell. The interrogation was not resumed until several days later.

"Do you know General Wagner, and did you often come into contact with him?"

"I know him quite well, and we worked together extremely closely."

"Do you know General Fellgiebel?"

"Yes, I saw him almost every day."

"What were your relations with General Stieff?"

"Good. He served under me for some time."

"Did you know Olbricht and Stauffenberg? Did you often have occasion to work with them?"

"Yes, from time to time."

"And so, you knew all of these people, and yet you claim that you knew nothing of their plans!"

"You seem, sir, to have no idea of the sort of responsibilities which my position involves; otherwise you wouldn't be asking me any of these questions."

"One of the defendants claims that he told you at the beginning of July that an attempt would be made on the Führer's life. What do you have to say to that?"

"I don't believe it. He must be mistaken."

"We shall see. . . . And what do you understand to be the underlying causes of the assassination plot?"

"Simply the way in which the situation has developed since 1941, since Stalingrad in particular, culminating in a crisis of confidence and an act of desperation at the eleventh hour."

"Could you be more specific?"

"You can't expect to take it all in at a glance, any more than you could sort out all the various cooperative links between the different branches of the high command. I'm willing to set it all down for you in writing, but that would take several days."

"Very well then," said the investigator.

At the beginning of September, Heusinger was brought face to face with a brilliant young colonel [1] who was now both a defendant and a state's witness. He confirmed that he had not breathed a word to Heusinger about the plot against the Führer but had simply communicated his impressions about the mood of the younger officers. Afterward he asked to speak privately with Heusinger; they were allowed a few moments together, but with a police officer standing by.

"General," the colonel began, "I'm going to be hanged tomorrow. I'm glad that I'll have this chance to speak with you—and this is the last conversation I'll have with anyone in this life. I've always had tremendous confidence in you, and I want to thank you for interceding on my behalf. Yes, I found out about that, you know."

"I did what I could, and I'm very sorry I wasn't successful."

"I'm paying the price now for not having told them what I knew. Tell General Zeitzler that I only found out about the assassination plot on June 30, 1944. I want him to know that. And I'm going to ask you, general, to convey my last farewells to my wife for me. I've written her a letter, but whether she'll get it or not is another matter."

"I'll do what I can. You can count on me."

"You've taken a great weight off my mind. Good-by, general. Till we meet in another world."

Heusinger was deeply touched by this last encounter with the young colonel. "Isn't there any chance of saving him?" he asked one of the police officials. "He didn't get involved in this business deliberately. He's a splendid fellow, a very valuable officer."

"Nothing can be done about it. He's implicated in the plot."

"But does it have to be the death penalty?"

"I advise you, general, not to try to do anything more for him. Your own case is still far from being cleared up, the charges against you are very serious, and you'd be taking the risk of attracting even more suspicion onto yourself."

"I was simply asking out of common humanity, out of pity for a comrade."

1. General Heusinger has requested that this officer not be mentioned by name.

After a few more sessions with his interrogators, the charges against Heusinger were dropped for lack of any conclusive evidence, though he was still to be detained in the Ravensbrück concentration camp, near the little town of Furstenberg. His orderly found out where he was being held and packed a suit of civilian clothes into a bundle, which he brought along with him to the camp. At the camp gates he told the sentry, "I want to see my general."

"What?" said the SS man. "You want to see your general? And you nothing but a private—or just who do you think you are?"

But the orderly was so insistent that the sentry finally let him pass. When Heusinger unrolled the bundle, he found a revolver wrapped up in a pair of pants.

"No," Heusinger said to his orderly, "I won't be needing this. Take it back with you, and take these [the torn, burnt remains of his uniform] back to my wife for me."

Heusinger was released in September 1944. Shortly afterward he was summoned to OKH headquarters at Angerburg, less than five miles from the Wolf's Lair, where he was informed by Guderian, OKH chief of staff since July 21, that the Führer was expecting him. He was shown into Hitler's private refectory, a drab, depressing little room furnished with a large round wooden table and a few chairs. When standing to greet the general, Hitler appeared to be seriously ill—he was stooped over, much more so than before the explosion, his left arm trembled convulsively, and he was a mass of nervous tics and twitches. He looked at Heusinger for a long time, then said, "I'm sorry, general, that you too had to be dragged into this investigation, and I'm sorry that you've been subjected to such treatment. . . ."

"It was a very painful experience for me."

"I imagine it must have been. Sit down, general. One thing that all this has taught me is that dying is very easy and very quick. . . . If I had never regained consciousness, I would not even have been aware of my own death. And if my life had ended then and there, I would have been released from all my worries, from the sleepless nights, and from a painful nervous affliction. A split second is enough to take you away from all this and deliver you to eternal rest and peace.

"One thing you must realize about this whole business is that it never disturbed me to be the target of an assassination plot. In my position I have to expect that sort of thing every day. How many have already failed, and how many more are hatching at this very moment? That doesn't bother me. But what has wounded me to the quick is that all the elements of both the left and the right that I thought had either been won over or put out of the way of doing any further harm have sensed that their time has finally come. I treated these gentlemen too well; I paid them their pensions, I no longer considered them to be dangerous, and I stopped worrying about them altogether. And what thanks do I get for it? They spring up again the moment they feel a shift in the wind, with every petty lordling from east of the Elbe right behind them. But I'm going to be ruthless in putting things back in order. I can't permit my work to be endangered once again by such a lunatic enterprise. I'm going to scourge them out, this little cabal, with a rod of iron, and they'll get no more than what they've asked for."

Hitler fell silent, as if he were expecting Heusinger to signal his approval of this program, but Heusinger did not say a word.

"I have the three-page report that you wrote in prison, and I thank you for it. It's the only coherent criticism of the measures that I've been forced to adopt during this war that I've ever read. I don't agree with you. I understand that the faction which opposed my decisions coalesced in 1942. But as chief of state I cannot consider everything exclusively from the military point of view. I couldn't lose sight of the political and economic consequences of my decisions, or their impact in the realm of propaganda. And in any case I couldn't always explain all the factors involved in every decision I made. Where would that leave us, after all?"

"Of course not," Heusinger replied. "But we mustn't forget that we have met with nothing but setbacks since Stalingrad. When a series of decisions results in as many defeats, it's only natural that this begins to give rise to an increasing amount of doubt and criticism."

Heusinger's analysis was scarcely to the Führer's liking, and his voice hardened as he continued. "Nevertheless I have every right to expect that my subordinates' confidence in me will overcome all such doubts. And I have all the more right to expect this when the situation becomes critical. . . . And just as I require the lowliest foot soldier to carry out his orders on the spot, blindly and unquestioningly, I require my generals to do the same."

Heusinger made another attempt to explain his position. "Most of the generals have had an extensive military education. When they take part in an operation, they are accustomed to put a great deal of work and a great deal of thought into it. They feel that they have a heavy responsibility to the men under their command. You would be hard put to forbid them to think, to turn them into unreasoning instruments of command, and to force them to act perhaps contrary to the dictates of their consciences."

"There you have it!" Hitler shouted back. "The legacy of Messrs. Fritsch, Beck, and Brauchitsch! I made a serious error when I entrusted those gentlemen with the formation and training of the officer corps. I thought that they'd be carrying out my program, but since I've been in command of the army myself, I've been forced to acknowledge a little more each day how much they deceived me. I've often regretted that I didn't carry out a purge of my officer corps the way Stalin did. I have to, I want to make up for that now. It's long past time. . . . I want them finally to learn to obey me blindly. What I ask of the Party and of the entire German people, the army must do also. It isn't the generals who must bear the responsibility, it is I and I alone, and if that doesn't suit them, then they're of no use to me at all."

The audience was at an end. Hitler got up, showed Heusinger to the door, and shook his hand. "Go now. You must rest, general. Go back to your family. Later, we shall see."

As soon as word reached the front that a bomb had been detonated at Rastenburg and that Hitler had survived unscathed, Hitler's GHQ was deluged with congratulatory messages and professions of continued loyalty from all the senior commanders of the Wehrmacht; Kluge's was one of the first to arrive. The police investigation which began the following day soon fanned out to cover the entire territory of the Reich; the eventual roundup spared no one, and anyone suspected of being an opponent of the regime was arrested, as well as those who were implicated, however remotely, in the plot itself.

A military tribunal, made up of Field Marshal Gerd von Rundstedt and a few Nazi loyalist generals, was convened to deal with the military conspirators, although this was just the first step—anyone convicted by the tribunal would be stripped of his military rank and handed over to the secular arm—the People's Court—to be tried and sentenced. The president of the People's Court was a notorious butcher, Dr. Roland Freisler—a former militant Communist who had seen the light and joined the Nazi Party in 1925. Freisler, dressed in dark-red robes, called the first session of the People's Court to order on August 1. The first batch of defendants included Marshal von Witzleben, Generals Hoepner, Hase, and Stieff, and Lieutenants Yorck von Wartenburg and Albrecht von Hagen—both close associates of Stauffenberg. None of the defendants expressed any regret during the two-day trial for having allowed themselves to become enemies of the Reich. The trial itself was a caricature of justice; Freisler badgered, browbeat, and insulted the defendants and did not make the slightest effort to preserve the fiction of the court's impartiality. The court-appointed attorneys offered no defense, except to appeal for a mitigation of sentence—death by firing squad instead of being hanged and then suspended from meathooks as Hitler had ordered: "I want to see them hanging like carcasses in a slaughterhouse."

The German press published pictures of the defendants which were reprinted all over the world: Marshal von Witzleben, one of the victors of the Battle of France, was dressed in a suit of civilian clothes that was much too big for him, with no tie or suspenders, and nothing but a piece of string to hold his trousers up; his fellow officers were decked out in the same scarecrow style. Whenever Witzleben stood up to speak in his own defense, he had to clutch at the waistband of his trousers to keep them from slipping down, a final humiliation that was too great for the marshal to bear.

Sentence was carried out two hours after the verdict was announced. They were all hanged slowly to prolong the agony, and on Goebbels' orders the entire proceeding was preserved on film.

Most of the architects of the various plots against Hitler were reunited for the last time in the Prinz Albrechtstrasse prison: General Oster, Admiral Canaris, Ambassador von Hassell, Count Herbert von Bismarck, Count Heinrich von Lehndorff (an associate of Tresckow's on the eastern front), Pastor Dietrich Bonhoeffer, and, ironically enough, General Fromm himself. The general, who had tried to save his own skin by sending Stauffenberg and Olbricht to their deaths, had been arrested because it was felt that he had been insufficiently energetic in putting down the abortive putsch at the Bendlerstrasse. After enduring lengthy torture sessions at the hands of the Gestapo, Fromm would be sentenced to death for cowardice and finally executed on March 19, 1945, in Brandenburg prison.

Although a number of the guards at the Prinz Albrechtstrasse were not SS men (a few of them were actually Communists) and did what they could to make their charges' lives more bearable, the prisoners were interrogated, and often tortured, in frequent and interminable relays, day and night. In August Count von Helldorf, the Berlin prefect of police, and his deputy, Count Fritz von der Schulenburg, were both hanged,[2] as was Otto Kiep, a member of a separate anti-Nazi group that had formed around Count von Moltke. Ambassador von Hassell,

---

2. Count Friedrich von der Schulenburg, the diplomat, who was Beck's close friend and former commanding officer during the First World War, was also executed on August 10.

Colonel Hausen, and Colonel Schmend followed them to the gallows in September. The executions continued through October, November, and December. There were some who managed to cheat the hangman: the Christian trade-union leader Max Haberman poisoned himself from fear that he would betray those who had sheltered him when he was a fugitive, and the Communist Franz Jacob, also afraid that he would crack under torture, hanged himself in his cell.

On the eastern front Major Fabian von Schlabrendorff was detailed to escort Tresckow's body back to Germany for burial in the family vault. The general had been so close to the Russian lines when he killed himself that it was naturally assumed that he had been killed in action; however, his role in the conspiracy was disclosed soon enough. Gestapo men broke into the crypt, removed the body, and brought it to Sachsen-hausen concentration camp, where it was burned before Schlabrendorff's eyes. He was arrested on August 17 and taken to the Prinz Albrecht-strasse.

Stülpnagel was finally released from the Verdun military hospital and brought first to Berlin, then to the concentration camp at Fursten-berg, where General Heusinger was briefly one of his fellow inmates. Stülpnagel was interrogated and tortured up to the end; he was finally garrotted on August 30. Count Helmut von Moltke, an outspoken oppo-nent of the regime, was also picked up in the dragnet, though he was not connected with the assassination plot. He was held in Tegel prison, and the prison chaplain allowed him to take communion for the last time, along with his wife, before he was executed on January 23, 1945. On April 9, 1945, Admiral Canaris managed to tap out a message to the occupant of the adjacent cell in Flossenburg prison. "They're sup-posed to hang me tomorrow." In fact he was garrotted with a violin string, in a grotesque ordeal that lasted half an hour.

Fabian von Schlabrendorff continued to deny that he had in any way participated in the conspiracy, which meant that he was subjected to the most atrocious tortures that Himmler's inquisitors could devise. His trial began on February 3, 1945, with the hanging judge Roland Freisler still on the bench. Suddenly the proceedings were interrupted by the wail of the air-raid sirens; Freisler scooped up the documents in the case and made for the shelter, but not quickly enough. The court-room sustained a direct hit, the floor collapsed, Freisler was buried in the rubble, and the Gestapo's dossier on the defendant Schlabrendorff was reduced to ashes.

When Schlabrendorff's case was finally called again, on March 16, the new president of the court, Dr. Krohne, presented a fresh bill of indictment against him, which was so vaguely worded that Schlabrendorff was actually acquitted. However, he was still detained in prison, then transferred to Flossenburg, where he was informed that he could expect to be shot all the same By the end of March, with the Russians approaching Berlin, the pace of the executions quickened every day; trials became even more perfunctory, or were dispensed with altogether. The victims of this last-minute killing frenzy included Fritz Goerdeler (brother of Carl Friedrich), General Fellgiebel, Generals Lindemann, Thiele, and von Thungen (all associated with Olbricht in the Valkyrie network in Berlin), and Bishop Otto Muller. There would in fact be several thousand summary executions before the collapse of the Third Reich; the SS guards usually first went through the gruesome charade of turning their prisoners loose before dispatching them with a bullet in the back of the neck.

Of course executions without trial were by no means confined to the last few weeks of the war. General von Sponeck—who had absolutely no connection with the conspiracy—was murdered in his cell a few days after July 20. Major Kuhn, the original custodian of the conspirators' stockpile of explosives, managed to escape through the Russian lines, but only because his brigade commander, General von Thieberg, had delayed carrying out the order for his arrest. Thieberg was sentenced to nine months' imprisonment, but the judgment was vacated on Hitler's orders, and Thieberg was cut down in his cell.

The trials and executions—with or without trials—continued virtually to the end; as the military situation grew more dismal and chaotic, prisoners were hastily transferred from camp to camp in the path of the advancing Allied armies. A number of conspirators were liberated before their captors could execute them, including Schlabrendorff, General Thomas, Pastors Niemoller and Gerstenmaier, and Hjalmar Schacht. In spite of the many occasions on which he had rebuffed, deserted, and "betrayed" the conspirators, General Halder had still found his way into a concentration camp, though he too survived the massacre at war's end.

In September, Heusinger had rejoined his family, who had taken refuge in the Harz Mountains, near the present East German border. He was kept under close surveillance by the Gestapo until the end of March 1945, by which time the Americans were already approaching. He left his family, and in the mountains he fell in with a small headquarters staff who had lost their troops and joined them in a long march toward the south, across Thuringia, Bohemia, and Bavaria. Heusinger was making for Friedrichshafen on Lake Constance, in the hope of crossing the border into Switzerland. Throughout April, as he recalls today, "I saw a number of German army units fighting bravely to the end in hopeless circumstances, and a people without food, close to despair, unable to believe that it was all over and the war was lost." His journey from Saxony to Bavaria brought him into daily contact with the ordinary people of Germany. One of his chance companions on the road south, an electrician in his fifties, remarked to Heusinger one day, "It seems to me, general, that we're going to lose the war."

"Here we are in March 1945," Heusinger replied, "and it's taken you until now to figure that out?"

This gives some indication of the extent to which the German people were still mesmerized by Goebbels' propaganda; they never broke out of step until the very end, and they remained convinced even then that the war might still be won.

15.

March 1945–May 1945: "In the Best Interests of the Nation"

Hitler had now completely withdrawn from the world, into a seclusion that was equally reminiscent of the cloister and the dungeon. He refused to acknowledge the reality of what was happening at the front, though he still continued to suspect that his subordinates were keeping something from him. He saw every officer of the Wehrmacht as a potential plotter and every general as a traitor—though he made a grudging exception to this rule in the case of his faithful junior partners, Keitel, Jodl, and Burgdorf.[1] Many of those in his immediate entourage attributed the pathological stubbornness and destructive bloodlust of his last days both to his isolation and to his rapid physical decline. His skin was washed-out and pale, his eyes dull and lifeless; in addition to the persistent tremor in his left arm he was now troubled by stomach cramps, and he was coughing and spitting constantly. Sometimes bedridden for two or three days at a time, he was also suffering from insomnia, so that the daily military conferences might not convene until three or four in the morning.

The conduct of the war itself had become a completely hypothetical exercise, a map-table fantasy in which orders were still relayed to armies that no longer existed. Hitler's characteristic concern with organizational details had finally become an obsession, which led him to dissipate his still formidable powers of concentration on insignificant trifles that were scarcely worth the notice of a battalion or company commander. Of his generals, Marshal von Manstein still commanded his respect (though he had not commanded an army group since March 1944). "One of our greatest strategists," Hitler said of him. "I would gladly give him twenty divisions if I had them."

From the time of Halder's disgrace in the fall of 1942 until April 21, 1945, two stenographers sat in at all the military conferences at

---

1. General Wilhelm Burgdorf, Schmundt's successor as head of the Army Personnel Office. [Tr.]

Hitler's GHQ. "It is without historical precedent," wrote Helmut Heiber, "to have stenographers present at a top-secret meeting, and to have every word that is uttered put down on paper. To have made such a decision would take no less than the boundless self-confidence and the ever vigilant suspiciousness of a Hitler."

These last, certainly, were two qualities that Hitler still possessed in abundance and the records of the last "daily briefings" (actually midnight harangues on familiar themes that often went on until shortly before daybreak) most often show him gloating over fallen enemies, speculating endlessly on the series of "miracles" that he constantly expected would come to redeem the Third Reich, and ventilating all the ancient grievances of his younger days—the Viennese tramp's contempt for the Slavs, the Italians, the Jews, and all the other lesser breeds of the Hapsburg dominions, the fanatical patriot's disdain for the cowardly generals at the front and the treacherous, backstabbing politicians at home—all mingled together with the usual alternation of stupefying banality with bravura passages of inspired lunatic banter.

To begin with, then, the "Bohemian corporal's" last laugh on the Prussian officer caste: "These empty-headed lordlings are a breed apart, with their arrogant airs, an animal plague on the nation, riddled with cowardice and effete notions. Sometimes I hate them even more than the Jews—who at least know themselves for what they are. They never want to be soldiers, whereas these others are constantly claiming that right for themselves as their exclusive prerogative. . . ."

The Italian commanders: "They have fifty thousand men down there under the command of the duke of Bergamo. . . . A duke of Bergamo, a duke of Pistoia, it has to be a duke! But when you actually meet these dukes, as I have, you see that they're all such chowderheads that you can truthfully say that they're nothing more than a lump of fish paste wrapped up in a ducal title."

The navigational prowess of Goering's Luftwaffe: "I heard them say too many times, 'We couldn't locate London.' It's disgraceful not to be able to find London! And then these same hapless imbeciles come back and tell me, 'Yes, my Führer, when the enemy bombers reached Dortmund, their radio guidance system enabled them to drop their bombs on buildings that were five hundred meters wide and two hundred and fifty meters long.' Idiots! And we still can't manage to find London, which is fifty kilometers in diameter and a hundred and fifty kilometers from the French coast!"

The Italian tanks: "It's been my observation that in every engagement they were always quick as lightning—to break down. Two or three days later there'd only be one of them left. The others were all back in the repair sheds."

On ensuring the stability of the western front: "We have to take care that courageous officers are assigned to defend our strong points, and not just windbags like that General von Schlieben, who was sent to Cherbourg, issued a blustering proclamation, then went out to the most advanced blockhouse, waited for the enemy to arrive, and ran up the white flag.

"I've made an unalterable decision. I have no interest at all in this damned seniority system—it's a question of men, and nothing else. It all depends on the man, and if I choose a junior officer to fill a difficult post instead of a divisional commander or a fortress commandant, then he'll be worth ten of them. These generals are a pack of yellow-bellies! In our country they're trained to think that it's perfectly natural for everyone else to give up their lives for them. But in fact they're already peeking over at the enemy lines and saying to themselves, 'What could happen to us after all? We'll be taken prisoner, we'll be treated with all the deference that's due to our rank, particularly those of us who are of noble birth, and then we won't have to have anything to do with this rabble on our own side.' This is intolerable, and that's why we'll have to review the roster of all these fortress commandants. This Cherbourg business should be a lesson to us. What a disgrace! And we mustn't let them stammer out some excuse to the effect that we shouldn't make too much of such-and-such an incident for fear of doing damage to the army. Or that it's better into the bargain to heap praise on an individual commander: that's what we've always felt to be the greatest of the criminal errors committed by the Italians—to turn a coward into a hero, some unprincipled bastard who actually behaves even worse than some bastard of a Communist, since *he* at least is fighting for an idea!

"We simply pass over these swine in silence, or if we do mention then, we try to praise them so it's not so obvious what a filthy mess they've made of things. It can't go on like this!" (The German press and radio had lionized General von Schlieben as "the valiant defender of Cherbourg," a hero who had held out to the bitter end.)

An unexpected commentary on the attempt of July 20: "It had a truly miraculous effect, inasmuch as the shock almost cured me of my nervous disability. I still suffer from a slight tremor in my left leg when the daily conference goes on for too long, but before the explosion my leg twitched even when I was lying down—but I don't mean to imply that that's the recommended treatment."

A tirade inspired by the appearance of the first batch of defendants before the People's Court: "When you see these people, they're a horribly degraded lot. At one time I stripped General Hoepner of his rank not only because he disobeyed a direct order but also because he was a man of drastically limited mentality. . . . It was apparent right away when the defendants stood in the dock what small-minded fellows they all were. The judges on the tribunal even asked how such men could ever become officers. Yes! How did they indeed? It was simply because I was forced to take what I could get."

And when all was lost, Hitler was still hopeful: "Each of the partners in the enemy coalition went into the war with the idea of putting something over on the others. The United States, the former colony, wants to inherit England's colonial empire before it sinks into the sea. Russia wants to acquire the Balkans, the Dardanelles, Iranian oil, Iran itself, and the Persian Gulf. England is trying to prop up her own position and to strengthen herself in the Mediterranean. In other words, there will come a time—and it may come at any moment, since history is made by mere mortals on the other side as well—when this coalition will disintegrate." And when Hitler learned of Roosevelt's death on April 12, 1945, he went into a transport ecstasy, since he was convinced that the miracle he had predicted had finally come to pass, just as it had in the days of Frederick the Great.[2]

One day Hermann Otto Fegelein, Hitler's Waffen SS liaison officer and the husband of Eva Braun's sister,[3] was singing the praises of SS General Hauser, who courageously exposed his person to enemy fire without the slightest regard for the consequences: "When an enemy shell passes overhead, and his ADCs throw themselves on their bellies, he yells out, 'What's the matter—you afraid?' "

Hitler replied, "So would I—I'd get down on my belly too, and I knew only one general who didn't do the same—he hadn't heard the shell coming."

The last of the transcripts that has survived covers the daily conference of March 23, 1945, the day on which the Allies finally crossed

2. The "Miracle of the House of Brandenburg" occurred in 1762, when the death of the Tsarina Elizabeth of Russia took Frederick's most formidable enemy out of the war and saved Prussia from being overrun by a coalition of hostile powers.

3. This did not prevent him from being arrested and stripped of his rank for attempted desertion, and finally executed a few days before the end in reprisal for the treachery of his chief, Heinrich Himmler. (See p. 244).

the Rhine in force. General Patton had reached the west bank on the previous night, sent assault parties across the river in rafts, and thrown a pontoon bridge across the upper Rhine near Mainz, at the same time that General Montgomery's forces had established a bridgehead on the lower Rhine. Hitler began by calling on imaginary troops to plug up the crumbling dike; his mind was filled with a disorderly procession of ideas, and he seemed to be watching his phantom legions passing in review. The daily conference had convened that day at three o'clock in the morning. After dealing with the current emergency as best he could, Hitler moved on to a critique of the various non-German formations in the Wehrmacht, beginning with the Ukrainians: "Either they're trustworthy or they're not. It would be idiotic for me to put weapons in the hands of a division that isn't trustworthy. I'd prefer to take their weapons away from them and use them to arm a German division. . . . The same thing goes for the Vlasov division. . . .

"The Hindu brigade is a practical joke. There are Hindus who won't kill a louse—they'd rather be eaten alive—so it's hardly likely that they'd kill an Englishman. That just seems ludicrous to me. Why would the Hindus fight more bravely to defend our country than they fought at home, even under the leadership of Chandra Bose,[4] to free India from the English? Why would they be any braver back here? I suppose that if we used the Hindus to turn prayer wheels, or some similar occupation, there'd be no stopping them then. But the thought of using them in a real, bloody battle is ridiculous. Since we hardly have a surplus of matériel at our disposal, these harebrained propaganda stunts are totally unacceptable. . . .

"They've also been peddling stories about a Galician division. If this division were to consist of Austrian Ruthenes, then we'd have no choice but to take their weapons away from them immediately. The Austrian Ruthenes were pacifists; they were lambs, not wolves. In the Austrian army during the last war they were a pathetic lot. . . . But we would just be deluding ourselves with speculations like this, as I don't have the arms that we would need to equip these additional divisions. It's ridiculous, in fact."

Nevertheless Fegelein's aide-de-camp persisted in beating this dead horse. "The Hindu brigade," he remarked, "has an effective strength of twenty-three hundred men. That's not to be dismissed lightly."

4. Indian nationalist militant who raised the Hindu brigade in Germany in 1943; he later organized a more formidable "Indian National Army" of three divisions under the auspices of the Japanese, which fought on the Indo-Burmese border.

"It would give the Hindus the greatest pleasure," Hitler replied, "if we told them, 'There won't be any need for you to fire a single shot.' And what would you propose to do with the Hindu brigade?"

Embarrassed, the SS officer stammered out, "I really couldn't say. They've been at rest for some time now."

"But they've never been in action!" Hitler objected.

"No, my Führer."

"As far as I'm concerned, a unit that's at rest is a unit that's seen heavy fighting and is allowed to stop and gather its strength. Your troops are always gathering strength, but they never fight."

Hitler had lost France as quickly as he had conquered it in 1940. His first response to this calamity was to recall Marshal von Rundstedt from retirement once again as his new commander in chief in the West, in September 1944. Rundstedt met with the Führer before setting out for the front. "There's a man for you!" Hitler exulted to Keitel. "He's exactly what I need." He began to make preparations for a massive counteroffensive through the Ardennes, and in December, a few weeks before the offensive was to be launched, his divisional commanders were summoned for a final personal exhortation from the Führer.

"It is essential to wrest the enemy's confidence in his ultimate victory away from him with an offensive onslaught that will prove to him at the outset that his prospects for success are nil. . . . We must also prove to our adversary that no matter what he does, he will never be able to count on our surrendering. That much is clear.

"I have had to make a number of extremely critical decisions in my lifetime. Only a man who is prepared to sacrifice himself and to devote himself singlemindedly to a cause, setting aside all personal considerations, could have acted as I have done. I am convinced that no one will arise in the course of the next ten, twenty, thirty, even fifty years who will exercise more authority over the nation or will exhibit such joyful ardor in action as I have. . . .

"Listen well, gentlemen. If we are still capable of striking a few resounding blows, this 'united front' that is being artificially maintained between the ultracapitalist and the ultra-Marxist states—this 'united front,' I tell you, may well collapse all at once with the crash of a thunderclap. . . ."

And in the opening days of the Battle of the Bulge the Allies believed that they were facing a renascent Wehrmacht, but in fact this was nothing more than the death throes of a moribund Reich. The offensive in the

Ardennes did not have enough strength behind it, even on such a narrow front, and the last German drive in the west was totally stalled by year's end.

"Rundstedt," Hitler told Keitel, "is too old. He's not agile or energetic enough to get from one end of the front to the other anymore."

The supreme commander who had already brought this armies to destruction still persisted in his policy of forcing his generals to take the blame for every setback—all the more so now that the end was approaching. In February 1945 Guderian told Ribbentrop that the war was lost, and Ribbentrop scurried off immediately to tell Hitler that his chief of staff was harboring these defeatist sentiments. Hitler's confidence in Guderian was great but not unlimited—he had never made him a marshal, after all. He sent for Guderian and warned him that this sort of talk was nothing less than treason, and if there were any more incidents of this kind, then his rank would not save him from the firing squad or his family from imprisonment. (Albert Speer, the maverick war production minister, was also present, and Hitler's words were intended for him as well.) In March Guderian was dismissed, and the day-to-day conduct of operations on the eastern front was entrusted to General Krebs.

On April 22, however, Hitler was finally forced to confront the fact that the Russian siege of Berlin could not be raised and that there would be no escape from his underground bunker beneath the Chancellery. It was only then that he admitted for the first time that defeat was inevitable—this wrenching admission was followed by another torrent of abuse aimed at the traitors in the entourage. Then, after announcing that he would never abandon the capital, he added, "It's no longer a question of fighting—we have nothing left to fight with. As far as negotiations are concerned, Goering would make a much better job of it than I could."

The following day Goering's chief of staff, General Keller, flew from Berlin to Berchtesgaden, where Goering had already installed himself with a remnant of his staff. Keller repeated Hitler's remarks to his chief, including his promise to stay in Berlin until the end and his cryptic reference to "negotiations." (According to General Heusinger, Hitler actually had planned at one point to withdraw to Berchtesgaden and conduct the national resistance from this "Alpine redoubt.") Goering was all too eager to pick up the torch, even before it was dropped, and he immediately sent off a telegram to Berlin, essentially asking for confirmation of Hitler's intention to abdicate in his favor and authorization for the opening up of negotiations with the Allies. "I shall act," the message concluded, "in the best interests of the nation and of our people. You know what my feelings are toward you in these most critical hours of my life. These are beyond the power of any words of mine to express. May God protect you, and in spite of everything may He hasten your way here. Your loyal, Hermann Goering."

In Berlin, Martin Bormann was quick to interpret this as an ultimatum, and to remind Hitler of the Reichsmarshal's previous suspected attempts to treat with the enemy. Hitler was inclined to agree: "A contemptible ultimatum! Loyalty and honor are gone, only bitterness and betrayal remain. Before the end they're all going to turn against me." For the present Goering was to be informed that this démarche constituted an act of high treason, but that his life would be spared in recognition of his past services. Bormann took it upon himself to order the chief of the SS contingent at Berchtesgaden to put Goering under arrest. The Reichsmarshal submitted his resignation—Hitler's telegram had not offered much of an alternative—even while volunteering the opinion that it was essential to open negotiations with the Allies. He added that he himself would be willing to fly to Eisenhower's headquarters personally. General Ritter von Greim, who was appointed to succeed Goering as chief of the Luftwaffe, found that his new command consisted of little more than a handful of planes with nowhere to land.

On the evening of April 28 Hitler learned of another premature attempt to supplant him as the political leader of the Reich. Several days earlier Himmler had met with a Swedish emissary, Count Bernadotte, at the Swedish legation in Lübeck. His surrender proposals were transmitted to the British and American (but not the French or Soviet) governments, who consulted among themselves and then rejected them. Hitler responded to this with an outburst of truly staggering proportions—an onlooker might have supposed that he was in the final throes of delirium tremens. The defection of the Reichsführer, whose apparatus of police terror had been a constant prop of the regime, was to become even more apparent in the few days that remained. Now only Goebbels was left.

At three thirty in the afternoon of April 30, 1945, Hitler and Eva Braun, his bride of a little more than thirty-six hours, committed suicide. This was Hitler's decision alone, and by midnight their bodies had been buried in a shell crater, set alight in a "Viking funeral," and vanished without a trace into the smoking rubble of the Third Reich.

One question that still remains, and which will always remain, is, Why did the high command do nothing to bring the war to an end before the military situation had become so desperate? One general, in this case Adolf Heusinger though he could be any other senior German commander, responds, "This will be the accusation that the world will always be able to level against us, tomorrow or at any time in the future.

"Let us backtrack a bit. The number of generals who were aware of all the problems we were faced with was severely limited. There were two different courses open to them: Faithful to their oath of allegiance, they could try to ward off catastrophe by offering the benefit of their accumulated wisdom—depending of course on the extent to which the supreme commander would listen to them. Or indeed by stepping outside the bounds of military discipline, they could resort to violence against their supreme commander. A great many officers in leadership positions adopted the first solution. They stood up to Hitler I don't know how many times, and they tried to oppose his free-ranging, untrammeled imagination with their own technical expertise and experience. They tried to divert him from the path of error, they presented one counterargument after another. He took shameless advantage of their discipline, the highest virtue of the military ethic, in a way that they were completely unprepared for.

"To be sure, there were a great many people who were captivated by Hitler or who followed him just to further their own ambitions. Others deliberately sequestered themselves in their private domains—the exercise of their commands. There were many who felt they had a moral obligation to remain at their posts, partly for the sake of the troops and also because they were unwilling to give way to other, more pliable men.

"But then there were the officers who raised these contradictions to such a pitch that Hitler did not hesitate to dismiss them. And finally there were those who asked to be relieved from active duty, though in fact Hitler refused all such requests during the last years of the war, since he considered this to be tantamount to desertion.

"Violence was the only alternative that was left. After Hitler's startling successes at the beginning this would certainly have touched off a civil war. Hitler enjoyed the confidence of the people, the entire German people. There were a few who still tried it in spite of everything, and that gave us the *attentat* of July 20. But even if Hitler had been killed, what would have been the chances that the putsch would succeed? In Germany the masses of the people were still behind their Führer.

In the army the rank-and-file soldier still had faith in him, to say nothing of the SS.

"The number of determined individuals involved was very small, it's true. But all through history it has always been just a handful of men who have been willing to take direct action under such circumstances. Let's not forget what such a decision entails for a soldier—an officer raises his hand, at the height of the conflict, against his supreme commander, who is waging a life-or-death struggle at the head of his own people. He makes his move, even though he is convinced that his murderous act can on no account prevent his country's unconditional surrender to the enemy. He still goes through with it, in the hope of sparing his people from even greater suffering. But he also knows that the people themselves, blinded and deafened by Goebbels' propaganda, will condemn him because they still believe in their Führer. And that's not all—most of the soldiers at the front believe that their only salvation lies in a concerted resistance to the external enemy. For them Hitler is still the symbol of the struggle and their talisman of victory. That is how an officer who was prepared to take action would have had to view the situation, and that in fact was precisely how the situation presented itself. . . .

"And that is still not all. This officer is flying in the face of all the principles of military discipline. How then is he to secure the obedience of his subordinates? He is destroying loyalty, so who will remain loyal to him? In the eyes of many of his comrades he is committing an assault on honor itself, so how could he possibly stake all his hopes on his troops' sense of honor? He has sworn an oath, though to be sure Hitler has defiled that oath, but does that mean that he is released from his obligations? He has reminded his men a hundred times of the sacred nature of their undertaking to do their duty. Two million German soldiers have gone to their death to uphold it. Should he forswear himself? The oath of allegiance is more than a matter of form—he has sworn before God.

"One might reply, But would God require him to respect such an oath? This then is the soldier's crisis of conscience. Everyone had to fight this battle in his own heart. There could be no resolution on principle that would be valid for everyone, only tragic and unresolvable contradictions between two different conceptions of duty. If he were faithful to one of them, he would be derelict in the other. Who was wrong? Such things are not for mere men to decide.

"A commander decides the destiny of his subordinates, whether he commands whole armies or a squad of thirty men. Each one of their lives is an entire world that he alone must bear on his shoulders. The decision, especially for an officer, was very difficult. Even so there are a great many people who would still condemn the German commanders out of hand. They would accuse them of having lost their nerve, of being afraid to face up to the responsibilities. Freedom of action and obedience are just as closely intertwined as destiny and responsibility."

Adolf Heusinger, in the statements in this book, provides, undoubtedly, the best rationale we'll ever have on why the German generals' plot never succeeded. He was not only a general himself, but more than any other general was able to observe Hitler and his irrational reasoning during the critical years. It is hoped that this account will give greater insight into the problems and psychological factors involved in the German generals' plot against Hitler.

Appendix: Interview with General Heusinger, Conducted by U.S. Army Intelligence, September 12, 1945

In May 1945 General Heusinger had reached the end of his long march. He was aware that he was still being pursued by SS execution squads—thanks to a chance encounter with another fugitive general, who told him, "You're on the list of the ones they're planning on doing away with before the war's over." His original plan of escaping to Switzerland had miscarried; instead he sought refuge on a small farm near Munich, where he gave himself up to an American patrol on May 10. At first he was taken to a POW camp at Augsburg, then to Heidelberg, and finally, in view of his rank and his extensive experience of the planning and execution of operations on the eastern front, he was transferred to the Military Intelligence Center at Oberursel, near Frankfurt. Here for the first time he met face to face with a high-ranking American officer, Lieutenant Colonel Oron J. Hale (in civilian life a professor of history at the University of Virginia).

The following document, obtained through the generous cooperation of Professor Hale and of George Wagner of the National Archives and Records Service, is an English translation of the first and most comprehensive of several debriefing sessions in which Heusinger participated. Here he discusses the General Staff's war preparations in the late thirties and the planning of Operation Barbarossa. (The interviewers are identified as Lieutenant Colonel Hale and Brigadier General R. C. Brock.)

QUESTION: Did the German Wehrmacht derive any valuable lessons from participation in the Spanish Civil War?

HEUSINGER: Tactically and strategically we learned nothing. The General Staff was not directly concerned. Experts from the Air Ministry and the Ordnance Office went to Spain to test and observe the performance of their matériel. The Russians did the same. The Air Force doubtless acquired valuable tactical experience, but the ground forces little. The German volunteer legion had a staff but it was mainly concerned with administration. It was not a command staff. General Warlimont was the first chief and he was succeeded by General Sperrle and finally General Richthofen. They may have advised Franco unofficially in operational matters, but I have no knowledge of that.

The matériel which was sent to Spain for testing was doubtless shipped by sea, either camouflaged as ordinary freight or sent in pieces and reassembled there.

QUESTION: Did the Belgian declaration of neutrality in 1938 have any effect upon German military planning?

HEUSINGER: I do not recall the declaration. The declaration of the Belgian king in 1939, after the outbreak of the war, that Belgium would defend her neutrality against any aggressor did not affect operational plans, as the directives for the campaign in the west were based from the beginning on the occupation of Holland and the march through Belgium. It may well be, but it is not a matter of knowledge to me, that Hitler thought that when Britain and France undertook offensive operations they would move into Belgium. Furthermore, this was supported, in part, by the current disposition of Belgian forces, which were concentrated on the German frontier while the Franco-Belgian border was, relatively speaking, unguarded.

QUESTION: To what extent were German tactical doctrines kept secret before 1939?

HEUSINGER: Only the usual classification for combat and troop training manuals was maintained. Such materials must have been in the hands of the military attachés. Since these manuals had to be distributed to the troops for training purposes, it would have been impossible to keep them secret.

QUESTION: In 1939 how long a war did the general staff estimate that Germany could conduct?

HEUSINGER: Naturally, that depended upon the number and strength of our opponents. In 1939 we estimated one year. The OKW envisaged a long war with the greatest doubt and apprehension. One heard repeatedly the warning "For God's sake no long war" (*Um Gotteswillen nur keinen langen Krieg).* In 1939 Hitler assured Brauchitsch that England and France would not declare war when Germany moved against Poland. The General Staff expected a war of two or three months' duration. After France and England declared war, the opinion was that it would last a long time, but no definite time was predicted. Both Brauchitsch and the chief of the general staff had grave doubts as to Germany's ability to conduct a prolonged struggle.

In the general planning it was estimated that we would require a four months' reserve of armaments and munitions to carry through the period of conversion to war production. At the outbreak of the war, however, we had only a two months' reserve. This gap was bridged during the inactive period of the war between the Polish and western campaigns.

QUESTION: Did technical difficulties delay the development and equipment of the Wehrmacht before 1939? Were there serious failures of German tanks during the march into Austria?

HEUSINGER: There were many difficulties in arming and training the new Wehrmacht. The tempo was forced by the political authorities. We lacked trained officers and NCOs. Design and development were hurried through and weapons put into mass production without the careful testing customary in the German army. The result was numerous failures when they were placed in the hands of troops. The old Model 81 infantry rifle was tested and altered over a period of seven years before it was issued to the troops. In the rearmament period everything was done in a tremendous hurry. Armament producers were often delayed in their deliveries by shortages of necessary machine tools and lack of skilled production personnel.

There were many tank failures in the march into Austria. At that time we had only the Mark I and II tanks, which we called "tin cans" *(Blechkisten).* There were few Mark IIIs, and Mark IV did not exist. These tanks were very primitive and there were countless breakdowns.

QUESTION: How did the general staff view the possibility of a French attack in 1938 at the time of the Sudeten crisis?

HEUSINGER: The general staff was of the opinion that a French attack in the west would have broken through, as our fortifications were not complete, nor were they in 1939, when the French could have broken through, although at heavier cost. The West Wall was completed only from Trier south to the Rhine in 1939. Northward it was incomplete and without any depth. After 1940 construction ceased. To a certain extent the West Wall was a bluff, like the Atlantic Wall. With regard to the latter it was impossible to fortify the entire coast and every military man must have concluded that a landing and a penetration of five kilometers would end all difficulties as far as fortifications were concerned.

QUESTION: Who were the outstanding strategical planners in the German general staff before 1939? Was there anyone who could be compared with Schlieffen?

HEUSINGER: No, there was no Schlieffen. In professional circles the following were the most highly regarded: Beck, Halder, Manstein, Heinrich Stülpnagel (shot on 20 July) [sic], Fritsch, and Brauchitsch. Also Rundstedt, although he was not as active in the War Ministry. General Beck was undoubtedly the greatest spirit in the general staff. However, he was always of the opinion that war would be a catastrophe and in this opinion he found a great friend in General Gamelin. In the general staff we always said that General Halder and General Manstein had received "the necessary two drops of the wisdom of Solomon." In the top level of the general staff, Manstein was regarded as the ablest and most original planner. That is also my opinion. However, there was no Schlieffen.

QUESTION: Who really originated the plan for the 1940 campaign in the west?

HEUSINGER: The first plan for an offensive campaign was formulated in November 1939. In substance it was a repetition of the 1914 Schlieffen plan. As the start of the campaign was delayed doubts arose as to the achievement of any surprise with this plan. The basic idea of the new plan—the breakthrough in the Ardennes, crossing of the Meuse, and the trapping of British, French, and Belgian forces in the north by pushing the tank forces through to the Channel—came to several minds at once. And in justice it should be said that one of these was Hitler's. However, General Manstein, then chief of staff to Marshal Rundstedt, deserves the greater credit. He worked out the plan and proposed its adoption. The order was given to the Operations Division in February 1940 to replan the campaign along the proposed lines. From February 1940 to May 1940 the plan was subject to the sharpest criticism. Among the critics was General Guderian, who described the plan as a "crime against Panzers." General Halder deserves the credit for defending the plan against all critics and insisting upon its execution. General Bock was also opposed to it and appealed to the chief of the general staff. Halder said once that he would stick to the plan if the chances of succeeding were only ten percent.

QUESTION: Why did Hitler take all the credit for planning the campaign in his Reichstag speech after the armistice with France?

HEUSINGER: Hitler was opposed to popularity for any of his generals or military leaders. Hitler did not want another Hindenburg. This was a considered policy, I believe.

QUESTION: If France and England had declared war on Germany in 1938, did the general staff think Russia would join then?

HEUSINGER: No, up to and including the Anschluss with Austria it was felt that the moves in foreign policy were German national questions based on legitimate claims. Even General Beck supported the Anschluss. There was no division of opinion among the general staff until the Sudeten crisis and the occupation of Prague. The danger was then clear, and opposition to the policy of adventurism developed.

QUESTION: Did the conclusion of the Russian nonaggression pact result in any changes in the plans for the Polish campaign?

HEUSINGER: Not at all. There was no time to change the plans.

QUESTION: From the standpoint of German operations did the capitulation of the Belgian army in June 1940 have an important effect upon the fate of the Dunkirk pocket?

HEUSINGER: It was, of course, a welcome relief to the German forces, which otherwise would have been prevented from exerting direct pressure upon the pocket from the north and the east. The British were of course already cut off from contact with the French on the south. Their evacuation might have been less difficult had the Belgians held on the flank, but for the latter the situation was hopeless. They could not have broken out, and their surrender would have been forced in two or three days.

QUESTION: Was resistance on the Belgian frontier in 1940 greater than had been expected?

HEUSINGER: It was about what we had anticipated. North of Liège resistance was heavier—more determined. But elsewhere about as expected.

QUESTION: How were General Weygand's defense measures, before the resumption of the German attack southward, regarded by the general staff?

HEUSINGER: We were definitely surprised at what he accomplished in so short a time. He devised and instituted at many critical points an antitank defense tactic which proved quite effective. Woodlots, villages, and farm buildings were established as antitank strongpoints, and these served as a chessboard defense in depth that gave our tank forces trouble. The 14th Panzer Corps was caught and held for two days in such a defense system. In the course of the war the development of successful defense against panzer forces followed this principle.

Strategically he took measures that Gamelin had failed to take when he brought all available troops out of the Maginot Line and moved them to the left wing to meet the weight of the German attack over the Seine. Operationally this was the correct move, which Gamelin had not made.

QUESTION: How well informed was the German High Command on the state of British defenses after Dunkirk?

HEUSINGER: Very well informed. All equipment of the expeditionary force was lost, and we knew that there were few reserves of men and matériel in the homeland. Never in modern times had Britain been in a more critical situation. Only a man like Winston Churchill could have brought the country through such a crisis. We had no plans for an invasion and no equipment and specially trained forces with which to undertake the invasion. Hence the delay, the hesitation, and finally Hitler's decision not to risk it. Whether we should have risked it is of course now only a matter of historical interest. Admiral Wagner, with whom I have discussed this question recently and who was then chief of Naval Operations, is of the opinion that it would have failed. I think it could have been done. Militarily, this was for us one of the lost opportunities of the war.

With regard to the air attack in August and September—the Battle of Britain—I can speak only from the standpoint of the army. It was not thought possible to conquer Britain from the air. The objective was to destroy British air power and gain control of the air. This failed. English aircraft were greater in number than estimated or Britain's production was higher than estimated. By the middle of September it was obvious that the attack against London would not be decisive. Our losses in aircraft from improved flak and other defense measures became too high in proportion to results achieved. The air attacks were then switched to new objectives—the production and armament plans became the targets with a view of knocking out or delaying British rearmament. But in my opinion these were only substitute objectives fixed after the failure to achieve the first main objective—to destroy the British air power and gain control of the air over London and the south coast.

QUESTION: When did the Operations Section receive the order to prepare plans for the Russian campaign?

HEUSINGER: In December 1940. There were previous discussions and preliminary studies outside our section, but the detailed study and planning began in December.

QUESTION: Did General Marcks have anything to do with the planning?

HEUSINGER: General Marcks, who was a general staff officer, commanded a division in the western campaign but was without an assignment in the autumn of 1940. While the Army High Command was at Fontainebleau, General Halder assigned General Marcks to make a study—not a detailed plan—of a campaign against Russia. In its main features it did not differ greatly from the final plan prepared by the Operations Section. General Hilpert also made a study which was examined and evaluated in the Operations Section. General Hilpert proposed a massing of force on the German right in Romania, placing the main effort in a wide encircling movement toward Moscow with limited advance and holding operations on the left and center. The plan was rejected because the railroad lines and connections through Romania would not carry the necessary volume of traffic.

Hitler's directive for the planning of the campaign fixed the objectives so rigidly that in effect it determined the main features of the plan. These objectives were: (1) Conquer and occupy the Ukraine as quickly as possible. (2) Establish contact with Finland at the earliest possible moment. These objectives dictated the simultaneous right and left blows of the German forces, which was the outstanding feature of

the final plan of the campaign. Different objectives, or a less rigid directive, would have resulted probably in a different plan.

QUESTION: Did Hitler or the general staff expect a Russian winter
campaign in 1941? Were any preparations made?

HEUSINGER: The original timetable called for the launching of the
campaign in May, with the objectives to be reached in five months—
that is, in October. But the campaign did not begin until late June,
bringing the terminal date into November. Originally, Hitler, the C in
C, and the chief of the general staff agreed that wherever they stood
in November, they would close down operations. However, they gambled
with the weather, which in the late autumn was favorable, just as it
was to Napoleon in 1812, and kept saying, "We can risk it." Then came
the bitter weather, and the German armies started to retreat.

As far as winter preparations were concerned, measures had been
taken by the supply services, but they were inadequate. Clothing was
prepared for a hard German winter, but it was inadequate for a severe
Russian winter. The transport failed because German locomotives were
not equipped for extremely low temperatures. Moreover the Russians
in their retreat destroyed all the water tanks and this created enormous
difficulties in train operations. The campaign should have been halted
earlier and necessary measures taken to hold the positions already taken.
When the German armies began to retreat, Hitler dismissed Brauchitsch
and personally took command. He always maintained thereafter that
he personally saved the German army from the fate that had overtaken
Napoleon's forces in the retreat from Moscow.

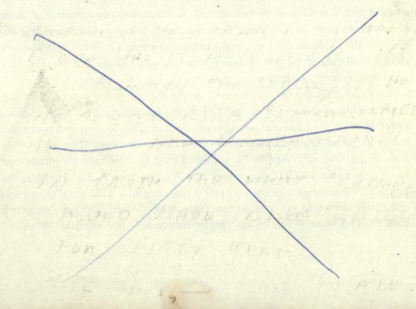

Glossary of German Military Terms and Nazi Party Organizations

Reichswehr: the German army was so called under the Weimar Republic (1919–1933); Hitler introduced the term *Wehrmacht* for the armed forces as a whole, including the navy *(Kriegsmarine)* and Goering's air force *(Luftwaffe)*, which had been severely limited and banned outright, respectively, by the terms of the Versailles Treaty. When the West German army was reorganized in 1950, it was renamed the *Bundeswehr* ("federal army").

OKH (Oberkommando des Heeres, "Army High Command"): the successor to the imperial and the Reichswehr general staff. After 1941 OKH was primarily responsible for the conduct of military operations on the eastern front.

OKW (Oberkommando der Wehrmacht, "Armed Forces High Command"): created by Hitler in 1938 as a counterweight to the old-line, predominantly Prussian staff officers of OKH. OKW included representatives of the navy and the Luftwaffe, and was responsible for military operations in the west, in North Africa, and throughout the Mediterranean. General (later Marshal) Wilhelm Keitel was OKW chief of staff from 1938–1945.

Abwehr (Abwehrdienst, "Self-Defense Service"): the chief German military intelligence service, directed by Admiral Wilhelm Canaris from 1935 until 1944 and most noteworthy for its involvement in several anti-Hitler conspiracies and in covert collaboration with the Allies.

Organisation Todt: a civilian engineering and construction corps organized along paramilitary lines by Dr. Fritz Todt (d. 1942) which was responsible for most of the Wehrmacht's principal fortifications and military installations, ranging in scale from the "western defense wall" along the French coast to Hitler's various command posts and field headquarters.

SS (Schutzstaffel, "Guard Detachments"): originally one of the several Nazi paramilitary organizations, after 1934 Heinrich Himmler's SS "state within a state" became the principal instrument of political repression and systematic terror in Hitler's Reich. Among its various branches were: The *SD* (Sicherheitsdienst, "Security Service"), presided over by Reinhard Heydrich until his assassination in 1942, later by Ernst Kaltenbrunner. The Party intelligence and espionage agency competed (successfully) with the Abwehr and ultimately absorbed most of its functions. The *Gestapo* (Geheime Staatspolizei, "Secret State Police") was chiefly responsible for internal "security," the SD for foreign intelligence operations and political surveillance, but both were active in France and throughout occupied Europe and both were commonly referred to as "the Gestapo."

The *Waffen SS* ("SS in Arms") were the Party's elite front-line combat troops. They wore the distinctive black uniforms of the SS, and their command structure—organized according to a special table of ranks devised by Himmler—was completely separate from that of the regular army. Originally open only to Germans of proven "Aryan" descent, Waffen SS divisions were later recruited from the "Nordic" occupied territories, including France, the Low Countries, Norway, Denmark, and the Baltic countries.

SA (Sturmabteilung, "Storm Troopers"): were essentially a rank-and-file party paramilitary organization, with none of the elitist pretensions of the SS. Though the SA had more than 2,500,000 members at the height of its power in 1934, its leadership was purged by the SS (with the active connivance of the army) and the SA lost most of its real political power and importance over the next few years.

[handwritten marginalia:] IRISH / INDIAN / BRITISH / SPANISH

Sources

* Full titles given in Bibliography. Comments in brackets are by the translators.

Chapter 1. July 20, 1944: The Wolf's Lair

Marie-Jeanne Viel, "Hitler et ses géneraux."
Heinz Linge, *Bis zum Untergang.* [Memoirs of Hitler's valet, who continued to idolize his former master until his death. Linge permitted only these highly colored reminiscences of Hitler's private life to be published posthumously.]
Interview with Frau Gertraud Junge, Munich, 1980.
Walter Frevert, *Rominten.* [An account of what was doubtless the most successful of Goering's many careers—that of master forester of the Reich and "king of the hunt."]

BERLIN

Interview with Frau Weichbrot, Berlin, 1959. (At that time the Stauffenberg brothers' former governess was still living in Berthold's villa in the suburb of Wannsee, which during the weeks before July 20, 1944, was the unofficial GHQ of the Valkyrie conspiracy.)
Interviews with Nina von Uxküll, Gräfin von Stauffenberg. (Countess von Stauffenberg and two of her sons—one of whom is currently a deputy in the West German Bundestag—first met with Eugène Silianoff at Bamberg in 1955. Further details of her account of the final days of the conspiracy were communicated by telephone in 1980.)

THE WOLF'S LAIR

Interviews with General Heusinger, Cologne, 1979–1980. (General Heusinger's eyewitness testimony, his notes, and personal papers furnished the basis for our account of the events of July 20 at Rastenburg.)
Zimmermann and Jacobsen (eds.), *20. Juli 1944.*
Hans Rothfels, *Die deutsche Opposition gegen Hitler.*
Interview with the son of General Paul von Hase (commander of the Berlin garrison, July 20, 1944), Bonn, 1961. [The elder Hase was charged by his

fellow conspirators in the Bendlerstrasse with securing the government
buildings in downtown Berlin, Goebbel's Propaganda Ministry in particular.
He was among the first batch of defendants brought before the People's
Court, along with Witzleben, Hoepner, Stieff, Yorck and others, and was
brutally done to death by the Gestapo on August 8, 1944.]

Interview with Frau Gertraud Junge, Munich, 1980. [Unlike her colleague, Frau
Christa Schröder, who was extensively interrogated by U.S. Army Intelligence in 1945, Frau Junge has apparently never allowed her impressions
of Hitler's household and of the events of July 20 to appear in print before.]

Chapter 2. July 20, 1944: Paris

Wilhelm, Ritter von Schramm, *Der 20. Juli in Paris.* [Like Stülpnagel, the author
was a career military officer in the Prussian tradition as well as a scholar
and historian.]

Interview with the daughter of Cäsar von Hofacker, Paris, 1956. (At that time
Fräulein von Hofacker was twenty-three years old, a secretary at the German
Embassy in Paris.)

Interviews with Mme Mercier, of the Comité d'histoire de la seconde guerre
mondiale, and M. Watelet, Curator of Perdiodicals, Bibliothèque Nationale.
Periodicals consulted include *Paris-Soir, Le Cri du Peuple, Le National populaire,
La Gerbe, Je suis partout, Paris-Midi, Berliner Lokal Anzeiger, Deutsche Allgemeine
Zeitung, Signal, Völkischer Beobachter.*

Interviews with Mme Arburger, Archives de la Préfecture de Police, Paris, Mme
Canavaggio, Archives Nationales, and Dr. Ernest Roskothen, former judge
of the German civil tribunal in Paris.

Chapter 3. 1934–1935: The Army Swears Fealty

Interview with Louis François-Poncet.

Interview with General von Witzleben, a cousin of Marshal Erwin von Witzleben.
During the thirties the younger Witzleben was an ADC on his cousin's staff
and a member of the circle which surrounded General Beck and which
became the nucleus of the "Prussian opposition." (General von Witzleben
first met with Eugène Silianoff on July 20, 1954—the tenth anniversary of
the Valkyrie conspiracy.)

Maxime Mourin, *Les complots contre Hitler.*

Gert Buchheit, *Ludwig Beck.*

Interview with Fräulein von Kotze, Institut für Zeitgeschichte (Institute for Contemporary History), Munich.

André François-Poncet, *Souvenirs.*

Chapter 4. 1936–1937: "They Call Him Hermann"

Interviews with Adolf Heusinger and Louis François-Poncet.
André François-Poncet, *Souvenirs*.
Walter Frevert, *Rominten*.
Michel Tournier, *Le roi des aulnes*.
Interview with Michel Tournier, de l'Académie Goncourt.

Chapter 5. 1938: "A Swine, But a Lucky Swine"

Maxime Mourin, *Les complots contre Hitler*.
Interviews with Adolf Heusinger and Mme François-Poncet.
Interviews with Frau Goerdeler and Fräulein Goerdeler, widow and eldest daughter of the most energetic of the civilian conspirators, Heidelberg, 1959. Fräulein Goerdeler generously allowed Eugène Silianoff to examine her father's private papers (which he had left in her charge when he went into hiding a few days before July 20, 1944): these included a complete, unpublished account of his clandestine mission to London in 1938.
Hans Bernd Gisevius, *Bis zum bittern Ende*. [The quotations follow the German edition rather than the English translation, which is considerably abridged.]
Jacques Bénoist-Méchin, Preface to *Hitler parle à ses généraux*.
Interviews with Ewald Heinrich von Kleist, Munich. Eugène Silianoff met with the younger Kleist on many different occasions during Silianoff's fourteen-year tour as *Le Monde* correspondent in Munich, 1955–1969. A descendant of the poet and novelist Heinrich von Kleist, a cousin of one of Hitler's marshals (commander in chief of Army Group Caucasus), as well as of Stauffenberg, and thus of Hofacker and a good many other of the conspirators, Kleist perfectly embodied the ideals and attitudes of vanished Junkerdom in a way that is best exemplified by the following exchange:
SILIANOFF: And what was your father's profession—I mean apart from his political activities?
KLEIST *(somewhat taken aback)*: His profession? He was lord of the manor, of course!
Ernst von Weiszäcker, *Memoirs*.
Interviews with Louis François-Poncet.
Interview with the widow of Admiral Canaris, Stuttgart, 1959. Silianoff was introduced to Frau Canaris through the good offices of the editor-in-chief of the German magazine *Rundschau*. She provided a vivid background briefing on her husband's character and private life—and the torments he later endured in Flossenburg concentration camp—but, as is typical of the inscrutable "Little Admiral," he had told her almost nothing of his career in the Abwehr and his role in the various military conspiracies in which he took part.

Interviews with M. Le Marec, Comité d'histoire de la seconde guerre mondiale, and M. Watelet, Bibliothèque Nationale. Periodicals consulted: *Le Figaro, Paris-Soir.*
Gert Buchheit, *Ludwig Beck.*
Bodo Scheurig, *Deutscher Widerstand.*

Chapter 6. 1939: First Soldier of the Reich

Interviews with Adolf Heusinger; Heusinger's diaries, notebooks, and personal papers.
Le Figaro, Paris-Soir, Le Matin, Match archives.
Raymond Cartier, *Histoire de la deuxième guerre mondiale.*
Eugen Kogon, *Der SS Staat.*
Helmuth Greiner, *Die Oberste Wehrmachtsführung.*

Chapter 7. 1940: "I Can Force Them to Obey Me"

Interviews with Adolf Heusinger; Heusinger's diaries, notebooks, and personal papers.
Interview with Henri Michel, president of the Comité international de la seconde guerre mondiale *(Le Monde).*
Jacques Chastenet, *Le drame final.*
Encyclopédie Visuelle Elsevier.
Historia Spécial.
Interviews with Louis François-Poncet and Mme Paul Stehlin.
Contemporary periodicals in the Bibliothèque Nationale.

Chapter 8. 1941: "We Have Nothing to Fear from the Americans"

Raymond Cartier, *Hitler et ses généraux.*
Interviews with Frau Goerdeler, Heidelberg, Lord Granard, Paris, and Adolf Heusinger, Cologne; soldiers' impressions of the front excerpted from letters preserved by Heusinger.
Encyclopédie Visuelle Elsevier.
Hugh Thomas, *The Murder of Rudolf Hess.* [The author is a British physician—not to be confused with the historian Hugh Thomas, author of *The Spanish Civil War*, etc.—and a former member of the quadripartite medical team who attended Hess in Spandau fortress. His conclusions, though ingenious, have not won widespread acceptance among historians.]
Walter Warlimont, *Im Hauptquartier der deutschen Wehrmacht.* [General Warlimont was Heusinger's opposite number at Rastenburg, OKW chief of operations.]

Chapter 9. 1942: "The Russians Are Done For"

Paul Carrell, *Unternehmen Barbarossa.* [*Hitler Moves East.*]
Maxime Mourin, *Les Complots contre Hitler.*
Interview with Adolf Heusinger; Heusinger's diaries, notebooks, and personal papers.
Fabian von Schlabrendorff, *Offiziere gegen Hitler.* [The lengthy quotations from Schlabrendorff's testimony given here and in Chapter 10 follow the original German, rather than the English edition (*The Secret War Against Hitler*), supplemented by personal communications with Eugène Silianoff, 1979–1980. Along with Stauffenberg, Schlabrendorff was one of the bravest and most resourceful of the military conspirators. He survived the war (thanks to a series of lucky accidents), resumed his interrupted career at the bar, and in 1967 was appointed a justice of the Federal Constitutional Court, the supreme court of West Germany, serving until his retirement in 1975. He died on September 3, 1980, at the age of seventy-three.]
F. W. Winterbotham, *The Ultra Secret.*
Interview with Frau Goerdeler, Heidelberg.

Chapter 10. 1942–1943: Stalingrad

Walter Görlitz, *Paulus and Stalingrad.*
Gert Buchheit, *Ludwig Beck.*
Ursula von Kardorf, *Berliner Aufzeichnungen.*

Chapter 11. 1943: Infernal Machines

Walter Görlitz, *Paulus and Stalingrad.*
Walter Frevert, *Rominten.*
Interviews with Michel Tournier and Adolf Heusinger; Heusinger's notebooks and personal papers.
Maxime Mourin, *Les complots contre Hitler.*
Fabian von Schlabrendorff, *Offiziere gegen Hitler.*
Interview with Nina, Countess von Stauffenberg, Bamberg. (The countess graciously conducted Eugène Silianoff on a personal tour of Bamberg, including the cathedral with its celebrated sculpted horseman— "*der Bamberger Ritter*"— the former barracks in which Stauffenberg began his military career (in a cavalry regiment called, confusingly enough, *die Bamberger Reiter*), and the archbishops' palace on a hill overlooking the old town. Her account of her husband's career has been supplemented by Bodo Scheurig's *Stauffenberg;* other details concerning Stauffenberg's activities in Berlin prior to July 20 and the Valkyrie conspiracy in its later stages were furnished by Frau Weichbrot and Fräulein von Hofacker.)

Interview with Ewald Heinrich von Kleist, Munich.
Bodo Scheurig, *Stauffenberg.*
Helmuth Greiner, *Die Oberste Wehrmachtsführung.*
Encyclopédie Visuelle Elsevier.

Chapter 12. 1944: "When the Oxcart Gets Stuck in the Mud"

Peter Hoffmann, *Widerstand.* [Easily the most comprehensive of the numerous
studies of the anti-Hitler resistance which have appeared since 1945; particularly valuable for its minutely detailed account of the complex, and often
highly confusing, activities of the various strands of the Valkyrie network
in Berlin, Paris, and elsewhere on July 20, including full texts of the communiqués which emanated from the Bendlerstrasse and from Hitler's GHQ
at Rastenburg.]
Werner Maser, *Adolf Hitler.*

Chapter 13. July 20, 1944: Exercise Completed

Interview with the son of General Paul von Hase, Bonn. (Herr von Hase, who
is now an official of the Federal government, confirms General Heusinger's
observation that to an officer of the old school such as General von Hase
it was unthinkable that any order issued to a subordinate could be disobeyed.) [The possibility that such an order would be countermanded by
the supreme commander, had not been taken into account—presumably
because Stauffenberg was still convinced that the supreme commander
was no more.]
Hans Royce (ed.), *20. Juli 1944.*
Zimmermann and Jacobsen (eds.), *20. Juli 1944.* [Both of the foregoing are
collections of articles published by the Bundeszentrale für Heimatsdienst,
the public-information agency of the Bonn government.]
Erich Kosthorst, *Die deutsche Opposition gegen Hitler.* [Also published by the Bundeszentrale für Heimatsdienst.]
Eberhard Zeller, *Geist der Freiheit.*
General Walter Warlimont, *Im Hauptquartier der deutschen Wehrmacht.*
Wilhelm, Ritter von Schramm, *Der 20. Juli in Paris.*

Chapter 14. After July 20, 1944: The Last Knights

Ernst Jünger, *Strahlungen.* [Ernst Jünger's wartime journals, though extracts are
quoted in various secondary sources, have yet to be translated into English
in their entirety.]

Interviews with Adolf Heusinger; Heusinger's notes, diaries, and prison recollections.

Interview with Fräulein Goerdeler, Heidelberg, and Mme Mercier and M. Le Marec, Comité d'histoire de la seconde guerre mondiale.

Chapter 15. March 1945–May 1945: "In the Best Interests of the Nation"

Hitler parle à ses généraux.
Raymond Cartier, *Hitler et ses généraux.*
John Toland, *Adolf Hitler.*
Interview with Adolf Heusinger.

Additional Interviews and Correspondence

Professor Oron J. Hale [See Appendix]; John Toland; George Wagner (Modern Military Branch, National Archives and Records Service); Robert Wolfe (director, Military Records Division, NARS); William H. Cunliffe (assistant director, Modern Military Branch, NARS); Dr. Hans Stercken (former director of the Bundeszentrale für politische Bildung, Bonn); Dr. Auerbach (director of the Librarians' Institute, Bonn).

Bibliography

[English titles given in brackets]

Brown, Anthony Cave, *Bodyguard of Lies*. New York, 1975.

Buchheit, Gert, *Ludwig Beck, ein preussicher General*. Munich, 1964.

Carell, Paul, *Unternehmen Barbarossa, 1941–1942*. Frankfurt, 1963. [*Hitler Moves East*].

Cartier, Raymond, *Histoire de la deuxième guerre mondiale*.

————, *Hitler et ses généraux, les secrets de la guerre*. Paris, 1952.

Chastenet, Jacques, *Le drame final*. Paris, c. 1965.

Encyclopédie Visuelle Elsevier, *Les généraux de Hitler et leurs batailles*. Brussels, 1976.

François-Poncet, André, *Souvenirs d'une ambassade à Berlin, 1931–1938*. Paris, 1946.

Frevert, Walter, *Rominten*. Munich.

Gisevius, Hans Bernd, *Bis zum bittern Ende* (2 vols.). Zurich, 1946. [*To the Bitter End*].

Görlitz, Walter, *"Ich stehe hier auf Befehl!"* Hamburg, 1958. [*Paulus and Stalingrad*].

Greiner, Helmuth, *Die Oberste Wehrmachtsführung, 1939–1945*. Wiesbaden, 1951.

Hagen, Hans W., *Zwischen Eid und Befehl: Tatzeneugenbericht von den Ereignissen am 20. Juli 1944*. Munich, 1959.

Hassell, Ulrich von, *Vom anderen Deutschland*. Frankfurt, 1964. [*The Von Hassell Diaries, 1938–1944*].

Historia Spécial, Hitler et ses généraux. Paris, 1978.

Hitler parle à ses généraux (preface by Jacques Bénoist-Méchin). Paris, 1964. [English translations of transcripts of daily conferences may be found in Felix Gilberg (ed.), *Hitler Directs His War*. New York, 1950.]

Hoffmann, Peter, *Sicherheit des Diktators*. Munich, 1969.

————, *Widerstand, Staatsstreich, Attentat*. Munich, 1969. [*The German Resistance*].

Irving, David, *Rommel, the Trail of the Fox*. New York, 1977.

Jünger, Ernst, *Strahlungen*. Stuttgart, 1960.

Kardorf, Ursula von, *Berliner Aufzeichnungen, 1942–45*. Munich, 1962.

Kogon, Eugen, *Der SS Staat und das System der deutschen Konzentrationslager*. Munich, 1946. [*The Theory and Practice of Hell*].

Kosthorst, Erich, *Die deutsche Opposition gegen Hitler zwischen Polen- und Frankreichfeldzug*. Bundeszentrale für Heimatsdienst. Bonn, 1957.

Kramarz, Joachim, *Claus Graf Stauffenberg: Das Leben eines Offiziers*. Frankfurt, 1965. [*Stauffenberg—The Life and Death of an Officer*].

Leber, Annedore (ed.), *Das Gewissen steht auf: 64 Lebensbilder aus dem deutschen Widerstand von 1933–1945*. Berlin, 1960.

Linge, Heinz, *Bis zum Untergang*. Munich, 1979.

Macksey, Major Kenneth J., *Panzer Division*. New York, 1968.

Maser, Werner, *Adolf Hitler, eine Biographie*. Munich, 1971.

Mourin, Maxime, *Les complots contre Hitler*. Paris, 1946.

Rothfels, Hans, *Die deutsche Opposition gegen Hitler: Eine Würdigung*. Hamburg, 1958. [*The German Opposition to Hitler*].

Royce, Hans (ed.), *20. Juli 1944*, Bundeszentrale für Heimatsdienst. Bonn, 1961.

Scheurig, Bodo, *Claus Graf Schenk von Stauffenberg*. Berlin, 1964.

———, *Deutscher Widerstand, 1938–1944*. Munich, 1969.

———, *Freie Deutschland: Das Nationalkomitee und der Bund Deutscher Offiziere in der Sowjetunion*. Munich, 1961.

Schlabrendorff, Fabian von, *Offiziere gegen Hitler*. Zurich, 1946.

———, *The Secret War Against Hitler*. New York, 1965.

Schramm, Wilhelm, Ritter von, *Der 20. Juli in Paris*. Munich, 1963. [*Conspiracy Among Generals*].

Shirer, William L., *The Rise and Fall of the Third Reich*. New York, 1959.

Thomas, Hugh, *The Murder of Rudolf Hess*. New York, 1979.

Toland, John, *Adolf Hitler*. New York, 1976.

Tournier, Michel, *Le roi des aulnes*. Paris, 1970.

Trevor-Roper, H. R., *The Last Days of Hitler* (2 ed.). New York, 1962.

Viel, Marie-Jeanne, "Hitler et ses généraux," *Historia Spécial*, no. 379 bis.

Vollmacht des Gewissens, Die, compiled by Europäische Publikation e.v. Frankfurt, 1965.

Warlimont, General Walter, *Im Hauptquartier der deutschen Wehrmacht, 1935–1945*. Frankfurt, 1962. [*Inside Hitler's Headquarters*].

Weizsäcker, Baron Ernst von, *Memoirs*. London, 1951.

Winterbotham, F. W., *The Ultra Secret*. London, 1974.

Zeller, Eberhard, *Geist der Freiheit: Der zwanzigste Juli*. Munich, 1952.

Zimmermann, Erich, and Jacobsen, Hans Adolf (eds.), *20. Juli 1944*. Bundeszentrale für Heimatsdienst. Bonn, 1961.

Index

Abetz, Ambassador Otto, 214, 215
Abwehr, 50, 64, 137, 163, 168
Allies, the, 176, 179, 180, 182, 183, 192,
    196, 206, 240, 241, 242
Alsace-Lorraine, 76
Anti-Hitler movement, 74, 167, 180, 181,
    185, 190, 193, 195, 196, 197, 199, 203
    after Stalingrad, 161
Anti-Nazi provisional government, 199
Anti-Semitism, 27, 39, 73, 238
Antonescu, Marshal, 148, 184
Armed Forces High Command. *See*
    Wehrmacht High Command (OKW)
Army Group Center, 182, 201
Army Group North, 204
Army Group South, 167, 188
Arthuys, M. Jacques, 26
Association of German Officers, 176, 177
Austria, march into, 53
Austrian Ruthenes, 241

Badoglio, 181, 183
Bagnères, Captain Jacques, 182
Bank of England, 50
Bargatzki, Walter von, 19
Battle of Britain, 96, 151
Battle of the Bulge, 242
Baumgart, Dr., 22, 27, 218
Beaverbrook, Lord, 101
Beck, General Ludwig, 20, 22, 23, 24, 25,
    40, 50, 53, 54, 55, 59, 100, 105, 125,
    157, 195, 203, 205
    anti-Hitler activity, 56, 61, 62, 63, 66, 67,
      69, 73, 77, 79, 83, 125, 137, 161, 182
    Blomberg's wedding and, 47, 48
    Czechoslovakia and, 57
    described, 36, 37
    Goerdeler and, 49
    Operation Valkyrie and, 5–7, 11, 12, 207,
      209, 211, 216
Belgium, 79, 88, 92
Benoit-Mechin, Jacques, 54
Berger ("Hitler's double"), 8
Berlin Olympics, 73
Bernadotte, Count, 244

Bismarck, Count Herbert von, 56, 233
Blomberg, Erna von, 47, 49, 51
Blomberg, Marshal Werner von, 34, 36, 180
    marriage, 47, 48
Blomberg affair, 47–49
Blomberg-Fritsch crisis, 1938, 171
Blumentritt, General, 23, 24, 25, 27, 28,
    29, 212, 213, 215, 216, 219, 220, 222
Bock, Marshal Fedor von, 1, 83, 86, 90, 106,
    109, 110, 115, 124, 129, 131, 135, 143
Bodenschatz, General, 8
Boeselager, Baron von, 164
Boineburg-Lungsfeld, General von, 20, 22,
    25, 27, 29, 212, 213, 214, 215, 216
Bomb raids
    on Berlin and Germany, 4, 15, 188, 200,
      234
    on London, 101
Bonhoeffer, Pastor Dietrich, 233
Borhoefferie, Dr. Kurt, 69
Bormann, Martin, 14, 24, 32, 140, 244
Bose, Chandra, 241
Brandt, Colonel, 9, 10, 165, 166
Brauchitsch, General Walther von, 49–53,
    57, 78, 79, 80, 143
    on Battle of Britain, 96, 97
    conspiracy attempts to recruit, 61, 62, 68,
      71, 73, 74, 77
    Russian compaign and, 103–105, 107–
      111, 113, 115, 116, 125
    western front and, 80–82, 87, 88–90
Braun, Eva, 1, 15, 240, 244
Brehmer, Brigadier General, 29, 30
British Secret Intelligence Service, 57, 58,
    134
Broich, Baron von, 172, 173, 183
Burgdorf, General Wilhelm, 237

Canaris, Admiral Wilhelm, 50, 55, 56, 57,
    105, 233, 234
    anti-Hitler activity, 69, 70, 73, 77, 83,
      163, 167, 168
    described, 64, 65
Cartier, Raymond, 84, 99
Casablanca conference, 174

"Case Green," 57, 64, 68
Caucasus, 126, 127, 129, 131, 134, 135,
    138, 142, 145, 156, 157, 177
Chamberlain, Prime Minister Neville, 59,
    61, 70, 71, 72
Chancellery, underground bunker of, 243
Chiang Kai-shek, 187
Christian, Gerda, 13, 15
"Christian conspiracy," 168
Churchill, Prime Minister Winston, 50, 58,
    59, 60, 101, 175, 177, 197
Committee for a Free Germany, 222
Compulsory military service, 38
Concentration camps, 38
Conservative Nationalist Party, 40, 55
Crimea, 184
"Crystal Night," 73
Czechoslovakia, 54, 55, 56, 57, 64, 68, 71,
    74

Danzig, 74, 75
Das Reich, 3
D-day, 197
Decker, Lieutenant Colonel, 113
De Gaulle, Colonel Charles, 89, 92
Delp, Father, 220
Doenitz, Admiral, 195, 213, 214
Donets Basin, 181
Dulles, Allen, 100
Dunkirk, 90, 91, 92, 151

"Eagle's Nest," 54, 72, 193, 194
Ebert, President Friedrich, 39, 40
École Militaire, 22, 25
Eisenhower, General Dwight D., 244
Elser, Georg, 84
Engel, Lieutenant Colonel, 2
England, 50, 57, 58, 87, 95, 96, 101, 134,
    151, 240
English Channel, 95
Enigma cipher machine, 134

Falkenhorst, General Nikolaus von, 87
Faulkenhausen, General Alexander von, 24
    conspiracy and, 125
Federation of German Trade Unions, 5
Fegelein, SS Captain, 8, 240, 241
Fellgiebel, General Erich, 3, 7, 11, 16, 120,
    197, 199, 228, 235
Fire and Blood (Jünger), 18
1st Guards Regiment, 25, 29, 218
Fischer, Corporal, 218, 219
Foreign Armies East, 186
Foreign news broadcasts, 70
France, 58, 69, 70, 71, 75, 77, 87, 88 127,
    128, 242
    battle of, 88–92, 94
François, General, 159

François-Poncet, Ambassador André, 32,
    33, 34, 40, 61, 68, 72, 73
François-Poncet, Louis, 32, 34, 35, 41, 43
    describes Christmas at Karinhall, 43–45
François-Poncet, Madame, 75
Frederick the Great, 1
Freisler, Dr. Roland, 232, 233, 234
Fresnes military prison, 30
Fritsch, General Count Werner von, 32, 55,
    61, 91, 125, 180
    Blomberg's affair and, 47, 48, 49
    described, 37
    Goerdeler and, 49
Fritsch case, 48, 49, 50, 51, 52, 53
Fromm, General Friedrich, 7, 11, 12, 20,
    23, 185, 203, 210, 211, 213, 233

Galen, Count Clement August von, 5
Gamelin, General, 40
Gehlen, 186, 187
General Army Office, 6, 184
George, Lloyd, 58, 60
George, Stefan, 5
Georgi, Major Friedrich, 210
German colonies, 75, 76
German Commanders, end of war and,
    245–247
German Democratic Republic, 176
German people, opinion of, 71, 77, 109,
    119, 130, 162, 189, 236, 245
German press, 70, 119
Gerstdorff, Colonel Baron Rudolf von, 164,
    167
Gerstenmaier, Pastor Eugen, 5, 235
Gestapo, 18, 34, 37, 50, 53, 55, 56, 57, 60,
    67, 73, 163, 167, 168, 189, 212, 214,
    217, 220, 221, 222, 224, 225
Giraud, General, 65
Gisevius, Hans Bernd, 50, 63
    Brauchitsch and, 50–52
Glass Bees, The (Jünger), 18
Glydenfeld, General von, 188
Gneisenau, Marshal Count von, 168
Goebbels, Joseph Paul, 24, 35, 42, 130, 154,
    189, 192, 209, 210, 233, 236, 244
Goerdeler, Carl Friedrich, 5, 39, 100, 105
    anti-Hitler activity, 49, 50, 51, 52, 64, 73,
    136, 137, 162, 205, 217, 220
    family of, 137, 138, 220, 235
Goerdeler, Fritz, 235
Goerdeler affair, 51, 52
Goering, Edda, 43
Goering, Emmy, 43
Goering, Karin, 41–43
Goering, Reichsmarshal Hermann, 3, 8, 47,
    53, 68, 69, 78, 101, 115, 151, 158, 159,
    167, 180, 193, 195, 196, 202, 213, 214,
    220, 243, 244

Goering, Reichsmarshal Hermann *(cont'd)*
art collection, 45, 46
conspirators attempt to recruit, 68, 69,
74
described, 40, 41
home Karinhall, 43–45
honors and titles, 42
Luftwaffe and, 91, 92, 97, 150, 154, 188,
189, 201
relationship to Hitler, 42
wives, 41, 43
Goethe and the Generals
(Weniger), 17
Granard, Lord, 101
Great Britain, 56, 57, 59, 60, 70, 71, 77,
87, 91, 92, 104
Greece, 97, 98
Greiffenberg, General von, 77
Greim, General Ritter von, 244
Gross Deutschland, 3
Gruhn, Fraulein Erna. *See* Blomberg, Erna
von
Guderian, General Heinz, 63, 88, 89, 91,
216, 243
Russian campaign, 106, 108, 109, 113,
119, 173, 179
Gunsche, Major Otto, 14

Haberman, Max, 234
Haeften, Lieutenant Werner von, 4, 6, 7,
10, 11, 199, 203, 211
Hagen Lieutenant Albrecht von, 232
Halder, General Franz, 48, 63, 65, 66, 79,
80, 105, 169, 188, 235, 237
anti-Hitler activity, 67–69, 71, 73, 74, 77,
78, 83
described, 63, 64
Hitler and, 140, 141, 143, 144
Russian campaign, 106, 110, 111, 114,
116, 118, 119, 120, 121, 122, 123, 124,
125, 126, 135, 136–141
summer offensive, 126, 127, 128, 129,
131, 132, 133, 134
Halifax, Lord, 59
Hamilton, Duke of, 100
Hammerstein, General Baron Kurt von, 32,
75, 221
Hanson, D. H., 58
Hardenberg, Count Hans von, 131
Hase, General von, 208, 210, 232
Hassell, Ulrich von, 5, 73, 75, 233
Hausen, Colonel, 234
Hauser, SS General, 240
Heiber, Helmut, 238
Heim, General, 146, 147, 148
Helldorf, Count Wolf von, 12, 69, 233
Henderson, Ambassador Neville, 56, 60
Hess, Rudolf, 69, 100, 101, 103

Heusinger, Lieutenant General Adolf, 8, 9,
10, 38, 75, 76, 80, 81, 86, 95, 97, 103,
132, 133, 192, 193, 195, 196, 200, 201,
202, 204, 205, 235, 236, 243, 245–247
anti-Hitler activity, 131, 199, 224–230
on battle of France, 92, 94
investigation of, 224–230
Operation Citadel, 178, 179
Russian campaign, 106, 107, 108, 109,
111, 115, 116, 120, 123, 124, 184, 186,
191
Schmundt and, 143, 144
Stalingrad and, 144, 145, 146, 151, 153,
154, 155, 156, 159
on the western front, 196, 197
Heyden, Lieutenant Colonel Bodo von der,
210, 211
Heydrich, Reinhard, 49, 74
Himmler, Heinrich, 1, 8, 11, 48, 49, 53, 69,
74, 110, 115, 163, 167, 168, 186, 187,
188, 189, 193, 195, 203, 213, 215, 220,
224, 244
Hindenburg, Colonel Oskar von, 35, 36
Hindenburg, President Paul von, 31, 32
death of, 34
described, 33, 34
opinion of Hitler, 35
political testament, 35
Hindenburg oath, 31
Hindu Brigade, 241, 242
Hitler, Adolf
Ambassador François-Poncet and, 72, 73
Army Group South plots against, 167
Beck and, 61, 62, 63, 66, 67
becomes *Führer,* 34, 35
Blomberg affair, 47–49
Brauchitsch and, 80–83, 87–90, 104
conspirators plan to arrest, 69, 162
Czechoslovakia, 54–57, 75
Dunkirk and, 90–92
at Eagle's Nest, 54, 72, 193, 194
Eva Braun and, 1, 15, 240, 244
final days, 237–247
first peace initiative, 78
foreign policy, 75, 76
Fritsch affair, 48–53
generals, officers corps and, 37, 66, 85,
115, 119, 122, 128, 179, 180, 238
Halder and, 140, 141, 143
Hess' disappearance, 103
Heusinger investigation and, 230–232
interview with Chamberlain, 61, 70
Italy and, 183, 184, 238
Jodl and, 138–140, 190
Keitel and, 61, 62
Kluge and, 163–166
Manstein and, 86, 87, 180, 181, 188, 237
military follies, 138

Hilter, Adolf *(cont'd)*
  Norway invasion and, 87
  November 8 and, 84
  oath of allegiance to, 31, 161, 162, 199,
    222, 245, 246
  "Operation Barbarossa," 98
  "Operation Blitz," 163–167
  Operation Citadel and, 172–175, 178,
    179, 181
  Operation Valkyrie, 6–11, 207–209, 213,
    214, 216
  palmists and astrologers and, 123, 124
  personal habits, 1
  personal staff, 2
  Rommel and, 133, 134
  Russian campaign and, 103–121, 124–
    126, 135–141, 184
  Soviet propaganda and, 175–177
  Soviet Union nonaggression pact, 76, 77
  Stalingrad and, 142–160
  succeeds Hindenburg, 31, 32
  summer offensive and, 126–132
  troops faith in, 192, 246
  view of United States and Britain, 99
  war with Poland, 77
  weapons and, 183
  at Werwolf GHQ, 134, 138, 139
  western offensive, 86–95
Hitler-Stalin pact, 76, 77
Hitler Youth, 70
Hoepner, General Erich, 68, 69, 171, 203,
    222, 232, 240
  Russian campaign and, 118, 119, 122–
    124
Hofacker, Lieutenant Colonel Cäsar von,
    19, 21, 25, 27, 28, 185, 221
Holland, 88
Hooven, Colonel, 177
Horn, Alfred. *See* Hess, Rudolf
Horst, Doctor, 27
Hôtel Continental, 30, 214
Hôtel Majestic, 17, 22, 219
Hôtel Meurice, 22, 25, 214
Hôtel Raphaël, 17, 212, 213, 214, 215, 217
Hoth, General Hermann, 106, 150, 154,
    155, 156, 172

Italy, 92, 180, 183

Jacob, Franz, 234
Jodl, General Alfred, 8, 14, 87, 88, 132, 181,
    197, 201, 202, 237
  Hitler and, 138–140, 190
  Rommel and, 133, 134
  Russian campaign and, 106, 107, 108,
    111, 112, 120, 145, 175, 178, 180
  summer offensive, 126–128
  Werwolf GHQ with Hitler, 138–140

Junge, Gertraud, 1, 13, 14, 15
Jünger, Ernst, 22, 218, 220
  books by, 18

Kaltenbrunner, Ernst, 225
Kantzow, Baroness Karin von. *See* Goering,
    Karin
Karinhall, 43–45
Keitel, Marshal Wilhelm, 3, 7, 8, 9, 10, 11,
    12, 24, 49, 61, 87, 88, 98, 140, 167,
    194, 195, 197, 200, 201, 202, 205, 207,
    216, 222, 237, 242
  Russian campaign and, 109, 119, 120–
    123, 159, 175, 177
  summer offensive and, 126, 127, 132
Keller, General, 243
Kempf, General, 172
Kharkov, battle of, 133
Kiep, Otto, 233
Kleist, Colonel von, 131
Kleist, Ewald Heinrich, 180, 210, 217, 221
Kleist, Ewald von, 57
Kleist-Schmentzin, Baron Ewald von, 55,
    56, 180, 190, 193, 194, 217
  mission to England, 57–61, 217
Kluge, Field Marshal Günther Hans von,
    21, 199, 202, 203, 221, 222
  anti-Hitler activities, 23, 24, 25, 27, 28–
    30, 137, 163, 164, 212, 213, 214, 216
  death of, 223
  Hitler and, 163–166
  Russian campaign and, 115, 118, 122,
    173, 182
Knochen, SS General, 30, 213, 214
Koch, Gauleiter Erich, 158
Korten, General, 10
Kortzfleisch, General, 211
Kraewell, Lieutenant Colonel von, 22, 30,
    213
Kramarz, Joachim, 200
Kranke, Admiral, 212
Krebs, General, 243
Kripo, 220, 225, 226, 228
Krohne, President, 235
Küchler, General, 187
Kuhn, Major, 235
Kursk, 172, 174, 178, 179, 186

Lagebaracke, 4, 7
La Roche-Guyon, 21, 22, 25, 27, 212, 221,
    222, 223
Leber, Julius, 5, 205
Leeb, Wilhelm Ritter von, 83, 106, 108, 143
Leftist groups, 130
Lehndorff, Count Heinrich von, 131, 233
Leipziger Gewandhaus, 39
Lenderfeld, Nina. *See* Stauffenberg, Nina
Lesdain, Jacques de, 223, 224

Liedig, Captain, 69
L'Illustration, 223, 224
Lindemann, General, 235
Linge, Heinz, 1
Linstow, Colonel von, 20, 25, 28, 212, 213, 214, 215, 219, 222
List, General Sigmund von, 101, 119, 136, 138, 156
Low Countries, invasion of, 88, 92
Luftwaffe, 78, 79, 91, 96, 97, 148, 150, 151, 154, 188, 194, 201, 238, 244

Maginot line, 79, 88
Manstein, General Erich von Lewinski von, 21, 86, 133, 148, 157, 162, 173, 179, 180, 181, 182, 188, 193, 194, 237
Marjane, Leo, 26
Maulaz, 221
Meissner, 33, 36
Mendelssohn, Felix, statue of, 39
Michel, Doctor, 20
Milch, General Erhard, 42, 156
Model, General Walther, 167, 172, 173, 177, 179, 180, 201, 222, 223
Mollendorf, Captain von, 7, 10
Molotov, Vyacheslav Mikhailovich, 98
Moltke, Count Helmut von, 233, 234
Mondel, 15
Montand, Yves, 26
Montgomery, Field Marshal Bernard Law, 241
Morell, Doctor, 123, 124, 164, 165, 193, 203
Muller, Bishop Otto, 235
Munich Conference, 71, 72, 73, 74
Murderer Lives at Number 21, The, 26
Murder of Rudolf Hess, The (Thomas), 103
Mussolini, Benito, 2, 7, 10, 11, 14, 15, 71, 72, 99, 174, 181, 209

National Committee for a Free Germany, 176, 177, 191
National Socialist ideology, 53, 55, 63, 76, 90, 101, 171, 180, 192, 224
Naval High Command, 105
Niemöller, Pastor Martin, 235
"Night of the Long Knives, the," 32, 63, 78
Normandie-Neimen Esquadrille, 182
Normandy beaches, 197, 213, 215
North Africa, 133, 134, 145, 146, 172, 177, 178
Norway invasion, 87
November 8 assassination attempt, 84, 85

Oath of Allegiance, importance of, 31, 161, 162, 199, 222, 245, 246

Oberg, General, 28, 30, 213, 214, 215, 220, 221
Oberhauser, General, 20
OKH, 11, 24, 66, 67, 77, 79, 91, 116, 165, 188, 193, 195, 197, 204, 217
OKW. *See* Wehrmacht High Command
Olbricht, General Friedrich, 6, 11, 12, 125, 162, 163, 165, 173, 183, 184, 193, 203, 228
Operation Valkyrie and, 207, 209, 210, 211, 216
"Operation Barbarossa," 98. *See also* Russian campaign
"Operation Blitz," 163–167
Operation Citadel, 172–174, 178, 179, 181, 182
Operation Valkyrie
aborted, 11, 12
assassination attempt, 6–16
conspiracy revived, 74
effect of America's entrance on, 125
executions after, 217–236
exercise completed, 207–217
final act, 210
first phase of, 207–209
modifications of, 6, 7
original planning, 6
in Paris, 17–30, 212–216
striking force of, 203
vacillation of Kluge, 23–30
Oranienburg, 38
Organisation Todt, 3, 4, 11
Oster, Colonel Hans, 56, 71, 80, 84, 105, 137, 162, 163, 165, 167, 233
described, 65, 66

Panther tanks, 174, 175
Papen, Franz von, 32, 35, 36
Paris
German entry, 92
wartime conditions in, 25, 26
Paris Soir, 26, 27
Patton, General George S., 241
Paulus, General Friedrich, 98, 135, 136
anti-Hitler activity, 140, 222
at Stalingrad, 145, 147, 150, 152, 154–160
People's Court, 232–235
Pétain, Marshal Henri Philippe, 92
Piaf, Edith, 26
Pieck, Wilhelm, 176
Podewills, Countess, 18, 20, 22, 218
Poland, war with, 77
Polish Corridor, 59, 75, 76
Popitz, Johannes, 220
Potsdam Regiment, 221
Prinz Albrechtstrasse prison, 233

Propaganda, 161, 175, 176, 177, 191, 192, 236
Propaganda Ministry, 142, 209, 210
Prussian Academy of Sciences, 67
Puttkamer, Vice-Admiral von, 8

Quirnheim, Colonel Albrecht Mertz von, 207, 211

Radio Berlin, 23, 24
Raeder, Admiral Erich, 53, 78, 95, 105
Rastenburg, 1, 2, 23, 110, 118, 120, 146, 159, 166, 178, 183, 185, 193, 202, 206, 209
Rath, Ernst von, 73
Red Army, 175, 176, 182, 186
Red Army General Political Bureau, 175, 176
Reich Central Security Office, 168, 215
Reichenau, Marshal Walther von, 58, 110, 112, 123, 124
Reich Press Chamber, 27
Reichswehr, 31, 32, 34, 36, 75, 158
Reinhardt, Django, 26
Remer, Major, 208–210
Replacement Army, 4, 7, 9, 190, 193, 205, 206, 207
Reynaud, President Paul, 92
Rhineland zone takeover, 38
Ribbentrop, Foreign Minister Joachim von, 58, 76, 133, 243
Richthofen, General Baron von, 152, 153
Röhm, Ernst, 32
Romanian army, 146, 147, 184
Romanian oil fields, 126
Rommel, General Erwin, 21, 23, 27, 86, 91, 101, 124, 133, 134, 143, 178, 180, 192, 205, 223
Roosevelt, President Franklin D., 99, 175, 177, 240
Royal Navy, 87, 95, 96, 101
Rundstedt, Field Marshal Gerd von, 21, 83, 84, 86, 90, 106, 108, 110, 180, 199, 202, 232, 242, 243
    Russian campaign and, 106, 108, 110, 111, 112, 115
Russia. See Soviet Union
Russian Army of Liberation, 187
Russian campaign, 103–111, 115, 119–141, 172, 188, 191, 201, 202, 205. See also "Operation Barbarossa"; Summer offensive
agitprop campaign, 140
Caucasus, 126, 127, 129, 131, 134, 135, 138, 142, 145, 156, 157
losses in, 116
Operation Citadel, 172, 173, 174, 178, 179, 181, 182

Stalingrad, 142–160, 172, 175, 177, 186, 191
suffering of German troops in, 112–114, 118
transportation problems, 121, 122
Russian POW camps, 157

SA, 32, 78
Saar plebiscite, 38
Sauckel, Gauleiter Fritz, 20
Saucken, Lieutenant von der, 210
Sauerbruch, Doctor, 34, 183
Sauken, Olga von, 185
Savich, General Edler von, 177
Schacht, Hjalmar, 52, 61, 65, 68, 235
Schauf, Sargeant Major, 218, 219
Schlabrendorff, Count Fabian von, 130, 136, 137, 162–167, 227, 234, 235
Schlieben, General von, 239
Schlieffen plan, 79, 86
Schmend, Colonel, 234
Schmundt, General Rudolf, 10, 123, 124, 132, 139, 143, 163, 167, 179, 194, 195, 196, 202
Schmundt, Major, 54
Scholl, Hans, 161
Scholl, Sophie, 161
Schörner, 180
Schröder, Frau Christa, 1, 13
Schulenberg, General Count Friedrich von der, 5, 37, 185, 233
SD, 20, 22, 27, 29, 30, 49, 168, 218, 220
Seniority system, 239
Seydlitz, General Walther von, 147, 148, 175, 176, 177, 191
Shaposhnikov, Marshal, 113
Sicily, 179
Siegfried Line, 54
Sonnemann, Emmy. See Goering, Emmy
Soviet Union, 2, 58, 75, 98, 101, 104, 240
attack on, 3
nonaggression pact, 76, 77
Speer, Albert, 243
Speidel, General Hans, 22, 25, 84
Sponeck, General Count Hans von, 116, 117, 124, 235
SS, 20, 22, 27, 29, 30, 32, 33, 69, 73, 78, 105, 117, 176, 187, 207, 208, 211, 214, 215, 220, 221, 246. See also Waffen SS
SS Totenkopf units, 78
Stahel, General, 202, 204, 205
Stalin, Josef, 110, 116, 129, 175, 187
Stalingrad, 142–160, 172, 175, 177, 186, 191
German prisoners, 175
Stauffenberg, Alexander, 168, 169
Stauffenberg, Berthold von, 5, 168, 169, 182, 184, 199, 206

Stauffenberg, Colonel Count Claus von, 222, 228
  arrest of, 11
  description of, 168, 169
  family, 220
  marriage, 170, 171
  Operation Valkyrie and, 4–16, 171, 182–187, 189, 190, 193, 197, 199, 203, 205–212
  religion and politics, 171
  wounds, 173, 174
Stauffenberg, Count Alfred Schenck von, 168
Stauffenberg, Frau, 199
Stauffenberg, Nina, 5, 6, 171, 173
Stehlin, Captain, 72
Steidle, Colonel, 177
Stieff, General Helmuth, 24, 25, 165, 166, 190, 203, 228, 232
Stophenberg, Hugo von, 168
Storm of Steel, The (Jünger), 18
Strasser, Gregor, 32
Stülpnagel, General Karl Heinrich von, 119
  anti-Hitler movement and, 18, 19, 20, 22, 23, 25, 27, 28, 29, 76, 80, 83, 125, 126, 212, 213, 214, 215, 216, 217
  attempted suicide and death, 218–221, 234
  description of, 18
  in World War I, 17
Sudeten Germany, 55, 71, 171
Summer offensive, 19, 126–134
Sundermann, Herr, 27
Swastika flag, 39

Teheran Conference, 177
Teuchert, Baron von, 19, 212, 221
Thiele, General, 235
Thomas, General Georg, 79, 235
Thomas, Hugh, 103
Thormaelden, Ludwig, 170
Thungen, General von, 235
Todt, Dr. Fritz, 2
Tresckow, General Henning von, 8, 145, 197, 221, 226, 228
  conspiracy and, 130, 131, 137, 162, 164, 165, 166
Tresckow, Major von, 91
Tukhachevsky, Marshal, 112

Uhlig, Heinrich, 84
Ukraine, 134, 138, 139, 143
Ukrainians, 241
Ulbricht, Walter, 176
"Unconditional surrender," 176, 177
Unger, Colonel, 213
United States, 56, 59, 125, 126, 145, 146, 240

Uxküll, Countess Caroline von, 168
Uxküll, Count von, 173, 183, 184

Vansittart, Sir Robert, 50, 58, 60
Vilna, 202, 204, 205
Vlasov, General, 187
Voss, Colonel von, 119, 221

Waffen SS, 3, 12, 30, 78, 87, 113, 116, 117, 191
Wagner, General, 197, 221, 228
Waldorf, Claire, 42, 43
Walzenecker, General, 14
Warlimont, General, 8
Wartenburg, Lieutenant Yorck von, 232
Wartenburg, Marshal Ludwig Yorck von, 159
Watt, Watson, 96
Wednesday Club, 67, 220
Wehrle, Chaplain, 5
Wehrmacht, 6, 24, 62, 76, 78, 87, 95, 97, 98, 123, 128, 133, 134, 145, 171, 179, 182, 186, 215
Wehrmacht High Command (OKW), 3, 49, 64, 78, 84, 91, 116, 118, 174, 178, 195
Weichbrodt, Frau, 182, 199
Weichs, Marshal von, 148
Weimar Republic, 33, 39
Weinert, Erich, 176
Weizsäcker, Baron von, 64
Weniger, Professor Wilhelm, 17
Werwolf GHQ, 2, 134, 138, 139, 143
Western Army Command, 21
Western front, 80–82, 86–95, 192, 193, 196, 201, 239
  D-day, 196, 197
  discussion of offensive, 79, 80
Western Naval Group, 212
Weygand, General, 65
"White Rose" network, 161
Wilhelm I, 33
Wilhelm II, 168
Witzleben, Marshal Erwin von, 5, 24, 25, 66, 95, 221, 222, 232, 233
  anti-Hitler and, 68, 69, 71, 74, 77, 84, 209, 210
Woeffler, Major, 70
Wolf, Frau Johanna, 1, 13
Wolf's Lair, 1, 13, 106, 112, 126, 133, 146, 174, 179, 193, 203, 205, 230
  attempt on Hitler's life at, 6–16
  described, 2
  permanent GHQ, 3
World War I, 17, 18, 99, 103, 123, 158, 159, 218

Yorck, Marshal, 168, 185

Zeitzler, General Kurt, 144–148, 150, 151,
    155, 156, 159, 184, 193, 195, 197, 200,
    202

Operation Citadel and, 172, 174, 175,
    177, 178–181
Zhukov, General Georgi, 113, 116
Zimmermann, Colonel, 24

937